THE LOST DECADE:
AMERICA IN THE SEVENTIES

THE DOLPHIN

General Editor: Tim Caudery

26

THE LOST DECADE:

AMERICA IN THE SEVENTIES

Edited by Elsebeth Hurup

AARHUS UNIVERSITY PRESS

Copyright: Aarhus University Press, 1996
Printed by Rosendahls Bogtrykkeri, Esbjerg
ISBN 87 7288 377 4
ISSN 0106 4487

AARHUS UNIVERSITY PRESS
Building 170
University of Aarhus
DK-8000 Aarhus C, Denmark
Fax (+45) 8619 8433

73 Lime Walk
Headington
Oxford OX3 7AD
Fax (+44) 865 750 079

Box 511
Oakville, Conn. 06779
Fax (+1) 203 945 9468

Editorial address:
The Dolphin
Department of English
University of Aarhus
8000 Aarhus C, Denmark
Fax (+45) 8942 2099
E-mail engtc@hum.aau.dk

Published with financial support from the Aarhus University Research Foundation and The
Danish Research Council for the Humanities.

ANSI/NISO
Z39.48-1992

Cover design: Elsebeth Hurup

Contents

Acknowledgements

I would like to thank the contributors, not only for the effort and enthusiasm that they put into writing and revising their manuscripts, but also for their patience when various circumstances prevented us from meeting the original deadline. My thanks also go to Karl-Heinz Westarp for his constant support and for daring to entrust a novice with the task of editing this volume; to Tim Caudery, the general editor of *The Dolphin*, whose equanimity and mildness of manner really should be bottled and made available at every supermarket; and to Bente Kragh who poured coffee and listened and stood by at all times despite her often hectic workday. Finally thanks are due to the University of Aarhus Research Foundation and the Danish Research Council for the Humanities, without whose generous financial assistance the present volume would not have been possible.

Elsebeth Hurup

Preface

The perfect Seventies symbol was the Pet Rock, which just sat there doing nothing.
Howard Junker, *Esquire* (Dec. 1977)

A 1991 article entitled 'The Return of the Seventies' stated that 'The 70s was the last innocent age – before AIDS, crack, Wall Street greed, and yuppies.'[1] Certainly no one in the seventies would have agreed that the decade was characterized by innocence. In fact, a commentary in *Esquire* in 1977 began: 'Up front, for starters ... the Seventies don't exist. There is no cultural pattern these days, nothing ever to be nostalgic about.'[2] The writer continued: 'At least that has been the myth: we agreed not to have the Seventies because we'd been had by the Sixties. Too much hype. Too many dreams abused. Too many killed, too many maimed and too many missing in action. Too much.' Another commentator speculated in 1978: 'Here on the brink of the '80s, it would still be risky to guess what people will mean when they speak of the '70s ten years from now.'[3] Describing the decade as 'elusive, unfocused, a patchwork of dramatics awaiting a drama,' he concluded that it probably was a historical pause that might not 'at the moment seem worth remembering' but he assured the reader that 'it will as soon as disaster drops among us again.' Judging from the above assertion of the seventies as an age of innocence he was right: the eighties brought enough disasters of their own to make the previous decade look like the good old days.

Historian Peter Carroll's title for his book on the decade, *It Seems Like Nothing Happened* (1982), is in perfect accordance with conventional wisdom but is, as he states, intended as irony.[4] Plenty of things happened. The problem of defining the seventies as a decade in its own right, however, stems in part from the fact that, as the cultural concept of decades goes, the chronological seventies may be divided neatly into two halves, of which the first half really belongs to the sixties. As Frank Trippett of *Time* put it, 'Once gone, and often before, every decade migrates into the vocabulary of folklore. There it persists as a sort of handy hieroglyph for conjuring up popular memories of a time' and further: 'As folklore, decades seldom observe the calendar's nice limits.'[5] Thus, the sixties, most often said to have started with the assassination of President Kennedy in November 1963, extended into the seventies, with either Richard Nixon's resignation in 1974 or the fall of Saigon the following year signalling the end of the decade. As the 1980s displayed the singularly good manners of showing up on time with the election of Ronald Reagan, the seventies were left with only five years to form a cultural identity.

One thing is folklore, another is history. In attempting to make sense of an increasingly complex world, the decade is a convenient device for historians and laymen alike to translate processes and events into a number of trends, which in retrospect are deemed characteristic of a certain period. Yet the danger posed by the decades approach is that history becomes a series of discontinuities, a process which obscures important lessons to be learned from history. It is inevitable that for the non-historian the distant past recedes into mythology, but as the twentieth century draws to a close it is startling to observe how rapidly also the not-so-distant past is transformed into a mythic entity – 'a foreign country,' as L.B. Hartley said, where 'they do things differently.'[6] Thus, when George Lucas's *American Graffiti*, one of the first films to address a growing nostalgia for the fifties, was released, the perceived gap between the setting of the film, 1962, and the time of its release, 1973, was so large as to provide a veritable culture shock. This, of course, was one of the main points of the movie; indeed it was the point of a number of the nostalgia movies that proliferated throughout the seventies.

The title of the present volume, *The Lost Decade: America in the Seventies*, refers mainly to the fact that the period has been somewhat ignored, wedged as it is between the two strongly configurated decades of the sixties and the eighties. But it also alludes to a certain feeling of 'lostness,' a national identity crisis which manifested itself in a variety of ways. The essays in this collection address only a small number of the issues and themes that occupied the nation in the seventies, but the guiding principle has been to show the diversity and dynamics of a decade that is popularly associated with a certain blandness and inertia.

Notes

1. Leslie Rubinkowsky, 'The Return of the Seventies,' *Personal Magazine*, 12 May 1991.
2. Howard Junker, 'Who Erased the Seventies?' *Esquire*, Dec. 1977, 152.
3. Frank Trippet, 'The '70s: A Time of Pause,' *Time*, 25 Dec. 1978, 84.
4. Peter N. Carroll, *It Seems Like Nothing Happened: America in the 1970s* (1982; New Brunswick: Rutgers University Press, 1990), ix.
5. Trippett, 84.
6. L.P. Hartley, *The Go-Between* (1953), opening line.

10

'That's What I Like about the South:' Changing Images of the South in the 1970s

*John G. Cawelti**

There is a huge emotional and historical chasm between 1947 ... when I first arrived as a very young man in New York, and the attitude toward the South at that point, and the attitude that prevails now.... there used to be a very distinct tangible hostility in certain areas of New York life toward people who came from the South.

William Styron (1977)[1]

I did not believe ... that the nation would unite indefinitely behind any Southerner. My experience in office had confirmed this reaction. I was not thinking just of the derisive articles about my style, my clothes, my manner, my accent, and my family.... I was also thinking of a more deep-seated and far-reaching attitude – a disdain for the South that seems to be woven into the fabric of Northern experience.... To my mind these attitudes represent an automatic reflex, unconscious or deliberate, on the part of opinion holders of the North and East in the press and television.

Lyndon Johnson[2]

The North; not north but North, outland and circumscribing and not even a geographical place but an emotional idea.... a volitionless, almost helpless capacity and eagerness to believe anything about the South not even provided it be derogatory but merely bizarre enough and strange enough.

William Faulkner[3]

Pat Conroy's *The Prince of Tides* (1986), highly successful as both novel and film, updates the long literary tradition of young Southerners coming to New York and then struggling to go home again.[4] But Conroy's version is different: not only can the Southerner go home again healed of his violent and traumatic past, but he brings to New York a love and warmth that restores his

---

* I'd like to express my gratitude to my friend and colleague Arthur Wrobel, who helped me immensely in revising this essay.

own family and shows a new sense of life's meaning to the psychiatrist who treats him. Converted to cultural allegory, Conroy's novel presents a vision of the South as a culture deeply flawed, even traumatized, by its terrible past, but whose very failures have caused it to develop a deep sense of the basic human values of love and family. This enables Conroy's protagonist, like the culture he represents, to heal his own wounds, and become a kind of exemplar for other American regional cultures which have heretofore not had to face up to tragedy and failure to the same degree as the South.

Certainly part of the success of Conroy's work resulted from its very moving embodiment of this compelling new myth of the South as flawed exemplar. In this paper, we will explore some of the ways in which this new myth of the South came to be established during the 1970s. In the course of this discussion we will look at two very different versions of this myth and at some of its problematic implications in terms of contemporary developments in Southern culture.

Several events and trends of the 1970s reflected the dramatic political and economic changes the American South was undergoing and, in addition, indicated that the imaginative space the South occupied in American culture as a whole was shifting significantly. During the late 1950s and early 1960s, the South had been primarily an arena of conflict over desegregation; the rest of the nation watched in fascinated horror as mobs of white Southerners, supported by the brutal machinery of white-dominated Southern law enforcement, attacked and beat civil rights demonstrators. The national televising of Sheriff Jim Clark, who embodied everyone's idea of a brutal slave overseer, as he set dogs and firehoses on helpless demonstrators in Selma, Alabama in 1965, seared the conscience of the country and reinforced the long-established image of the South as the land of lynching and violence.

However, by the mid-1970s the locus of racial conflict had shifted from the South to Northern and Western cities like Los Angeles, Boston, Detroit, and Chicago. Though the South remained massively segregated in many ways, the blatant patterns of Jim Crow, especially in public accommodations, were rapidly disappearing while Southern African-Americans were making substantial gains in political power with the election of black officials and legislators. To many, the South seemed to have accepted desegregation more wholeheartedly than many areas of the North. In effect, the events of the 1970s made Americans realize that they could no longer assign the responsibility for racial conflict and hatred in America solely to the South.

In addition, once the overt conflict over desegregation had died down in the South, a broader recognition of the degree to which, in the aftermath of World War II, the South was undergoing a dramatic economic transformation brought about a decline in the image of the poverty-stricken Old South. In its place emerged the newly prosperous Sunbelt. Yet, ironically, what emerged in the forefront of the nation's consciousness was less this radical transformation of the Southern economy than a sense of the South as representing fundamental American cultural and moral traditions which were in danger of being destroyed by economic and technological change and which were already largely lost in the urban industrial North.

The election in 1976 of Jimmy Carter was a key instance of the new cultural significance of the South. Carter was the first representative of the Deep South to be elected president in well over 100 years and his election led to a sudden outburst in the national media of what some referred to as 'Southern Fried Chic.' Among the media events of the time was the enormous attention given to the President's brother, Billy, who was presented as a beer-swilling, pot-bellied redneck, a characterization which aroused a great deal of affection and which reflected the transformation of the redneck from foulmouthed racist degenerate to good old boy. Significantly the media rarely noticed that ol' Billy was an extremely acute businessman who proved more than capable of taking over the family enterprise.

Carter's election led to a presidency which failed, however. Perhaps, as we shall see, the new mythology of the South was partly responsible by leading Americans to misperceive Carter's program and then to react against him. However, Carter's election was not a unique national response to political leadership from the South. Earlier, the country had elected Lyndon Johnson before him and was later to turn to Bill Clinton. Both were strongly flavored by their Southern backgrounds, in spite of Johnson's personal conviction that the country would not long trust a Southerner as president. Even George Bush had many Southern connections as a longtime resident of Texas, though his style was not as clearly Southern as that of Johnson, Carter and Clinton. In addition, the traditional association between Southern politicians and the Democratic party remains strong and there does not seem to be any serious Southern Republican presidential contender waiting in the wings despite substantial Republican gains in the region.

But the mid-1970s had several other signs of the South's changing image. On television, reruns of the perennially popular *Beverly Hillbillies* continued to delight audiences with gentle ridicule of the pretensions and suburban fantasies of an affluent urbanized America; this show prospered by transplanting the leading characters of Al Capp's beloved Dogpatch into sophisticated California, the ultimate embodiment of the postwar American dream of suburban happiness. Clearly related to the long tradition of hillbilly-city slicker comedy,[5] the *Beverly Hillbillies* developed a theme that would be central to the new mythology of the South – the idea that in their very simplicity hillbillies possess a down-to-earth honesty and a dedication to family which can solve the problems of rootless alienation and false materialism which afflict modern America.

The Waltons, one of the most popular television series of the mid-seventies, developed this theme more seriously as did the greatest television success of

1977, the mini-series inspired by Alex Haley's 1976 bestseller *Roots*. Though *Roots* was very different in its powerful condemnation of slavery and racism, both programs centered on groups associated with the South and subject to oppression and marginalization, in one case African-Americans, in the other Appalachian mountaineers or 'hillbillies;' these programs represented times that were particularly challenging or difficult for these groups. *Roots* spanned slavery and the time of reconstruction, Jim Crow, and the Ku Klux Klan, while *The Waltons* was set during the Depression era when even whites were desperately impoverished. Both shows also centered around families attempting to maintain their traditions and values in the midst of troubled times and, especially in the case of *Roots*, in the face of terrible threats from the society itself. Yet, in spite of all these difficulties, the two families maintained their integrity, surmounted poverty and oppression and passed on their wisdom, love and deep sense of morality to a younger generation. Significantly, in these series 'family values' were not only associated with a troubled South, but with marginal groups. Later as the 'family values' movement reached its moral and imaginative nadir in the ugly self-righteousness of the 1992 Republican convention, this association was lost and 'family values' had become a hollow slogan of affluent white suburbanites, North and South alike. However, in the 1970s, the new myth of the South gained force from the idea that many important traditional values were best preserved in a 'backward' region among the poor and downtrodden.

This view was congruent with important cultural developments in two other areas: religion and music. The 1970s saw a great surge in the growth of television evangelism, before the Bakker and Swaggart scandals raised questions about the movement. Television evangelism was particularly associated with the South and its long tradition of protestant oratory and revivalism, but the new technology of cable television made possible the nationalizing of a Southern form of revivalism that had earlier been limited to the periodic crusades of a few great preachers like Billy Graham. In the 1970s many protestant ministers expanded into television, gradually building a large and powerful movement that, by the middle 1970s, was beginning to flex its political muscle. Some liked to refer to this movement as the 'silent' or 'moral majority' to suggest that it represented an American consensus of long-standing moral and religious traditions which had lost or not yet found its voice. With its long feeling of subjugation to the nation's other regions the South was particularly susceptible to such appeals, though many other Americans of the 'silent seventies' seemed to share a similar feeling that what was going on in Washington or New York or Los Angeles was profoundly threatening to the traditional American way of life. Ironically, in a country that once traced its religious heritage to the New England Puritans, the flamboyant South became increasingly associated with traditional religion. While John F. Kennedy's Catholicism nearly cost him the 1960 election, Jimmy Carter's 'born-again' Baptist Protestantism probably helped him win the support of numbers of conservative voters who otherwise opposed much of what he stood for.

Just as television evangelism swept the country in the 1970s, so did 'country music' which also had powerful associations with the South. In terms of popular music, the 1960s had been, above all, the era of rock and roll, with New York, Los Angeles, Motown (Detroit) and even London as the musical centers. Wild orgiastic mass concerts culminated at Woodstock, rock and roll's archetypal musical extravaganza. During the 1970s, Nashville became an increasingly important musical center and its Grand Old Opry on television along with other programs of country music and humor like *Hee-Haw* entered the mainstream of entertainment.

Once scorned by many non-Southerners as 'hillbilly music' country music had gradually increased in popularity since its beginnings as modern popular music in the 1930s, but its surging popularity in the late 1960s and early 1970s was unprecedented. By the mid-1970s, country music had become a major form of national popular music and was well on the way to eclipsing jazz and even rock and roll in mass popularity. The appearance in 1975 of one of Robert Altman's most successful movies, *Nashville*, reflected the national interest in country music when several of the movie's non-Southern stars composed and performed their own country style songs.[6]

Country music with its 'down-home' Southern flavor suggested shifting cultural constellations and themes. It appealed to a broader range of Americans not only geographically but across age groups. Popular music since the 1920s had been largely a music for young people – the two major musical revolutions of jazz-swing and rock and roll had made generational conflict a major aspect of their cultural rhetoric. But country music pleased older Americans because of its relative simplicity and harmoniousness compared to rock and roll's dissonance and orgiastic quality. Country music also appealed to long-standing traditions rather than to change and novelty: its style and instrumentation remained highly traditional even when its musicians increasingly adapted electronic amplification and other new instrumental techniques. The way performers dressed and even the styles of dancing it fostered had strong traditional overtones. No matter how encrusted with rhinestones, the costumes were clearly derived from traditional Western or Southern models. The dominant themes of the music were different too. Where rock and roll dealt mainly with passion, sex, drugs, alienation, and the faults of American culture, country music's lyrics concerned the failure of family, touching often on cheating, adultery, divorce, and the failure of love. In addition, country music had a strong religious element not only in itself but in the closely associated tradition of gospel music, which also grew out of Southern black and white religious traditions.

Significantly, the single most popular musician of the sixties and seventies, Elvis Presley, bridged the traditions of country music and the new rock and roll, the latter strongly shaped by African-American popular music. Until his death in 1977 at his mansion in Memphis, Tennessee, Elvis retained his connection with the South in spite of the fact that the locus of his performance was in the new national media centers of Hollywood and Las Vegas. Elvis' amazing success represented a new kind of Southern incursion into the national mainstream, and his early death and the cult of his memory came to rival that of major national figures like John F. Kennedy. When the world was startled in mid-1994 by the announcement of the marriage of Elvis' daughter to Michael Jackson, the most popular African-American singer in history, there seemed an eerie appropriateness to this union of black and white American bloodlines, as if the musical synthesis of the South and the North, black and white, which had originally given Elvis his power, was now being carried still further.

Just as Southern-flavored country music achieved increased national cultural prominence in the 1970s through its association with values of family, tradition, and simplicity, Southern cooking gained increased national and then international visibility through the spread of Kentucky Fried Chicken and the popular advertising symbol of the industry's founding father, Col. Harlan Sanders. Cultural associations between the South and a certain kind of hearty, 'finger-licking' down-home food go way back into the past as in the case of the Southern-connected brand names and advertising rhetoric used to sell Aunt Jemima pancakes and Log Cabin Syrup. But just as country music's national popularity depended upon new recording and performance techniques and on television, the globalization of Southern fried chicken reflected the development of the fast food industry and its elaborate new technologies of organization, distribution, and merchandizing.

In such cases, the aura of tradition cultivated by the South's mythologists tends to deconstruct itself in layers of irony. Kentucky Fried's famous image of the Colonel derived from the plantation patriarch and the confederate warrior, yet in the course of the later 1960s when KFC was rapidly expanding into both national and international markets the Colonel's image was reprocessed into a benevolent symbol of traditional wisdom and goodness, its connection to Jim Crow and white supremacy surviving, if at all, only in the color of his beard and clothing. Though fried chicken may have originated in the South,[7] it had become widespread throughout rural America and had certainly shed any distinctly Southern aura. What made KFC's chicken different and 'finger-lickin' good' was the Colonel's invention of a new processing technology using a pressurized cooker to create an especially tender version of the traditional fried chicken. To compound the ambiguities, not only is fast food the very antithesis of 'home cooking' but the mass production of chickens has become one of the important new trends in Southern agribusiness and a major force in the transformation of the Southern rural economy. Nonetheless, Kentucky Fried Chicken and the Colonel helped to reinforce the new image of the South as the last bastion of family, heritage, and rural values in a country feeling increasingly separated from its 'roots.'

Myth One: The South as Last Stronghold of Traditional American Values

Jimmy Carter's election to the presidency, the new media images of the Southern family, black and white, the rise of television evangelism and country music, and the spread of Kentucky Fried Chicken and other traditional Southern 'down-home' foods suggest the extent to which the myth of the South had undergone a process of revitalization and transformation. These assorted images represented the emergence of a new mythology of the South as traditional exemplar for the rest of the country. However, this new mythology developed in two related, but ultimately quite different directions one of which is rapidly being undercut by recent cultural trends, while the other may have more permanent impact at least in literary and intellectual circles. The South is now often seen on the popular level as the last bastion of traditional Americanism, but the more complex and interesting version of the South as exemplar portrays Southern history as carrying a tragic and ironic burden.

The idea that 'people at large see in [the South] the reflection of that status quo for which they long' and that the Southern 'gospel of individual salvation ... appeals to persons throughout the land who struggle with the torment of littleness, trying to gain some sense of instant worth and welcome from an indifferent civilization that is too complex for their coping,'[8] expresses the first and most popular version of the new Southern mythos.

Jimmy Carter successfully projected this image in his mid-1970s campaign for the presidency, while the media, fascinated with things Southern, reinforced it after his election. The first major component of the new myth, Carter's association with farming, made him a representative of rural America and of its tradition of honesty, simplicity, family, and local heritage. Even though in the 1970s fewer and fewer people actually lived on farms, Americans still deeply believed in the moral superiority of farm life. The myth of rural life was associated with traditional patterns of life, with a particular locality, and with a concern for family and its preservation, values which the mobility, rapid changes, and high divorce rate of modern American society seemed to be rapidly eroding. Jimmy Carter was, as it happened, a very committed family man whose devotion to his remarkable mother and highly intelligent wife was notable. In addition, his loyalty was severely tested when his brother Billy received a good deal of criticism. Interestingly, Bill Clinton showed a similar loyalty years later when he encountered criticism for his eccentric mother, his powerfully intelligent wife, and his wayward brother.[9]

Locality was very important in the Carter campaign. For a time the formerly obscure Plains, Georgia, became famous as the Carter family homestead. The emphasis on Plains affirmed the theme of dedication to particular places, which had long been evoked as a particular characteristic of Southern culture. Family loyalty and local heritage, honesty and rural simplicity, were themes further reinforced by Carter's well-known religious conversion and his apparently sincere belief in the evangelism associated with Southern protestantism. The South as the remaining bastion of 'old time religion' in America was another important element in the newly positive view of the South which many Americans came to hold in the 1970s. This can be contrasted with the ridicule of Southern fundamentalism in the 1920s as exemplified in the media circus which Northern and Eastern reporters made of the Dayton, Tennessee 'Monkey Trial' of 1925. With the upsurge of fundamentalism and of television evangelism in the 1960s and 1970s, the new myth of the South as the last bastion of American traditions gained another important mythic dimension.

The Carter presidency also linked itself to another important American tradition which at first glance seems strangely at odds with rural traditions, the heritage of New Deal liberalism and social reform. Postwar prosperity had led to a series of Republican victories and an increasing criticism of New Deal liberalism and reform. On the other hand, people in rural America well understood how much they had benefitted from New Deal agricultural supports, rural electrification, and regional development projects like TVA. Thus, while certain New Deal programs such as the support of labor unions, industrial regulation, deficit spending, and high taxes remained anathema, there was much about the New Deal which nobody wanted to change. In addition, under Franklin D. Roosevelt America had waged its greatest war in history to emerge as a dominant global power.

Carter himself actually wanted to shift the emphasis of American policy and expenditure from its increasingly futile attempts to maintain global domination to a new domestic agenda of reform, and for a time it seemed as if the national revulsion against Vietnam would support such a program. However, rather than acknowledging the many signs that American moral and political omnipotence was seriously eroding, Americans, and particularly Southerners, resisted this knowledge. The Iranian hostage crisis was a crucial test for Jimmy Carter. His apparent weakness and indecision in foreign affairs, not his image as Southerner, brought Carter down and led to the election of Ronald Reagan who promised to reinvigorate American moral traditions and restore America's threatened position of global leadership in the Cold War.

Reagan and his image makers recognized the great American yearning for anything resembling tradition and they successfully cobbled together an odd but temporarily effective melange of Western and Southern mythical traditions

18

that drew extensively on the way these traditions had been translated into Hollywood icons like John Wayne. Reagan's election and the image his administration projected gradually undercut the South's special claim to be the last bastion of American tradition.

In addition, as the 1980s and the 1990s continued the process which John Egerton refers to as 'the Americanization of Dixie,' it became harder to credit the myth that the South represented the values of family, stability, locality, and heritage any more than the rest of the country. In fact, this myth seemed increasingly difficult to sustain not only in the present, but in the past, for revisionist historians investigating the Old South have increasingly cast doubt on the region's distinctiveness. The 1980s ended with a sunbelt South that had as low a proportion of farmers and as many divorces as any other area of the country, while in the 1990s the new concern for domestic violence and abuse revealed that the Southern family shared traditions of spouse and child abuse that deeply challenge its claim to represent stability, security, and heritage in family life. Though the advocates of religious fundamentalism are becoming increasingly shriller and more authoritarian in their attempts to enforce orthodoxy of belief and behavior,[10] revelations of corruption and hypocrisy continue to cut into the credibility of the religious establishment. Even Kentucky Fried Chicken seems to have lost much of its Southern connection as it has become a global food-chain owned by a multi-national corporation. At the present time the archetypal KFC franchise of television ads is located in an anywhere Midwestern town and managed by an African-American. In short, whatever residues of its own traditions the South may retain as it enters the next century, its mythical status as the last bastion of traditional values in a rapidly changing America seems doomed to deconstruction.

Myth Two: Southern History as Tragedy

However, another version of the new myth of the South, though mainly influential among literary and intellectual elites, will probably prove to be more important to future redefinitions of the significance of the South in American culture. This myth, that of the South as tragic exemplar, had one of its earliest major expressions in the 1920s and 1930s through the work of a unique group of Southern intellectuals, the so-called Vanderbilt Fugitive-Agrarians. This group included a number of individuals who would later be defined as leading writers of the 'Southern Renaissance,' most notably John Crowe Ransom, Allen Tate, Robert Penn Warren, Andrew Lytle, and Donald Davidson. In 1930, this group formed the nucleus of the Southern 'agrarian' manifesto *I'll Take My Stand,* which was an important transition between older Southern ideologies such as that of the idyllic plantation and a newer conception of the South as representing a more complex tradition.

19

This anthology certainly did not keep the South from going the way of the rest of the country toward the erosion of a rural culture. Though at the time of the publication of *I'll Take My Stand* 45% of Southerners still lived on farms, by 1970 that had dropped to a mere 5%. However, more than their commitment to any particular socio-economic system, the Fugitive-Agrarians shared a view of the South, its history, and its relationship to American culture which became widely influential as members of the group fanned out across the country to become nationally known writers, critics and teachers in such non-Southern institutions as Yale, Minnesota and Kenyon College. Their vision contributed significantly to the developing conception of the South as tragic exemplar and created an important thematic linkage between this new myth of Southern culture and some of the central ideas of literary and artistic modernism.

Allen Tate once summed up the idea of the South shared by his Fugitive-Agrarian colleagues as:

> a sort of unity of feeling, of which we were not then very much aware, which came out of – to give it a big name – a common historical myth.... The South afflicted with the curse of slavery – a curse like that of Original Sin, for which no single person is responsible – has to be destroyed, the good along with the evil. The old order has a great deal of good, one of the 'goods' being a result of the evil; for slavery itself entailed a certain moral responsibility ... This old order in which the good could not be salvaged from the bad, was replaced by a new order which is in many ways worse than the old.[11]

The Agrarians believed that the old order was deeply flawed but that it still offered a vision of coherence and order largely lost to modern society. In their concern for the loss of this vision they resembled many of the leading American and European modernist writers and intellectuals, such as Yeats, Eliot, Pound, Mann, and Proust. A similar sense of things was reflected on a less sophisticated level in uncertainty felt by many people bewildered by the manifold social, technological and cultural changes of the twentieth century. This congruity between the new myth of the South and some of the central cultural themes of modernism doubtless paved the way for the spread of the new myth in the 60s and 70s.

The Southern writers and critics shared with these powerful literary voices, and particularly with Eliot, a critique of modern society and a view of the significance of literature which under the rubric of the 'new criticism,' would spread from modernist poetry, fiction and criticism to college and even high school classrooms around the country, influencing the way literature was taught for decades after World War II. A disproportionate number of the leading American 'new critics' were Southerners and the writers and students influenced by their ideas were some of the most important writers and intellectuals of the 1970s.

Robert Wooster Stallman summarized the cultural critique of the Fugitive-Agrarians as based on modern society's *'loss of a tradition, the loss of a culture, the loss of a fixed convention, the loss of a world-order'* (*A Southern Vanguard* [28]) (Italics Stallman). Lamenting the loss of a coherent society, the modernist writers and the new critics turned to the work of art, treating it as the last remaining expression of a unifying myth which had once ordered society. Poets and novelists developed new structural techniques such as the use of mythical archetypes and the deployment of layers of historical and literary allusions which would enable poems and novels like Eliot's *The Waste Land*, Joyce's *Ulysses* and *Finnegan's Wake*, Pound's *Cantos*, and Faulkner's *Absalom, Absalom!* to create richly ironic formal patterns and universalizing myths transcending the realistic and naturalistic representations of society characteristic of the later nineteenth century literature. The 'new critics' some of whom like Eliot, Tate, and Warren also created influential works of poetry and fiction, developed new modes of analysis and interpretation to explain the difficult coherence of the literary work. One of the most important aspect of the 'new critical' project became that of replacing discussion of the literary work as a representation of society or of the writer's own feelings with an image of the work as a complex order of its own.

The Fugitive-Agrarian appeal to a lost tradition of unified culture both reflected and reinforced the sense of loss and belatedness associated with the modernist critique of materialistic industrial culture. Certainly part of its power derived from the fact that its image of the earlier South provided a dramatic historical analogue to the modernist critique. The Fugitive-Agrarian attack on industrialization and the erosion of rural life fostered by the New South movement trenchantly exposed the 'lost cause' rhetoric which New South apologists had used to establish a mythical lineage between Southern industrialists and an idealized antebellum South.[12] The New South leaders had tried to justify the dislocations caused by their attempts to industrialize a traditional agricultural economy (and the labor exploitation and racism which went along with it) by throwing the glorious mantle of the antebellum Southern culture around their shoulders. However, the Fugitive-Agrarians clearly recognized that the modernization of the South was actually eroding the key elements they associated with Southern tradition, its emphasis on land, family, locality, and tradition. Their work and that of most of the other major figures of the Southern Renaissance of the late 1920s and 1930s, emphasized the fundamental conflict between an increasingly modernized, materialistic South and the Southern tradition, a conflict which resulted in a profound sense of loss and dislocation. Faulkner brilliantly expressed this division in the archetypal conflict between his Compson brothers: Quentin is a sensitive romantic who, a generation later, might have enlisted in the Fugitive-Agrarians. Coming to maturity in 1910 his desperate quest for honor, coherence and tradition can only lead him to suicide by drowning – as if he finally allows himself to be submerged in the forces which are destroying him; his brother Jason, an ardent exponent of New South commercialism survives the destruction of his family, only to carry on a futile and impotent existence.

This Fugitive-Agrarian version of the new myth remained close to the ideology of the Lost Cause in its portrayal of the antebellum South as a kind of agrarian paradise, lost not so much through its own faults as through the overwhelming power of the materialistic North. Though they, too, celebrated the Lost Cause and the gallantry of a hopelessly outnumbered and outgunned South in its principled last stand against Northern invasion, the Fugitive-Agrarians were decidedly more ambiguous about the antebellum South, slavery, and the Confederacy, an ambiguity reflected in some of the group's major literary works, like Tate's own despairing 'Ode to the Confederate Dead' and his horrified portrayal of lynching in 'The Swimmers' or in Warren's early novel *Band of Angels*. Indeed, as the writers of the Southern Renaissance became more of a presence on the national scene in the 1950s and 1960s, many of them became even more critical of the South's traditional racist attitudes.[13]

However, the impact of one major writer, William Faulkner, who was only distantly connected to the Fugitive-Agrarians, was largely instrumental in the transformation of the myth of the South on the national level. Though his major work was done largely between 1928 and 1942, Faulkner remained relatively little known, his work largely out of print, until the early 1950s when the success of the Viking Portable Faulkner, the 1949 Nobel Prize, and the large audience which saw the film version of his *Intruder in the Dust* began Faulkner's rise to the literary preeminence which he had attained by the 1970s.[14] By the mid-1970s, Faulkner had eclipsed his nearest rivals, Ernest Hemingway and F. Scott Fitzgerald, as the leading American novelist of the twentieth century.

Faulkner viewed the South in a darker and more tragic way than most of the Fugitive-Agrarians had conceived it.[15] His great *Absalom, Absalom!* (1936) was published in the same year as Margaret Mitchell's nostalgic romanticization of 'Tara' and 'Twelveoaks,' but it fell largely on deaf ears while *Gone With the Wind* became one of the most popular novels and films of all time. Only much later did the reading public recognize the importance of Faulkner's revelation of the human tragedy implicit in the plantation society and the racial exploitation and inhumanity which it entailed. Faulkner also contributed significantly to the demythologizing of the Lost Cause. The absurdity of the mystique of military gallantry and honor had been a central theme from his first novel *Soldier's Pay* (1926). Faulkner's critical treatment of the related themes of Southern honor and racism was particularly trenchant because he had such a deep understanding of the psychological dynamics of these cultural myths and of the powerful hold that they had on many Southerners. Yet, at the same time he felt increasingly that the double legacy of the Lost Cause and of racism was a terrible curse and burden which Southern society had to bear and, if it was to survive, somehow to expiate. In his two major works of the 1940s, *Go Down, Moses* (1942) and *Intruder in the Dust* (1948), Faulkner struggled inconclusively to work out a resolution of white guilt and racial conflict in the Southern past and present. In *Go Down, Moses*, his central character Ike McCaslin descends from an antebellum plantation founder who had created, as Faulkner's own great-grandfather may have done, a black as well as a white family line. The burden of this inheritance comes home when Ike discovers in family ledgers that the black (McCaslin)-Beauchamp line is a result not only of miscegenation but of incest, carrying with it the guilt of sexual exploitation of one's own children as well as of African-American slave women. In fact, many of Faulkner's most powerful treatments of racism involve the threat or actuality of incest, and reverberate with the terrible sexual obsessions and the inextricable hate-love relationship that were part of the system of Southern racism at its peak in the late nineteenth and early twentieth centuries.

Ike McCaslin tries to free himself from this burden of guilt by giving up his inheritance, an admirable gesture in some ways, though Faulkner portrays Ike's renunciation as ultimately futile. The system of exploitation and inhumanity goes on, and even as an old man Ike McCaslin remains haunted by the McCaslin family's black-white genealogy when he encounters a young woman descended from the black (McCaslin)-Beauchamp line who has loved and had a child with a descendent of the inheriting white (McCaslin)-Edmonds line. There is deep pathos in the eighty-year-old Ike's unsuccessful attempt to overcome his horror of miscegenation and to acknowledge his kinship to the new child. Ike demonstrates a moral strength and understanding that, in another society, might have made him a great patriarch; under the circumstances, however, he is trapped by the tragic burden of the Southern heritage and must end his life, childless, with a sense of impotence and despair.

Intruder in the Dust is set in 1940, which makes it almost contemporaneous with its telling. In writing the novel Faulkner tried to carry the story of the McCaslin family down to the present time and to imagine a resolution of the Southern racial crisis resulting from the changed attitude of a younger generation who, he hoped, would be less prejudiced toward blacks yet still be able to affirm the central values of the Southern heritage. This hope is enacted in the character of sixteen-year-old Chick Mallison who, four years earlier, had reluctantly assumed a moral obligation to the black patriarch Lucas Beauchamp, one of the central characters in *Go Down, Moses*. Though black, Lucas is ironically the last direct descendent of the founder of the McCaslin family and plantation. As the novel opens, Lucas is believed by everyone, including Chick, to have murdered a white man in cold blood, but Chick's sense of obligation to Lucas makes him participate in the terrifying exhumation of the murdered man and the establishing of Lucas' innocence. In the course of the

23

novel, Chick's uncle, Gavin Stevens, a recurrent Faulkner persona representing upper-middle-class Southern liberalism, becomes a spokesman, at unfortunate lengths according to many readers, of the view that the South's history obligates it to resolve its own racial problems, because this is the only way the terrible cultural split between black and white can be resolved. This was a position that Faulkner himself seemingly espoused for a time at the height of the Civil Rights-Desegregation crisis of the 1950s.[16]

However, Gavin Stevens' very insistence on the South's ability to deal with its own problems has a hollow ring, and Faulkner's horrifying portrayal of the community's fascinated anticipation of a lynching as the foredestined and inescapable outcome of the murder of a white by a black man rings more powerfully and persuasively than either the actual resolution of the story in Lucas' almost comic exoneration or the somewhat hysterically optimistic conclusions Gavin Stevens draws from it. Like many of Faulkner's later books, *Intruder in the Dust* ends on a less tragic note than his earlier masterpieces, but the view of the Southern heritage as profoundly tragic and perhaps ultimately inescapable, remains a dominant note. Indeed, the two figures who stand out most prominently and memorably from the two family sagas which were in many ways the culmination of Faulkner's career, that of the McCaslin-Edmonds-Beauchamps and that of the Snopes's, are the defiantly independent black, Lucas Beauchamp and the betrayed poor white, Mink Snopes.[17] These two characters jointly symbolize the central dilemmas of Southern history, the related tragedies of white inhumanity to African-Americans, and of the impoverishment of poor whites, along with the destruction of the land. Thus, in Faulkner, the Fugitive-Agrarian pastoral myth of the agrarian paradise lost through a combination of original sin and the intrusion of the materialistic forces of modernism became a darker and more complex vision of a guilt-ridden South deeply implicated in its own destruction.

A vision of the South remarkably similar to Faulkner's was brilliantly articulated in terms of historical discourse by C. Vann Woodward, the most influential Southern historian of his generation; Woodward's vision of 'The Irony of Southern History' was in its way as influential in shaping the development of American history writing in the 1960s and 1970s as Frederick Jackson Turner's 'The Significance of the Frontier in American History' was to an earlier period. Woodward first presented his concept of the real message of the Southern heritage in a series of essays and addresses in the 1950s and then as a collection of essays, *The Burden of Southern History*, in 1960; it was revised in 1968 and reprinted again in 1991, testimony to the lasting power of this treatment of the Southern tradition.[18]

Woodward argued that the South had promulgated a series of myths to conceal the tragic and ironic truth of its own history from itself and from the victorious North. However, he felt that these myths had increasingly lost their believability. The ideologies of Cavalier origin, of the benevolent plantation, the Lost Cause, and finally, the self-justifying saga of Reconstruction and White Supremacy with its ignorant blacks and rapacious carpetbaggers and scalawags had become 'faded historical myths' which were, he averred, 'weak material for buttressing Southern defenses, for time has dealt as roughly with them as with agrarianism and racism' (13).

Woodward went on to express the hope that the deep Southern consciousness of history, which he believed was an important part of the Southern cultural tradition, would eventually make Southerners increasingly aware of the reality of that history which 'includes large components of frustration, failure, and defeat. It includes not only an overwhelming miliary defeat but long decades of defeat in the provinces of economic, social, and political life. Such a heritage affords the Southern people no basis for the delusion that there is nothing whatever that is beyond their power to accomplish' (19). Woodward ventured to hope that this legacy of tragedy and defeat might make the Southern heritage an important and even redemptive counterpart to the national legend of American innocence and the themes of success and progress and invincibility which had led Americans to become morally complacent and to feel dangerously superior to the rest of the world. Americans, Woodward felt, badly needed the lessons of irony, of failure, and of a healthy sense of limitation that the Southern past had to offer, for 'National experience and the myths [of success and victory, innocence and virtue] based on it have isolated Americans to the degree that they qualify in foreign eyes as the 'Peculiar People' of modern times, quite as much as Southerners qualified for that dubious distinction in the last century. It is a dangerous isolation. If there were ever a time when Americans might profit from the un-American heritage of the South, it would seem to be the present' (230).

Woodward himself notes wryly that the South in more recent years has seemed to become even more American than the rest of the country in its unthinking patriotic fervor and moral complacency. He is surely correct that in many ways the contemporary South has increasingly put the heritage of defeat, guilt, and limitation behind it in its pursuit of sunbelt prosperity.[19] Though the 'burden' of Southern history does not seem to weigh very heavily on the shoulders of most contemporary Southerners, Woodward's ironic vision and Faulkner's tragic myth of Southern history were highly influential among American writers, scholars, and other intellectuals in the 1970s and continue to be central themes in writing about the South. Indeed, this ironic and tragic view has become increasingly influential in the treatment of American history in general, particularly in the post-Vietnam era. It was, for example, the dominant note of Ken Burns' television series on the Civil War which premiered in 1990. In that series, the Southern novelist and historian Shelby Foote, whose own history of the Civil War was heavily influenced by the Faulknerian vision, became to a considerable extent the voice of the series, articulating this theme of the war as a great historical tragedy in which both

North and South were transformed in ways that went far beyond their original purposes or wishes.[20] It might even be said that Foote helped engineer, at last, a sort of Southern victory in that great American conflict.

Of course, this view of American history was not exactly a new vision. Its emphasis on the tragic ironies of Southern history and their revelation of human limitation and failure seem remarkably close to that final understanding of the Civil War as a national tragedy which Abraham Lincoln expressed so movingly in his second inaugural address. Lincoln's vision reflected his Southern origins and his long residence in the North as well as the burden of being responsible for the nation in its most dangerous hour. It's appropriate that some of his central themes would reemerge in Southern writers and historians and be widely influential among Northern intellectuals at another moment of national crisis, the height of anti-Vietnam agitation and an upsurge in urban racial violence which marked the late 1960s and early 1970s. The deep uncertainty of that time began with the anti-Vietnam War demonstrations of the mid-1960s and the Watts riots of 1965, intensified through the 1967 march on the Pentagon and the 1968 assassinations of Martin Luther King and Robert Kennedy, and culminated in the uneasy and ambiguous Vietnam cease-fire, the Watergate scandals, and the resignation of President Nixon in 1973. These events decisively undercut the image of American omnipotence abroad and of the basic integrity and stability of the national government, and left Americans anxious about the future to a degree they had not been since the Great Depression of the 1930s.

The unacknowledged defeats and regular government lies of the Vietnam War and the fear of domestic violence engendered by racial conflict and African-American despair in the aftermath of the Civil Rights movement made the promise of America seem increasingly questionable. In response, thoughtful Americans became more fascinated by the one great tragic failure of earlier American history, that of the South; they were drawn to the new myth of the South so powerfully expressed by our greatest twentieth century novelist and one of our most influential historians, both of whom had portrayed the Southern experience of evil, limitation, and tragedy as an important corrective to the national tendency to see American history as a panorama of righteous accomplishment, inevitable progress, and international redemption.

Southern Literature, African Americans and the Holocaust

Faulkner, Woodward, and the other Southern writers who shared their vision were an important part of a larger postwar cultural recognition which expressed in many ways a more qualified sense of the meaning and promise of America. During these years, Southern writers rose to national preeminence, reaching a peak in the late 1960s and early 1970s with the canonization of

Faulkner and the arrival on the scene of a whole new generation of Southern voices. At the very same time, two other groups of American writers moved from the margins of American culture to an unprecedented centrality. The literary impact of Jewish-American and African-American writers was, like that of Southern writers, significantly disproportionate to their representation in the population as a whole. This highly significant cultural change first became apparent in the 1950s with the publication of two remarkable and interestingly similar novels, Ralph Ellison's *Invisible Man* (1952) and Saul Bellow's *The Adventures of Augie March* (1953). These influential *Bildungsromanen* portrayed the encounter of African-American and Jewish-American protagonists with the racism and anti-semitism of white America; narrated in a complex, ironic and highly allusive style, these novels were very different from the more politically-oriented social criticism of earlier black and Jewish writers like Richard Wright and Michael Gold.[21]

The success of these novelists helped create an audience for a galaxy of Jewish- and African-American writers, including Bernard Malamud, Philip Roth, Toni Morrison, Ernest J. Gaines, Alex Haley, Alice Walker, Ishmael Reed, John Edgar Wideman, and Leon Forrest. These writers shared many concerns and themes with Southern writers like William Styron, Walker Percy, James Dickey and Robert Penn Warren. Together, they dominated the mainstream of American literature during the 1970s and 1980s.[22]

Culture, like politics, makes strange bedfellows, and at first glance it seems hard to believe that Southern writers and African-Americans, to say nothing of Jewish-American writers, would have very much in common. Indeed, there is enormous diversity and difference in vision both between and within these groups. However, during the late 1960s and 1970s these writers articulated a vision of America and of human life in general which acknowledged the sense of limitation, failure and irony that characterized the period more powerfully than any other American novelists. Significantly all of these writers represented regional and ethnic subcultures which had historical traditions dominated by defeat, suffering and exploitation by more powerful cultures, and had historically occupied a minority or marginal position in American culture. Having long confronted the tragic limitations of life, these cultures responded by developing a strong sense of humor and satire, a sort of gallows humor in the face of apocalypse. In an age which responded particularly to what became known as 'black' humor or the 'drama of the absurd,' these writers occupied the center. Moreover, these subcultures, each with strong religious traditions and a particular attachment to family and religious community, were acutely aware of the erosion of these traditions.

Ralph Ellison ended *Invisible Man* with his protagonist wondering whether his own difficulty in discovering the truth either of himself or of America was not solely a problem for African-Americans. 'Who knows but that on the lower frequencies, I speak for you,' he had his protagonist narrator conclude

27

in one of the most often quoted passages from the fiction of the time. Saul Bellow concluded his *Augie March* in a similar way with Augie suggesting that America needed a different kind of Columbus to rediscover it. In the historical and cultural context of the 1970s, when Americans were traumatized by the Vietnam War, increasing urban violence, an epidemic of drugs, the anarchic rebellions of a younger generation, and the increasing decline of traditional ideas of the family, Southern, Jewish-American and African-American writers regenerated the myth of America. For them America became both a symbol of the ironic failure of human dreams and an arena for exploring the conditions of guilt, responsibility, survival and, ultimately, self-affirmation. By representing the tragedies of Southern, African-American and Jewish history in literature, the major writers of the 1960s and 1970s created an important group of American literary fictions which sought a new under-standing of America not as the culmination or redemption of history but as a country which had survived nearly global catastrophe to gain another chance. In this context questions of guilt, responsibility and acknowledgement became critical, and the role of cultural traditions, which had themselves survived the greatest of evils, became crucial.

Two important novelists, who made major contributions to American literature during the 1970s, illustrate how important the relationship between Southern, African-American and Jewish themes became for the creative life of the decade. Virginia-born William Styron emerged from the tradition of the Southern Renaissance particularly as it was embodied in William Faulkner and Robert Penn Warren. Toni Morrison, an African-American from Ohio, was strongly influenced by Faulkner (she wrote a master's thesis on Faulkner and Virginia Woolf) but also incorporated an African-American fictional tradition which included the Harlem Renaissance, the naturalistic fiction of Richard Wright and the postwar novels of Ralph Ellison and James Baldwin. The increasingly visible heritage of fiction and poetry by African-American women such as Zora Neale Hurston, Margaret Walker and Gwendolyn Brooks was also an important presence in Morrison's work. However, the careers of both Styron and Morrison underwent a major transition when they fictionally interrogated the 'burden' of Southern history by immersing themselves in the exploration of African-American slavery.

After writing through the influence of the Faulkner of *The Sound and the Fury* in his first novel *Lie Down in Darkness* (1951) and exploring divergent directions in his two novels of the early 1960s, Styron found his own voice and a new level of literary accomplishment in his highly controversial *The Confessions of Nat Turner* (1967), one of the first and still one of the few attempts by a white writer to create a sustained black narrative persona. This creation was bitterly assailed by African-American critics and their sympathizers in one of the major literary controversies of the late 1960s and early 1970s. Styron was sufficiently touched by the furor that he not only responded to his critics through essays and interviews, but went on to explore some of the deeper motives underlying his creation of Nat Turner in his major novel of the 1970s, *Sophie's Choice* (1979). In this novel, which remains his most powerful creation, Styron drew on a tragic story of the Holocaust and its survivors to meditate on the sense of historical guilt and tragedy which had led him to the story of Nat Turner.

Racism and its devastating impact on its victims had been central themes of Morrison's fiction from the beginning, but in her first two novels the settings were Northern and showed less concern for either the historical context or for the dramatic representation of racial conflict. Instead, racism manifested itself in these novels as an aspect of the inner consciousness of the characters, who struggled with a diminished sense of self and a powerful impetus toward self-denial. Morrison embarked on a major new direction in her third novel, *Song of Solomon* (1977). In this story, her middle-class black protagonist is driven to search for a way out of the impasse of his life by acknowledging and recovering his family past. As he journeys geographically and imaginatively into the South and the history of slavery, he discovers that his family history of oppression and suffering offers him not a burden of guilt, but a vision of transcendence.

Like many Southern intellectuals and writers born in the first half of the twentieth century, William Styron became part of the migration of gifted Southerners to the North.[23] Born and raised in Virginia and educated at Duke University, Styron moved to New York City after his service in World War II and eventually settled in exurban Connecticut. But it was as a schoolboy in the Tidewater South that Styron first encountered the story of Nat Turner's 1831 rebellion. By the time he had decided to become a writer he had already determined that he would someday try to write that story.[24]

When he turned his full attention to the recreation of Nat Turner in the early 1960s several factors shaped that process. We have already mentioned Styron's deep indebtedness to Faulkner in his early novels for many aspects of form and theme. Faulkner's own portrayal of slavery as the terrible burden of Southern history was reflected in Styron's vision of Nat Turner. He also probably drew on certain of Faulkner's key African-American characters, perhaps most importantly the Joe Christmas of *Light in August*, whose terrible ambiguities about whiteness and blackness are reflected in Styron's portrayal of Nat Turner's interior struggle.

Stanley Elkins' 1963 book on slavery, which was one of several revisionist studies attacking the more sympathetic interpretation of slavery characteristic of the work of U.B. Philips and other Southern historians, also triggered Styron's work. The earlier twentieth century apologists for slavery had amassed materials purporting to show the responsibility and benevolence of most slave owners. Very moved by the revisionist portrayals of the great inhumanity and degradation implicit in the institution of slavery, Styron drew on the new myth of the South as tragic exemplar to articulate his sense of horror. Indeed, it reveals much about the mood of this period that a revised edition of C. Vann Woodward's *The Burden of Southern History* was published within a year of *The Confessions of Nat Turner*.[25]

Styron realized that his attempt to create a black persona might be rejected by African-Americans, but he felt the deep obligation to make the attempt in any case:

> The Negro may feel that it is too late to be known, and that the desire to know him reeks of outrageous condescension. But to break down the old law, to come to *know* the Negro, has become the moral imperative of every white Southerner. (*This Quiet Dust* 14)

Styron's horror at the postwar revelations of the Holocaust also shaped his depiction of Nat Turner. To his mind, the burden of America's historical guilt for the institution of slavery and its unresolved consequences in the continued oppression of blacks parallelled European civilization's responsibility for anti-Semitism and other ethnic hatreds which had made the Holocaust possible.

Finally, the most immediate influence on Styron's work in the mid-1960s was the conflict raging in America about school desegregation, integration of public accommodations, voting rights and greater economic equality for African-Americans. The flame of the Civil Rights movement was a light by which Styron was challenged to read the Nat Turner rebellion. As he remarked later 'when I began to think about writing that novel back in the 1940s when I was a kid, I had no inkling of how it would play out in terms of the events of 1967 and 1968 when the whole country was inflamed.'[26] More than anything else the seeming discrepancy between Styron's tormented Nat Turner and the new image of militant, politically conscious and unwavering black leadership so important to the Civil Rights movement led to much of the controversy about *The Confessions of Nat Turner*.

There is a very complex relationship between *The Confessions of Nat Turner* (1967) and *Sophie's Choice* (1979). The latter, though written later, is actually the fictional account of how a young Southerner's involvement in the tragic fate of a survivor of Auschwitz inspired him to write a novel about Nat Turner.[27] *The Confessions* became an immediate best-seller and was, at first, very positively reviewed by distinguished critics and scholars, both white and black, such as Alfred Kazin and John Hope Franklin. Soon after its initial success, however, the novel was bitterly attacked by younger African-American writers and scholars abetted by the redoubtable American Marxist theorist Herbert Aptheker who had carried out one of the few substantial studies of slave revolts up to that time.[28] African-American critics dismissed Styron's Nat Turner as little more than a Southern white intellectual's racist projection; they wanted to see Nat Turner as a political leader rather than a tormented prophet, as a happily married black man hating all whites rather than one who ambiguously idealized white women, and as a man of action rather than an anguished intellectual. Styron responded that nobody, black or white, had paid much attention to Nat Turner until his novelistic recreation and that the historical record was so uncertain and unreliable about Turner's actual character and motivations that his inventions were perfectly legitimate exercises of the artistic imagination.

The controversy had a considerable impact on the reception of Styron's novel when it ran into this early form of what would now probably be characterized as an appeal to political correctness.[29] Culturally, the controversy was significant in the way it revealed how important the reconstruction of the Southern past had become as an arena for redefining the meaning of American history, particularly in relationship to race. Styron was not the only writer about slavery to face criticism for trying to express a sense of white guilt about the Southern history of slavery. Elkins and other revisionist historians of slavery were encountering similarly rough going from black scholars as well as from more conservative white historians. Traditional Southern historians objected that such analogies as the one Elkins had so powerfully drawn between Nazi concentration camps and Southern plantations were much overdrawn and did not acknowledge the care and responsibility which white masters extended to their slaves. Black critics, on the other hand, were angry at what appeared to be the assumption that the oppression of slavery had forcibly shaped African-Americans into docile Sambos and Mammys; instead they wanted to insist that blacks had not only been able to maintain their sense of individual integrity and dignity in the midst of such oppression, but had gone on to create a rich and vital underground culture to sustain them. The integrity of the black family in slavery and after emancipation became a major issue in the course of this debate and Styron was frequently faulted for making his Nat Turner a sexless and nearly virginal bachelor with an idealistic fascination for white women despite some evidence that he had a wife and perhaps even children on another plantation. In this context, it is easy to see why Alex Haley's *Roots* with its strong affirmation of the persistence and integrity of black families became one of the great successes of the 1970s.

Perhaps Styron's Nat Turner aroused so much anger at the time because a racially divided public was still not yet ready to accept a white man's version of a tragic black hero as an embodiment of the human predicament. In the previous decade Ralph Ellison had been praised for doing what Styron tried to do in the 1960s in that he had created a black hero who had a very universal human quality. Though Ellison had been criticized by a few readers for being too archetypal, Styron was denounced for his portrayal of Nat Turner's internal struggle between outrage at white oppression and the sense of guilt and emptiness which afflicted him at the violence and killing he had unleashed. Styron's examination of the human struggle between life-denying guilt and life-affirming responsibility was viewed by militant younger blacks as a white racist projection. They felt that Styron actually shared the stereotypical view of black moral weakness which he had put into the mouth of the character he based on the white transcriber of Nat Turner's confession, the obscure attorney Thomas Gray:

> All such rebellions are not only likely to be exceedingly rare in occurrence but are ultimately doomed to failure, and this as a result of the basic weakness and inferiority, the moral deficiency of the Negro character.[30]

Certainly this was not Styron's view but that of a kind of white racist from which the author clearly distanced himself. In fact, *The Confessions* does suggest that much of Nat's ambiguity and hesitation about killing whites, as well as his sense of separation from the mass of his black followers reflected slavery's psychological oppressiveness which had forced blacks to internalize feelings of dependency, self-hatred, and guilt. However, at the historical moment of the late 1960s, when the Civil Rights movement had peaked and black leaders were beginning to talk again about black power, pride, and separatism, any white version of a black hero was likely to arouse great suspicion. Thus, Styron's attempt to see a nineteenth century black revolt in the existential terms of guilt and responsibility was doomed to widespread rejection.

By the later 1970s it was increasingly possible for African-American writers to engage some of the same issues that Styron had struggled with in *Nat Turner*; in the mid-1970s, Toni Morrison made a major breakthrough in this direction. Styron, however, took the theme of the tragic burden of the past in another direction.

Styron's *Sophie's Choice* and Morrison's *Song of Solomon*

> If slavery was the great historical nightmare of the eighteenth and nineteenth centuries in the Western world, slavery's continuation in the horror we have come to call Auschwitz is the nightmare of our own century.
>
> William Styron, 'Hell Reconsidered'

Styron turned in *Sophie's Choice* from the horror of African-American slavery to the catastrophe of the Holocaust and, specifically, to the tragic story of a Polish Catholic victim who survived that terror. In *Sophie's Choice* Styron articulated more explicitly the dialectic between the 'irony of Southern history' and the terrible twentieth century burden of the Holocaust, issues that were only implicit in *The Confessions*. As Styron sees it there are two possible responses to the tragedy of history: either giving way to a sense of guilt which paralyzes and ultimately destroys or acknowledging a personal responsibility which can lead to survival, self-affirmation and perhaps some sort of wisdom. Styron explores this dialectic through the encounter of three characters: Stingo, an aspiring young novelist from the South, feels obscurely guilty that his first novel is being financed by a family heritage which came from the long-ago sale of a young slave named Artiste. He broods on the fact that Artiste was unjustly sold to a sure death in the inferno of the Deep South, an injustice he is reminded of by a contemporary miscarriage of justice in the case of a young African-American. Sophie is a Polish Christian who has survived Auschwitz but has lost her faith because of her overpowering despair and desolation over the loss of her two children. Nathan Landau is a brilliant but schizophrenic American Jew whose mad death wish overwhelms Sophie's ebbing will to live when he convinces her to join him in suicide.

Nathan and Sophie are both victims of what became known through the experience of those who had escaped the Holocaust as survivor guilt. Burdened with guilt for not being killed, some survivors seemed doomed to spend the rest of their lives feeling morally bound to the dead and thus unable to redeem their own lives. Sophie represents the total victimization implicit in the Nazi vision of a slave society, since she is not only Christian but comes from a Polish family which was deeply committed to German values and anti-semitism before the Nazi invasion. Her most unbearable burden comes from the fact that she was forced to choose which of her children would be allowed to survive on her arrival at the camp, even though she knows that the child who was momentarily saved almost certainly perished later.

Nathan, who, in his sane moments, is a highly gifted and delightful person, reflects in his self-destructive madness another kind of survival guilt: the anguish of those who feel that they have escaped destruction by the mere chance of birth in more fortunate circumstances. Stingo comes to recognize his own complicity in this web of guilt and responsibility, for there is a clear parallel between his legacy from slavery and Nathan's security as a Jewish American; in both cases, safety and happiness have somehow implied the suffering of others. This sense of guilt is too overpowering for Nathan and it destroys him and his beloved Sophie. Though Stingo dreams of saving Sophie by taking her back to the rural South, becoming a gentleman farmer and the author of a book about Nat Turner, this solution is too optimistic and too facile. Sophie is irresistibly drawn back to Nathan and to death and Stingo is left bereaved and alone, wondering if there is any hope for the world: 'the suffering Stingo whom I once inhabited, or who once inhabited me, learning at firsthand and for the first time in his grown up life about death, about pain, and loss, and the appalling enigma of human existence, was trying [to affirm] the only remaining – perhaps the only bearable – truth. *Let your love flow out on all living things*' (560). But even this may be only a vain hope in a world in which even the survivors are destroyed by the evil which they have momentarily escaped:

For did not Auschwitz effectively block the flow of that titanic love, like some fatal embolism in the bloodstream of mankind? Or alter the nature of love entirely so as to reduce to absurdity the idea of loving an ant, or a salamander, or a viper, or a toad, or a tarantula, or a rabies virus – or even blessed and beautiful things – in a world which permitted the black edifice of Auschwitz to be built? I do not know. (561)

Toni Morrison also wrote from the beginning about the burden of racist oppression and its destruction of redeeming love by the imposition of guilt and self-hatred on its victims. Her first book dealt with the way in which racism creates self-loathing in those whose black physical bodies represent ugliness as conceived in racist terms. In her second novel a black survivor of World War I and American white racism creates an annual holiday, National Suicide Day, as a taunting invitation to his fellow African-Americans to end their torment by destroying their empty selves. Morrison's third novel was a major breakthrough in the historical interrogation of the heritage of African-American slavery and would lead directly to her most powerful work to date, *Beloved* (1987).

Song of Solomon also begins with a suicide, in this case, an unintentional one. An African-American life insurance agent, convinced that he can fly, leaps off the roof of a white hospital the day before the protagonist of the novel becomes the first black child to be born in the same hospital. Though in a literal sense Mr. Smith, the insurance agent learns as he leaps 'that only birds and airplanes could fly,' his act, which took place in the depths of the Depression in February 1931, is full of symbolic significance for the rest of the novel.[31] Though his flight is actually a fall, Mr. Smith's demise is hymned by a 'singing woman [who] wore a knitted navy cap pulled far down on her forehead' (5). The song she sings is an old and mysterious children's song, 'O Sugarman done fly away,' which evokes the legend of the magical African who, captured and delivered into slavery, found the power to fly back to Africa. But Mr. Smith is weighed down by the blue silk wings he mistakenly thinks will propel him 'to the other side of Lake Superior,' (3) and by his lifelong association 'with illness and death, neither of which was distinguishable from the brown picture of the North Carolina Mutual Life Building on the back of their yellow cards' [the insurance receipts he gives out to the poor blacks from whom he weekly collects a pittance] (8).

The novel's protagonist enters into life in the wake of Mr. Smith's death and eventually encounters the true meaning of the 'Song of Solomon;' but to do so he must embark on a complex quest into his family past in the slave South. 'Milkman' (Macon) Dead is the son of a black middle-class businessman who has married the daughter of a successful black doctor and prospered by buying rundown properties which he rents at exorbitant rates to blacks. Unlike the pathetic Mr. Smith who has aspired to middle-class respectability but has never quite attained it, Macon Dead Sr. is one of the leading black businessmen in this unnamed Northern city. But the price of his success has been the total rejection of his slave heritage and black folk culture. Like Ralph Ellison's Invisible Man before he realizes his true condition, Macon Dead has tried to enact 'the black rite of Horatio Alger' by adopting white middle-class values of conformity, respectability, and monetary success as the driving motives of his life. He has imposed these same values on his children and the result is a family life of such stultification and rigidity that it justifies the name of Dead which was given to his father when, after the Civil War, he 'agreed to take and pass on to all [his] issue the name scrawled in perfect thoughtlessness by a drunken Yankee in the Union Army' (18).

Milkman's quest begins as a young man when he meets his father's sister Pilate, a bootlegger, and the head of a household of free-living women. Pilate, is, in fact, the 'singing woman' who carries the song and who had performed it during Mr. Smith's attempted flight. She represents the underground tradition of African-American oral culture which flourished in the oppressive world of enslavement and which has continued in the folk culture that members of the black bourgeoisie, like Macon Dead, have repudiated. Pilate's sense of freedom and her refusal to accept the repressiveness and conventionality of middle-class life are very attractive to the young Milkman and he begins a process of imaginative enlargement which will eventually make it possible for him to accomplish his quest. His search begins with clues about a family treasure and leads to the mythical figure of a slave named Solomon, who founded Milkman's family in America and then disappeared, supposedly having flown back to Africa. Milkman's journey takes him to a small town in Virginia named Shalimar after the legendary Solomon. Here he encounters a village of kinsmen and is initiated not only into the truth of his history but into a deeper and richer vision of life. In the end, Milkman learns that the real meaning of the legend of flight is not physical as Mr. Smith thought, but imaginative, and that the real flight is not into the future, but into the past – to make connections, to acknowledge the ancestors and to reestablish the wholeness of self by accepting and celebrating one's true heritage. Whether this recovery of the past will be sufficient to overcome the terrible force of black rage and nihilism which are as much a part of Milkman's heritage as the inventive vitality of folk tradition remains uncertain at the end of *Song of Solomon*. At the novel's conclusion, the burden of the past reasserts itself when Milkman's friend, Guitar, symbolizing the violence and desire for revenge generated by centuries of oppression, destroys Pilate. This act puts into doubt the sufficiency of Milkman's new strength to encompass the destructive force of history's tragedy and guilt. Like Styron, Morrison remains uncertain whether the affirmation and acknowledgement of our responsibility for history will be enough.

The Tragic South and the American Dream

> It was not a story to pass on.
>
> Toni Morrison, *Beloved*[32]

The tragic history of the South as recreated by the historians and novelists, white and black, of the postwar period offered thoughtful Americans of the 1970s and 1980s a deeper sense of the ironic ambiguities of the American dream, a greater awareness of the racial and ethnic conflicts that had often been overlooked in the celebration of American democracy, and a realization of the degree to which oppression and suffering were as much a part of American history as progress and prosperity. However, it was far from certain that most Americans would choose to acknowledge these discoveries. The South, itself, seemed remarkably able to disassociate itself from its heritage of evil and defeat when it tasted the new prosperity of the sunbelt and hastened to assure itself that once put on the right track by the Civil Rights movement, it was really doing a better job of granting meaningful opportunities to African-Americans than the ghettoized North with its fearful 'black underclass.' A new version of the Lost Cause found expression in both North and South through the increasing interest in reenactments of Civil War battles in which the social and political issues of the war, and its basis in the conflict over slavery, were subordinated to a celebration of the bravery and endurance of the soldiers on both sides. In spite of the novelists and historians who continued to investigate the tragic history of slavery, it sometimes seemed as if the majority of the public would prefer to forget that history, making it 'not a story to pass on.'

But this is the pessimistic view, based on what one hopes are the more superficial expressions of popular culture. If it is true that the long-term meanings of a culture are expressed in its greatest and most powerful literature, then the myth of the South as tragic exemplar and the deeper literary exploration of the heritage of slavery and racism it helped articulate has made possible a new and deeper criticism as well as reaffirmation of the promise of America. This new kind of reaffirmation recognizes America's flaws, mistakes, and limitations and acknowledges that much of American history has been dark and tragic, yet still seeks to celebrate the dream of human betterment. Such a conception of America has been one important outgrowth of the myth of the South as tragic exemplar. This vision of Southern history has flowed together with the similar consciousness of much modern Jewish and African-American writing. As an expression of this spirit let me close by citing a passage from the 1988 revision of Leon Forrest's 1973 novel *There is a Tree More Ancient than Eden.* Forrest is an African-American novelist from Chicago whose family lineage is impeccably Southern – from Mississippi and New Orleans. In 1988 he added to his 1973 novel a concluding sermon on the death/crucifixion of Martin Luther King preached in an after-hours tavern in the midst of Forrest's fictional version of Chicago's black ghetto by the bizarre figure of the 'six-foot seven inch Pompey c.j. Browne.' In the peroration of his sermon 'Oh Jeremiah of the Dreamers' Browne turns to the future of King's legacy and calls on us to seek anew the promise of the American dream:

> Yet I hear Martin's voice still to fight on, crying forth in the wilderness demanding of the Lord remembrance: Honor, Honor unto the Dying Lamb of our learning lanterns – the frontier of the shrouded dream. Thank God Almighty I'm free at last: but free to uncover what freedom beyond the mountain top's metamorphosis? Is paradise without politics? What beyond the sprouting maggots of the Soul's morning metamorphosis? What is that Yonder? What unshrouded, unsheathed chariot is that Yonder? That the foundling, transported in a chariot of Chains reaches out to touch?[33]

Notes

1. In a 1977 conversation with Louis Rubin and Robert Penn Warren, who agreed with this assessment. Louis D. Rubin (ed), *The American South: Portrait of a Culture* (Baton Rouge: Louisiana State University Press, 1980), 310.
2. Quoted in Rubin, *The American South*, 162.
3. Faulkner, *Intruder in the Dust* (New York: Random House, 1948), 152-153.
4. A few samples: Thomas Wolfe's *You Can't Go Home Again*, William Styron's *Lie Down in Darkness*, and Walker Percy's *The Last Gentleman*. A non-fiction example: Willie Morris' *North Toward Home*.
5. Some would trace this tradition to the very beginning of American drama in Royall Tyler's *The Contrast* (1787) and it certainly played a significant role in 19th century humor and Mark Twain.
6. The 1970's fascination with country music led to a number of excellent movies about the lives of country singers including *Coal Miner's Daughter* (Loretta Lynn – 1980) and *Sweet Dreams* (Patsy Cline – 1985). It also made a number of country singers like Dolly Parton, Johnny Cash, Kenny Rogers and Kris Kristofferson into important movie stars.
7. Cf. John Egerton's speculation on the Southern origins of fried chicken in *Southern Food: At Home, On the Road, In History* (New York: Knopf, 1987).
8. H. Louis Patrick, a Presbyterian minister in Charlotte, N.C., quoted by John Egerton in *The Americanization of Dixie: The Southernization of America* (New York: Harper's Magazine Press, 1974), 198.
9. One might even speculate that what often seemed to be excessive criticism of the Carter and Clinton women was partly inspired by the feeling that they seemed to be in conflict with the traditional images of female domesticity and male supremacy and patriarchy associated with the rural tradition.
10. A good example is the Southern Baptist convention which has been taken over by conservatives and is in the process of trying to wipe out any pockets of liberalism remaining within its purview. This has the appearance of a systematic campaign and is evident in efforts by conservative fundamentalists, at the Southern Baptist Seminary in Louisville, to drive out more liberal professors.
11. Cited in Rubin, *The American South*, 296-297.
12. There are several excellent studies of the myth of the Lost Cause, including Rollin

Osterweis, *The Myth of the Lost Cause 1865-1900* (Hamden, CT.: Archon Books, 1973), and Thomas J. Connelly and Barbara L. Bellows, *God and General Longstreet: The Lost Cause and the Southern Mind* (Baton Rouge: Louisiana State University Press, 1982). I've also profited greatly from Susan Speare Durant's dissertation *The Gently Furled Banner: The Development of the Myth of the Lost Cause, 1865-1900* (unpub. Ph.D. dissertation; Chapel Hill: University of North Carolina).

13. Compare Robert Penn Warren's defense of segregation in *I'll Take My Stand* to his later views as expressed in, for example, *Segregation: The Inner Conflict in the South* (New York: Random House, 1956).

14. Just as an example, the library of the University of Kentucky lists 71 books on William Faulkner published between 1970 and 1980. The earlier decades show: 1960-1970 49; 1950-1960 18. Before 1950 there were virtually no book-length studies of Faulkner. In contrast to the 71 books on Faulkner listed between 1870 and 1980 there were, in the University of Kentucky library, 43 on Hemingway and 22 on Fitzgerald in the same period.

15. The 1930 'Agrarian' anthology *I'll Take My Stand* was still pervaded by a residual adherence to the myth of the Lost Cause and the fantasy of an antebellum paradise. The 1947 *A Southern Vanguard: The John Peale Bishop Memorial Volume* (edited by Allen Tate), which was a sort of Agrarian emeriti collection was much less so. In their later work, some of the former Fugitive-Agrarians developed a much darker view, notably Robert Penn Warren. Even *A Southern Vanguard* was headlined by Malcolm Cowley's prize-winning 1945 essay 'William Faulkner's Legend of the South,' one of the first sustained analyses of Faulkner's 'tragic fable of Southern history.' This essay, written while Cowley was working on the *Viking Portable Faulkner* (1946), introduced Faulkner to a new generation of readers and began his emergence as a major American novelist. In spite of some minor points which current readers would probably disagree with, Cowley's essay remains a brilliant analysis of Faulkner's tragic myth of the South.

16. These views upset many Faulkner admirers, including James Baldwin who wrote a bitter criticism of Faulkner's stand, 'Faulkner and Desegregation' which originally appeared in *Partisan Review* in 1956 (reprinted in *Nobody Knows My Name: More Notes of a Native Son* (New York: Dell, 1961). Faulkner later retracted or qualified some of the statements he was accused of making and it is clear that some of his critics overexaggerated his commitment to white supremacy and the rejection of any sort of Federal intervention in the desegregation crisis.

17. The Snopes family is the subject of a trilogy, *The Hamlet* (1940), *The Town* (1956) and *The Mansion* (1959) while the McCaslin-Edmonds-Beauchamp line is present in *Go Down, Moses* (1942) and *Intruder in the Dust* (1948). The five novels have some interlocking characters, particularly Gavin Stevens, who appears in all the novels and through whom these novels are also linked to Faulkner's first major work with a racial theme, *Light in August* (1932).

18. Woodward and other historians later expressed some reservations about the potential effectiveness of the 'burden.' Cf. Woodward's own 'A Second Look at the Theme of Irony' printed in the revised edition of *Burden* in which he notes that 'the irony of history had caught up with the ironist – or gone him one better' (230). His concern was that the South, instead of learning from its long experience of limitation and defeat, had become the nation's most enthusiastic supporter of American imperialism and 'the national myths of invincibility and innocence.' Earlier, he had hoped that the Southern experience might serve as a corrective to such complacencies. Cf. also Woodward's *Thinking Back: The Perils of Writing History* (Baton Rouge: Louisiana State University

Press, 1986) and the discussion of Woodward's views in Michael O'Brien's *Rethinking the South* (Baltimore: Johns Hopkins University Press, 1988). O'Brien insightfully notes the deep conservatism which is intertwined with Woodward's version of liberal populism, a combination which also seems to characterize the special quality of Faulkner's social and political vision.

19. Cf. the commentaries of John Shelton Reed (*Whistling Dixie: Dispatches from the South* 1990; *The Enduring South: Subcultural Persistence in Mass Society* 1972) and John Egerton who disagree about the extent to which the Southern tradition is being eroded by 'the Americanization of Dixie,' but who agree that the past is being perverted and corrupted by the new temptations of Sunbelt prosperity. As Egerton puts it, 'the South and the nation are not exchanging strengths as much as they are exchanging sins; more often than not, they are sharing and spreading the worst in each other, while the best withers' (*Americanization of Dixie,* xx). A pathetic indication of how meaningless the Southern heritage and the myth of the Lost Cause have become is the current struggle in South Carolina to continue using the Confederate flag as the official state symbol, an effort which is clearly more concerned with the perpetuation of racism and sexism than it is with the understanding and recognition of history.

20. Shelby Foote's excellent history *The Civil War: A Narrative* (3 vols; New York: Random House, 1958-74) and his *Shiloh: A Novel* (New York: The Dial Press, 1952), had been pervaded by the spirit of Faulkner. Though the Burns Civil War series had a number of contemporary scholarly commentators including the impressive African-American historian, Barbara Fields, it was Foote's personality and his perspective which dominated the series, just as the tragic ironies of the Civil War were Burns's primary theme in his treatment of the great conflict.

21. Cf. Richard Wright, *Native Son* (1940) and *Black Boy* (1945), and Michael Gold *Jews Without Money* (1930). One fascinating novel of the early 1930s, Henry Roth's *Call It Sleep*, originally published in 1934 and significantly not reprinted in paperback until 1976, foreshadowed the work of Ellison and Bellow, but it was a lone orphan with no progeny. For further discussion of the rise of Jewish and African American writers to national centrality see my essay 'Literature, Race and Ethnicity in America,' in W.M. Verhoeven (ed), *Rewriting the Dream: Reflections on the Changing American Literary Canon for Jan Bakker*, Costerus New Series 83 (Amsterdam: Rodopi Press, 1992).

22. The increasing success of Jewish and African-American writers paved the literary way for other minority groups and for more forceful feminist voices to come to the fore in the multi-cultural 1980s and 1990s, and also helped bring about a large-scale deconstruction and recreation of the American literary canon to include representative women, Native American, Latino, and Asian-American writers both in the present and in the past. This trend has caused massive revisions in the literary anthologies used to teach American literature, changes which will probably have a considerable impact on the cultural consciousness of the next generation.

23. Among these were Thomas Wolfe, Katherine Anne Porter, Allan Tate, Robert Penn Warren, Cleanth Brooks, John Crowe Ransom, Stark Young, Richard Wright, Ralph Ellison, Truman Capote, Gore Vidal, and Mary Lee Settle. Willie Morris was part of the later phase of this Southern expatriation and he discusses his motives and feeling about the move in the significantly titled *North Toward Home*.

24. Styron has discussed the origin of *The Confessions of Nat Turner* many times, notably in the essays 'This Quiet Dust' and 'Hell Reconsidered' collected in *This Quiet Dust and Other Writings* (New York: Random House, 1982). Many years later he gave a

similar account in 'An Interview with William Styron,' *Sewanee Review*, 99:3 (Summer 1991), 463-477.

25. The original edition of *The Burden of Southern History* was published in 1960, the revised edition in 1968. Styron continued to adhere to this view of Southern history. In a 1991 interview he cites Woodward and goes on to say 'as a nation we've never had the horrible catastrophic invasions such as the Russians suffered over and over again or even as the British suffered during World War II with the incredible bombardment. The south did suffer that sort of experience, and that's why I think it fostered more of a tragic sense than other regions.' 'An Interview with William Styron,' 469.

26. *Ibid.*, 468.

27. *Sophie's Choice* (New York: Random House, 1979), 459-60, 491.

28. The black response was codified in a volume edited by John Henrik Clarke, *William Styron's Nat Turner: Ten Black Writers Respond* (1968) which included essays by Lerone Bennett, Alvin Poussaint, Vincent Harding, John Oliver Killens, John A. Williams, Ernest Kaiser, Loyle Hairston, and Mike Thelwell.

29. The controversy is by no means over as is indicated by a recent article on *The Confessions of Nat Turner* and novelistic responses to it by Mae G. Henderson in '(W)riting "The Work" and working the rites,' *Black American Literature Forum*, 23:4 (Winter 1989), 631-661.

30. *The Confessions of Nat Turner* (New York: Random House, 1967), 84.

31. *Song of Solomon* (New York: New American Library, 1978), 9.

32. *Beloved* (New York: Penguin, 1988), 275.

33. *There Is a Tree More Ancient Than Eden* (Chicago: Another Chicago Press, 1988), 213-214.

Declension and Renewal: New England's Shifting Mood in the 1970s

David E. Nye

> An American
> is a complex of occasions,
> themselves a geometry
> of spatial nature.
>
> – Charles Olson[1]

The New England American is a complex of occasions built up over 350 years and spread out over the complex geometry of six states, from the rough Atlantic coast of Maine to the quieter reaches of Long Island Sound, from the White Mountains of New Hampshire to the tumbled hills of western Connecticut.[2] The white population found, like the Native-Americans before them, that there were really two regions, the mountainous and inland north (Maine, New Hampshire, Vermont), which is difficult to farm due to poor soils and a short growing season, and the more fertile hilly southern and coastal regions (much of Massachusetts, and all of Connecticut and Rhode Island). But even these areas were not competitive once the rest of the nation was settled. It has been at least a century since New England last sought to feed itself, and part of its complex geometry is the tracery of old walls and sunken foundations now hidden beneath thick foliage, vestiges of an agricultural life that has faded away. In the upland valleys, abandoned mills; in the towns abandoned railway stations; and on the coasts abandoned canneries. If its population was relatively uniform and agricultural when Crèvecoeur described it in the eighteenth century, since then it has absorbed constellations of immigrants and passed through several phases of industrialization. New England is old enough to have suffered many defeats and to have reinvented itself several times already. The story of the region in the 1970s, inasmuch as any such truncated piece of time can be called a story, is a characteristic one of decline and renewal. The story of declension was the narrative that seemed most obvious at the time, and will be treated first. The region's rebirth was a more subterranean process scarcely visible for much of the decade, but unmistakable in retrospect.

The 1960s had been a good period for New England, beginning with the election of John F. Kennedy as president, which signaled a boom in the regional economy and a rekindling of idealism, particularly among younger voters. To be sure, the mood darkened after the wave of riots in the ghettoes of the nation and the assassinations of two Kennedys and Martin Luther King, but few would have believed, at the beginning of the 1970s, that a surging Keynesian economy under the leadership of a liberal president were both things of the past. Seen from New England, the vastly unpopular and contentious presidency of Richard Nixon seemed merely an aberration made possible by division in the Democratic Party that had been nowhere more apparent than within New England itself. Most assumed the Roosevelt political coalition would still prove serviceable in the future, once a suitable candidate was found to lead the existing Democratic majorities in both houses of Congress. But the experiences of growth and of a liberal presidency would both turn out to be mirages on the historical horizon.

The seventies were to be uncomfortable, a time of adjustment and diminished expectations, a great sea change in American life. Nixon's election was not an aberration, not merely a backlash against the hippies and the anti-war movement, not a freak right-wing usurpation of leadership, but rather the index of a decisive shift away from liberalism in the nation as a whole, particularly in the South, but also elsewhere. New England's presidential electoral votes went overwhelmingly to Republicans in 1972, 1976, and 1980. This shift apparently originated in economic stagnation, but its sources were far more complex and elude full explication. The spiritual malaise of the 1970s deepened as the decade continued. The dour economic mood was reinforced by Watergate. The malingering end to the Vietnam War infuriated the right, tortured the left, and disconcerted anyone trying to find, much less occupy, the middle ground. Neither the fiasco of Nixon's abdication nor the collapse of the Saigon government were much discussed during the amnesia of the Ford interregnum. At the time of Carter's election, self-confidence briefly returned, but soon faltered when it became clear that a Democrat in the White House did not bring new growth to the economy. Americans watched as he proved helpless before OPEC, the Iranian Revolution, economic stagflation, the continuing crisis of the cities, and finally the hostage crisis. By the end of the decade New England was not only voting more conservatively, it was chastened in mood and down-sized in expectations. Its once unquestioned cultural leadership was a thing of the past, and it looked to a future in which other regions clearly would continue to grow in power and influence, as could be measured in electoral votes, population, and other hard indicators.

Moreover, New England was America's most expensive region. In 1979 Boston had been the most costly city in the country for the previous three years. Hartford and Portland, Maine, were also among top ten.[3] An urban family of four, living on what the Bureau of Labor Statistics called an 'intermediate' income, required $22,117 in Boston compared to a national average of $18,622, with most southern cities below that figure.[4] Furthermore, American family income stagnated during the 1970s. Measured in constant dollars, median family income had increased 40% in the 1960s, and the rise continued until 1973, when the first oil crisis halted the economy in its tracks. For the next two years real family income actually sank, then rose slowly until 1979, before sinking back to its 1970 level by 1981.[5] The long boom that had started in the 1950s had clearly ended. (Ronald Reagan would be elected in good part because he promised a return to rapid growth, cheap energy, and relaxed government regulation.) The overall stagnation was an average, however, hiding the fact that some areas grew rapidly, while New England's economy stalled. The most obvious cause seemed to be the high cost of oil. But there were other, long-term causes as well. The Vietnam War severely unbalanced the budget, stimulated the production of weapons that had little long-term use in the economy, and reduced government investment in infrastructure, housing, and education. In 1973 the Nixon Administration devalued the dollar for the second time in two years, making imports, notably oil, more expensive. Other immediate effects were to increase the competitiveness of American exports and to make foreign travel more expensive. More devaluations were to follow, weakening a family's buying power not just for oil but for all imported goods, including foreign cars, French wine, and luxury items. A people whose income, measured in constant dollars, had doubled between 1950 and 1973, were ill-prepared to accept an actual decline in buying power.

This decline was not shared equally among the regions. Once the industrial center of the United States, New England, New York, Pennsylvania and New Jersey suffered stagnation by any measure. During the decade Houston's population grew by 45% and bank deposits quadrupled. No major city in the Northeast grew at all, and New York was virtually bankrupt in 1975. Carter's cuts in defense spending during the Carter years hurt Connecticut's aircraft and helicopter plants, arms manufacturers, and naval ship yards. New England's textile mills and shoe factories continued to close, and many moved production south. In part lower taxes elsewhere were an incentive, as the region had the highest effective business tax rate in the country, double that of any southern state.[6]

As the center of population moved to the West and South, crossing the Mississippi River in the middle of the decade,[7] political power ebbed away with it, the population shift reducing representation in the House of Representatives. The population of the nation as a whole grew by 23 million, but virtually all of the increase came to the South and West, where the growth rate was 20% or more. By comparison, the New England and the Middle Atlantic regions had the same population at the end of the decade (49.1 million) as at the beginning.[8] The composition of this population had changed, however, through both in and out migration. The elderly and the poor were less likely to move to the sunbelt than the young and the skilled. Making matters worse, the high welfare benefits of the Northeast made it attractive for the poor and unemployed. By the end of the decade, the cities of the Northeast had been drained of many mobile workers, while their proportion of unmarried mothers, for example, had increased. Indeed, Hartford even adopted a system where the poor and unemployed could do cleaning and other routine work as a substitute for paying their delinquent property taxes.[9]

In a booming economy, such expedients would not have been necessary, but in the 1970s the Northeast often seemed an extension of the rust belt that began in the foundries and automobile plants of the Middle West. Compared to the South and West, it had older industrial plants, stronger unions, and higher energy costs. In cities, the decline looked even worse than it was because of the general urban deconcentration and the increasing preference for suburban shopping malls, giant discount stores on cheap land outside of town, and services along major highways. These changes devastated the downtowns of smaller cities, where stores were often empty and new construction was rare. The largest – Boston, Worcester, Hartford – swam in debt and were forced to curtail many municipal services.[10] The middle class moved out, not merely into suburbia, but into the countryside, ready to commute ever longer distances in exchange for the slower pace and quiet amenities of rural communities. The 1970s witnessed the refurbishing of the idyllic image of the New England village, with its white clapboard homes surrounding village greens dominated by a white church spire. Living in the country seemed ever more appealing, as did the lure of the professionally preserved past. Visitors poured into the idealized New England community at Old Sturbridge Village, Mystic Seaport, the 'authentic copy' of 'Plimoth Plantation,' and other historic sites.

Yet was a region focused on the past *passé*? The region that had produced transcendentalism and pragmatism, that had long seen itself as the intellectual center of the nation, faced a crisis of identity. Once it had seen itself as the core of American intellectual life, colonizing other regions with clergymen and teachers. Its history, from the Mayflower to John F. Kennedy, had seemed to represent the American experience. In the 1970s, however, the region began to seem idiosyncratic. Its politicians, notably Senators Muskie from Maine and Kennedy from Massachusetts, failed in their quest to be nominated for the presidency. Its writers, who once believed they spoke for the nation, were ill-disposed to write as regionalists. Its universities found themselves challenged both by newer private schools elsewhere (Rice, Emory, Stanford) and by land-grant institutions in the South and Mid-West with lower tuitions and ambitious faculties. If Boston still had a significant publishing culture, New York remained the center of publishing, and the leading writers mostly did not come from the Northeast (though some chose to live in western Connecticut, near New York, for tax reasons.) When Edmund Wilson and Mark Van Doren both died in 1972 there were no comparable figures to replace them, in a literary culture that was increasingly plural and marked by racial and gender divisions. When Robert Lowell died in 1977, there was no heir apparent. And when the Boston Atheneum, venerable Brahmin institution, found itself deep in debt, its only recourse, despite public protest from the city of Boston, was to sell its portraits of George and Martha Washington for $5 million.[11] The collapse of anything resembling a genteel literary culture was not, of course, the fault of New England alone, but rather a sign of the democratization of education and the coming to literary consciousness of disparate groups, including Jewish-, African- and Native-Americans, and by the rise of the counter-culture, which challenged any form of elitism.

Nor was this a comfortable decline. Oil prices shot up again in the Carter years. Supplies became uncertain, and living in the cold Northeast became a definite liability. Heating oil became twice as expensive, and gasoline was not always available. A malaise gripped the region. Still worse, the sky-high national interest rates reached 18% by the end of the Carter years, in a curious form of stagnation and inflation that defied conventional economic logic. Under these conditions, businesses profited more investing in the money market than they could through manufacturing. Worst of all, following the lead of California, voters staged a tax revolt at the end of the decade, forcing many cuts in services. In Massachusetts, voters pushed through 'Proposition $2^1/_2$' that limited government spending and forced closing of some schools and curtailment of services.

Just as importantly, the Nixon years witnessed a resurgence of ethnic consciousness, as Polish, Italian, Irish, and other white immigrant groups asserted their cultural difference from the mainstream. In part a reaction to Black militancy, the new ethnicity also expressed the rejection of the melting-pot ideal. Not all of the expressions of this new consciousness were positive. If the older ethnic groups celebrated the Polish culture that had produced Copernicus[12] or the Italian culture embodied in the Renaissance, they also often attacked count-mandated busing of school children to achieve racial balance. In Irish South Boston a group called Restore Our Alienated Rights (ROAR) demanded a halt to forced integration. In both 1974 and 1975 angry mobs stoned school buses and beat African-American students. Led by City Council member Louise Day Hicks and encouraged by President Ford's open disagreement with forced busing, the Irish poor showed that the North could be as militant about maintaining segregation as the South had been in the

1950s and 1960s. Ku Klux Klan speakers were welcomed in Boston, and the image of the North's moral rectitude was shattered.[13]

As William Polenberg has pointed out, disillusionment with the United States apparently encouraged people to look to their ethnic roots for sources of identity. The resurgence of ethnic difference was also linked to the Vietnam War. The patriotic feelings white ethnic Americans had cherished during World War II and after sought a new outlet. How could they invest their identity in the gradual pull-out from Vietnam? the invasion of Cambodia? or the horrors of the My Lai Massacre, which was widely publicized by court martial proceedings during the summer of 1971? much less the outright desertion of South Vietnam to defeat in 1974? Little wonder that between 1969 and 1972 census takers discovered 27 million 'new' self-declared white ethnics.[14]

During the early part of the decade, the antiwar movement had been strong in New England, particularly in college towns. Vigils, marches, protests, and sit-ins occurred throughout the region, often polarizing town and gown. For example, in the spring of 1972 students and faculty from several schools invaded Westover Air Base in Chicopee. Such actions triggered a strong conservative reaction among many ordinary citizens. Once the war ended, despite the disgrace of Watergate, in the 1976 presidential election all the New England states except Massachusetts cast their electoral votes for Gerald Ford. In part, this was no doubt due to unease with a southern Democratic Party candidate, but it was also a vote for moderate Republicanism and against the culture of protest associated with the Democrats.

This shift to the Republicans in New England had little to do with religious fundamentalism or far-right political movements. Rather it was a middle-class vote against higher taxes or increasing the size of the welfare state, a rural vote against the Washington bureaucracy, whose growth had become associated with the Democrats, and a frustrated vote against high oil prices. Underlying it all was status anxiety, as it became increasingly difficult for either the skilled working class or the middle class to preserve their income level and pass it along to their children. The most obvious aspect of the problem was what came to be called de-industrialization, or the process of closing factories in New England and instead relying on overseas plants or facilities in less expensive parts of the country. While the move to a service and high-tech economy looked reasonable in aggregate figures, the skilled worker from an abandoned New England shoe factory seldom found a position that paid as well, and often proved to be unemployable. De-industrialization was a long-term process, but it was felt more acutely in the stagnant 1970s than before. Between 1958 and the middle 1970s 675,000 workers disappeared from New England's mills, many of which were simply abandoned. Plant closings meant, in human terms, that people had to settle for poorly-paid service jobs instead of the union shop. Two adults working full time at

46

McDonalds or in a supermarket made as much as one skilled mill hand.[15] Even families that avoided such drastic drops in their income faced the rising cost of college tuition, during a time when their income did not keep pace with inflation. By 1973 a middle-class income made a family ineligible for a scholarship, yet it no longer could pay the cost of a private college. The economic escalator of the 1960s had gone into reverse, and families had to run as fast as they could to stay in the same place. When oil shortages forced New Englanders to stay home on weekends in underheated houses, it was little wonder that they began to turn against Jimmy Carter, who was unfortunate enough to have inherited from Richard Nixon a weak economy and vulnerability to OPEC.

This, then, is the story that most New Englanders told themselves during the 1970s, with the help of newspapers and the television news. The 1970s were a bad time, a time when people lost control to foreign oil cartels, a time of economic stagnation, high inflation, urban decay, political corruption, military defeat, and international humiliation. A time when the region lost ground to the rest of the nation.

Yet New Englanders retained a sense of tradition, strong cultural institutions, and a high-tech industrial base. If no longer at the center of American economic and cultural life, New England remained a vital and resourceful region that by 1984 had lower unemployment, more sought-after universities, and higher house prices than most of the rest of the nation. The 1970s was a time of readjustment, when the area began to transform itself. Many of the politically disaffected of the counter-culture moved to Vermont, whose political culture was radicalized to the point where an avowed socialist would later be elected mayor of its largest city. The rest of northern New England became increasingly fashionable as a vacation area, drawing crowds in the summer for its cool temperatures and outdoor activities, which included active art and music festivals. The roads filled up in October with tourists looking at the autumn colors, and skiing resorts did a booming winter business. The long New England coastline likewise proved a marketable asset, notably Cape Cod, New Hampshire, and southern Maine.

Counteracting flight to the suburbs, New England's cities were able to lure a new generation back to urban life, with schemes of gentrification that revitalized selected urban areas, while displacing the poor. When high interest rates in the late 1970s made new home construction too expensive for most, tax incentives and grants encouraged the rehabilitation of neighborhoods. In 1966 there had been 2,500 historic preservation groups in the United States; by 1976 there were more than 6,000. New England benefitted disproportionately from this renewed interest in history, for the simple reason that its buildings were on average older than in most other regions. Boston's renovation of Fanueil Hall and Quincy Market transformed a vegetable market into a trendy area of boutiques and restaurants. Lowell revitalized its downtown, by turning its empty mills into an industrial park and historic district administered by the National Park Service. In the process, the city attracted $26 million in local, state, and federal money.[16] Developers were drawn to historical preservation by new tax write-offs, and home buyers realized that property values in historic districts outpaced inflation. As a result, Boston's Beacon Hill and Back Bay areas became chic once again, and many smaller cities rushed to have old buildings designated as landmarks. In New Haven, Wooster Square, once threatened by industrial blight and encroaching slums, became a 'thriving enclave' after it was declared a national landmark in 1970.[17] Overall, in 1976, 'more Americans repurchased old houses than bought new ones' for the first time since the 1930s, and New England was a trend leader.[18]

In the Boston area the technological revolution of the computer was felt sooner than anywhere else except Silicon Valley in California, due to the synergy of skilled workers, cutting edge educational institutions, and local capital. Hartford remained the national capital of the insurance industry, and Connecticut's machine makers and skilled workers remained an asset few other regions could match. But the most significant development, without doubt, was visible between 495, the interstate highway that served as Boston's outermost ring, and Route 128. Along and between these two parallel freeways there sprang up a host of high-tech companies, such as Wang, Control Data, Digital Equipment, and Data General. Such industries stimulated one another, and Boston soon came to boast vigorous computer user groups, a museum of computing, software developers, and a nationally important computer show. In just two years, between 1976 and 1978, Massachusetts added 47,000 jobs in engineering, computing, and other high-technology areas.[19] Tracy Kidder made computer designers heroic figures in his best-selling *The Soul of a New Machine* that chronicled the creation of a new piece of hardware at Digital Equipment, and told the story of the corporation's success, with chapter titles such as 'The Wars' and 'How to Make a Lot of Money.'[20] At Tufts, scientists and engineers were collaborating to create the CAT scanner. At MIT huge grants supported research into metallurgy, computer applications, genetic engineering, cryptography, chemistry, and into pure research whose implications no one yet understood.

Knowledge has long been one of the most important products of the New England, and in the seventies its colleges and universities retained their national reputations. Despite dire and apparently infallible predictions, based on a drop in the birth rate that had begun in the late 1950s which portended down-sizing and the closing of some institutions, in fact, few colleges closed. Families were more willing than ever to sacrifice huge sums to send their children to elite schools – Harvard, MIT, Yale, Amherst, Dartmouth, Bowdoin, Tufts, Trinity, Williams, Wellesley, Smith, Mt. Holyoke, and many more – in hopes of preserving or enhancing their class status.

In this story of rebirth, New England built upon traditional strengths in advanced technology and education, harvesting many Nobel Prizes in the process. The northern landscape likewise proved to be a tourist bonanza, as was the 'nostalgia industry' that focused on historic homes and reconstructions.

Literature does not mirror life, and few writers set out to write the history of a decade. Certainly one cannot find many traces of either of these stories in the often intensely personal poetry of Elizabeth Bishop, John Ciardi, Robert Creely, Robert Lowell, Charles Olson, Ann Sexton, and Richard Wilbur, all of whom one might claim as New England poets, all active in the 1970s. However, the work of several novelists fleshes out these statistics and trends. Russell Banks' *Affliction* describes Lawford, New Hampshire, a small town in northern New England whose traditional sources of economic life have all but dried up. Its mills have closed, and it is 'someplace halfway between other places, a town people sometimes admit to having been from but where almost no one ever goes. Half the rooms in the big white colonial houses that face the river and the high dark ridge in the west have been emptied and sealed off against the winter with polyurethane and plywood, imprisoning in the remaining rooms elderly couples and widows and widowers abandoned by their grown children for the smarter life in the towns and cities.'[21] Those who do not leave Lawford are regarded as failures, notably the narrator's brother and central character, Wade, who has several part-time jobs and lives in a trailer outside town. Banks' achievement in the novel is to make Wade a sympathetic character, despite his violence, drinking, and muddle-headed failures to solve his problems, which originate in his complex relationship to his family, and which culminate in two murders. Yet, even as Wade falls apart, the town is slowly undergoing a transformation, led by two local entrepreneurs, who see that its very isolation is an asset. They establish a successful vacation resort, with 17 miles of ski trails, fancy lodges and over one hundred condominiums, breathing new life into the local economy.

The town's history is subordinate to the family drama, in which a son cannot escape his heritage of parental alcoholism and violence. Nevertheless, the realistic descriptions of Lawford and its residents are useful social history. For example, among the old houses in town,

> Here and there a particularly well maintained and – discounting the greenhouse, the sauna in the barn and the solar heat panels – lovingly restored mid-nineteenth century farm house accommodates the complex social, sexual and domestic needs of a graying long-haired man and woman with an adolescent child or two in boarding school, svelte couples who have come north from Boston or New York City to teach at Dartmouth, twenty miles south, or sometimes just to grow marijuana in their large organic gardens and live off inherited money in the region's dead economy. (10)

In one such sentence, Banks suggests the tensions between such couples and the long-time residents, which are not merely economic differences but fundamental matters of cultural style, measured in architecture, hair length,

49

cuisine, intellectual interests, and preferred forms of pleasure. Here is the familiar tension between city and country, between northern and southern New England, but translated into the specific details of a time and place.

John Updike performs a similar transcription of divergent cultural styles as part of the background to *Roger's Version*.[22] Set in Boston and Cambridge, the novel contrasts the urbane and somewhat jaundiced views of a professor of divinity with an earnest mid-western computer science student who wants to prove the existence of God ('purposeful intelligence') through computer analysis of physics and the 'Big Bang' theory. In this social comedy, Updike reasserts the superiority of urbanity, doubt, and irony, of Harvard and the New England intellectual tradition. At the same time, however, he undercuts any pretensions to moral superiority, as the professor commits adultery with his niece, who lives on welfare in a project. The description of a walk down into her area of town is a *tour-de-force*, detailing the contents of store windows, the names of small businesses, the mixture of races, the incongruous mixture of styles. As the narrator walks further from the university, poverty increases until he reaches houses that

> had given up pretensions: the yards were weedy to the height of a man's knees, and bottles and cans had been tossed into them as if into a repository. The façades were unpainted even where curtains or a tended flower box at an upstairs window indicated habitation. The owners had slipped away, whether through misfortune or an accountant's unscrupulous calculations, leaving the buildings on their own, like mumbling mental patients turned out into the street. (58)

A stunning contrast to the professor's elegant neighborhood near Harvard Square, this is a place of diminished welfare and cut-back services, which literally did turn mental patients loose in the streets and called it 'mainstreaming.' The unemployed niece lives in a relic of the Great Society, a 'yellow brick Camelot of low cost housing' which stinks of urine.

As was the case with Banks' novel, these contrasts are not the focus of the novel, but rather serve to accent the moral and aesthetic tensions that animate it. Either story might have been told in another setting, perhaps, but they would not have been quite the same. New England 'is a complex of occasions, themselves a geometry of spatial nature,' such as the culture embedded in Lawford, New Hampshire or Cambridge, Massachusetts. A ski resort is only possible in the former, and the computer revolution only in the latter. Wade's displacement and suffering would have a completely different texture, were he moved to a Cambridge tenement, transforming his story in the process.

These narratives are wedded to the places and the times of their telling, though this in itself hardly ensures a celebratory tone. On the contrary, Banks' *emigré* narrator asserts of Lawford, that 'We know better than anyone, precisely because we have fled in such numbers, that those who refused or were unable to leave no longer exist as a family, a tribe, a community. They are no longer a people'(6). While this is too harsh as an assessment of New England small town life, it does express a widely shared sense of loss, and a recognition that the little mill towns along the fall line, with their work ethic and sense of community, have irrevocably been transformed into resorts.

One of the final scenes in the Updike novel is a luncheon date between the niece and the adulterous professor of divinity, in which he agrees to pay her plane fare out of town. They sit in a slowly revolving restaurant at the top of a skyscraper, gazing out at Boston, the Charles River, and Cambridge. The skyscrapers themselves were the decade's additions to the Boston skyline, perpendicular proof that the city had abandoned its stubborn insistence on a more horizontal, European look, and accepted at last the American vertical city. A novel written at the turn of the century would have celebrated that view as proof of the triumph of modern civilization, trumpeting the vast panorama in the language of the technological sublime.[23] Indeed, the narrator does see that 'on high the river looked much broader – grander, more primeval – than it felt as you nipped across one of the bridges in a car.' He realizes that 'this city spread so wide and multiform around and beneath us: it was more than the mind could encompass, it overbrimmed the eye.' But he is also aware of decentering and loss. The university 'almost vanished in the overview' and was far 'less conspicuous than a number of riverside factories' that he had 'never noticed before, with their acres of flat gravel roof and their admonitory smokestacks.' The air is hazy and he cannot discern the Divinity School; his own house seems at best a 'dim patch of scum on the hazy pond.' (322-323). With this grand but indistinct perspective, he pays off his niece/mistress, and goes comfortably home to his wife. New England was still 'a complex of occasions' in 1980, but the 'geometry of spatial nature' had become fuzzy, and it was no longer seen close up, but glimpsed from a skyscraper's rotating restaurant.

Notes

1. Charles Olson, 'Maximus to Gloucester, Letter 27 [Withheld]' in A. Poulin (ed), *Contemporary American Poetry*, fourth ed. (Boston: Houghton Mifflin Company, 1985), 404.
2. This essay is based in part on personal recollections of the region where I was born. In 1970 I was in graduate school in Minnesota, but by 1974 I had returned to the area as a teacher. My parents and siblings remained in Connecticut and Massachusetts throughout the 1970s.
3. *Facts on File* 1979, 990.
4. William Ryan, *Equality* (New York: Pantheon, 1981), 13. These figures are for the 48 contiguous states, excluded Hawaii and Alaska.
5. See David E. Nye, *Contemporary American Society*, second ed. (Copenhagen: Academic Press, 1993), 154.
6. Barry Bluestone and Bennett Harrison, *The Deindustrialization of America: Plant*

Closings, Community Abandonment, and the Dismantling of Basic Industry (New York: Basic Books, 1982), 186.

7. *Statistical Abstract of the United States,* 1992 (Washington: U.S. Government Printing Office), 9.

8. *Ibid.,* 21.

9. *New York Times,* October 16, 1977, XXIII, 18:1.

10. *New York Times,* Jan 18, 1971, 18:5 [Boston] and *New York Times,* Feb. 20, 1977, XXIII, 20:4 [Hartford].

11. The sale originally was arranged in 1979 with the Smithsonian, but after protests about the loss of Boston's heritage, the paintings were sold to the Boston Museum of Fine Art, with funds raised by a special committee, including Senator Edward Kennedy.

12. Ted Szulc, *Innocents at Home: America in the 1970s* (New York: The Viking Press, 1974), 213.

13. Peter N. Carroll, *It Seemed Like Nothing Happened: The Tragedy and Promise of America in the 1970s* (New York: Holt, Rinehart and Winston, 1982), 176-177.

14. William Polenberg, *One Nation Divisible* (Harmondsworth: Penguin, 1980), 243-244.

15. Bluestone and Harrison, 95.

16. For a survey of historical preservation, see Michael Wallace, 'Reflections on the History of Historic Preservation,' in Susan Porter Bensen, Stephen Brier, and Roy Rosenzweig, *Presenting the Past: Essays on History and the Public* (Philadelphia: Temple University Press, 1986), 189.

17. *New York Times,* August 7, 1977, XXIII, 4:1.

18. Wallace, 188.

19. Bluestone and Harrison, 93.

20. Tracy Kidder, *The Soul of a New Machine* (Boston: Little, Brown, 1982).

21. Russell Banks. *Affliction* (New York: Harper and Row, 1989), 11.

22. John Updike, *Roger's Version* (New York: Alfred A. Knopf, 1987).

23. On the geometrical sublime, see David E. Nye, *American Technological Sublime* (Cambridge: MIT Press, 1994), chapter 4.

Searching for an Old Faithful America: National Park Tourism in the 1970s

Robert Matej Bednar

> Again the road brings us close to the brink of Millard Canyon and here we see something like a little shrine mounted on a post. We stop. The wooden box contains a register book for visitors, brand-new, with less than a dozen entries, put here by the BLM – Bureau of Land Management. 'Keep the Tourists out,' some tourist from Salt Lake City has written. As fellow tourists we heartily agree.
>
> Edward Abbey, *Desert Solitaire* (1968)

On July 5, 1976, The *New York Times* ran an article assessing the national mood on the occasion of the nation's Bicentennial. The author declared that 'outside the official observances of the 200th celebration of freedom, there is an undercurrent of uncertainty about what succeeding Fourths of July hold for future generations of Americans.' The author reported that people interviewed around the country 'expressed a mild disorientation about the state of American life, as though the national compass had been lost as the country moved through a confusing series of internal and external shocks.' These 'shocks' – identified in the article as Watergate, Vietnam, the oil embargo, 'stagflation,' the civil rights movement, women's liberation, 'the changing nature of family life,' and forecasts of ecological exhaustion – had 'changed the basic pattern of life for millions of Americans and challenged assumptions that had never been questioned before.' As a result, the author argued, the dominant mood in America was one of 'malaise.'[1]

Much to the dismay of many Americans, the National Parks – which traditionally had been valued for the fact that they were landscapes *separate from* the modern American social landscape – were not immune to these trends. Indeed, as we will see, the parks served as some of the main stages on which the drama of 1970s 'cultural anxiety' was played out, because many Americans turned to the National Park 'wilderness' landscapes for respite from their confusing everyday social world; they went to the National Parks searching for an Old Faithful America to re-orient themselves by. Ironically, however, these searchers encountered parts of that contentious social world again in the wilderness as well. Those searching for an 'Old Faithful' America in the National Parks to provide a contrast to the new America were constantly disappointed; those who sought to purify the parks of the influence of the new trends found themselves embroiled in rhetorical conundrums separating 'appropriate' and 'inappropriate' behaviors and facilities in the parks.

National Park Service (NPS) policies underwent important shifts during the decade, most of which leaned towards the preservation side of the organization's historical preservation/use dialectic, but never far enough to make preservationists happy and always too far for the others involved in the debates. National Park visitors in the 1970s were frequently warned that what they would encounter in the parks was 'a transitional amalgam of compromises between the old and the new that will cause vexation among both the "Chevrolet set" and outdoor purists.'[2] This description could be applied to American society in general in the Seventies, as Americans seemed to be in a state of limbo, caught in the middle of two strongly identified decades and two very different views of the future of America. To use two symbolic phrases (from Neil Young and Ronald Reagan, respectively) that encompass the distinction between the 1960s and 1980s, in the 1970s America was still reeling with the realization that they were living in a time 'After the Gold Rush,' but they also were not quite ready to 'wake up' to the coming 'morning in America' engineered by conservatives in the 1980s.[3] By the end of the 1970s, even the National Park Service itself seemed to have its own case of 'malaise.' A *New York Times* reporter observed in 1980 that the Service 'appears to be going through a kind of crisis of the spirit that arises from profound changes in its size and mission, major changes in the duties of Park Rangers, and budgetary and management problems.' Traditional duties remained for Rangers, but in addition, they now had to deal also with new social classes, subcultures, and ethnicities who did not have the same 'respect for the resource' as their more traditional constituency. Consequently, the author wrote, 'today a ranger may also have to act as a narcotics agent, a traffic cop, a community relations officer or a garbage collector.'[4] Because America itself was disoriented, America was demanding more and more from its National Parks, and the strains were showing everywhere.

This is a story about those strains. It is a story about people struggling to determine what the National Parks would and should mean in a rapidly changing America, and a story about people struggling to determine how those meanings would and should guide tourist behavior and experiences in the parks in the 1970s and beyond. The battle to define appropriate park behavior took shape as a *cultural* conflict, much as the tensions between American subgroups in society at large in the 1960s and 1970s were also informed by concerns over generations, classes, races, etc.. In telling this story I use the words of the people struggling with these problems in the context of the cultural conflicts at the time – late-1960s through early-1980s journalists, historians, preservationists, Park Service officials, environmental behavior researchers, anthropologists and cultural critics – so what emerges in this essay is a story both about the strains and about the way people talked about those strains as they were unfolding.[5]

In the 1970s, many Americans participated in this conflict in the parks themselves as visitors, and those who did not at least witnessed it in the form of a continuous flow of press reports about the pressures of 'overcrowding' in the parks focusing on the popular 1970s question, 'Are We Loving the Parks to Death?' At the center of this conflict was the question not only of *how many* people should be 'allowed' in the parks, but *which ones*, and *which uses* should be 'allowed' once the visitors were there.[6] As Joseph Sax wrote in his preservationist polemic *Mountains Without Handrails* (1980), 'most conflict over National Park policy does not really turn on whether or not we ought to have nature reserves (for that is widely agreed) but on the uses that people will make of those places.'[7] The conflicts were characterized by extensive discussions re-evaluating 'the state of the parks' in relation to the 'original intent' of both the legislation that had created Yellowstone National Park one hundred years before, and the 1916 'Organic Act' that had created the National Park Service.[8] The debates proved once again that, even from the beginning, the problem for the National Park Service has always been a semantic one with practical consequences: what does it mean when we say that the Park Service is charged with both conserving resources and 'providing for their enjoyment'? Conserved from what? For what? How? For whose enjoyment? How is it provided, etc.?[9] The most frequently asked question of the decade was similar to the one posed in the May 1972 *National Geographic* special issue celebrating the centennial of the founding of Yellowstone National Park: 'When does providing for "the benefit and enjoyment of the people" have to stop because of the heavy burden it places on preserving the environment?'[10]

Debate about the parks has always been concerned with the 'intrusions of human artifacts on the park landscapes,' but by the 1970s these debates became more pronounced because of the palpable impact of automobile-centered planning and the consequent visitation pressures.[11] As Linda Graber argued in *Wilderness as Sacred Space* in 1976, public lands can absorb all sorts of uses when these uses are not visible to other users, but when 'use pressure' grows – as it did dramatically after World War II – determining appropriate and inappropriate uses becomes more urgent.[12] Soon after the war, there was a phenomenal surge in American tourism in general and tourism in the National Parks in particular. The reasons for the surge were many, not the least of which was the somewhat intangible psychological one that people were reacting to the release from a suppressed desire to see America that had been promoted by the late-1930s 'rediscover America' movement but thwarted by the privations of both the Great Depression and wartime rationing. Some more tangible reasons included an increasing amount of leisure time for a broader range of American society; more efficient national highway systems that allowed for longer trips (particularly after 1956, with the inauguration of the Interstate Highway System); a proliferation of tourist information in the form of magazines, USGS topographical maps, and travel guides (especially the newly-completed WPA guides to the states); and the rising popularity of outdoor recreation due in part to the availability of camping technologies that had been adapted from wartime military production, such as application of aluminum, plastic, synthetic rubber, and nylon for tents, sleeping bags, insulated clothing, rafts, and hiking boots.[13]

In the midst of the post-war domestic travel surge, the National Parks were overwhelmed by a new influx of visitors. In 1956, the same year as Congress passed the Federal Interstate Highway Act, in part to deal with similar problems, the Park Service director, Conrad Wirth, initiated a sweeping plan to overhaul the infrastructure of the parks to cope with the actual and projected continued rise in visitation. He called the project 'Mission 66' because he hoped to complete it by 1966 in time for the fiftieth anniversary of the National Park Service.[14] By the late 1960s, the legacy of Mission 66 was an entrenched battle between preservationists and pro-development forces over the way the parks should be managed. Preservationists criticized Mission 66 from the beginning of its implementation because they saw it as 'a travesty upon the "true" mission of the National Park Service, which was to preserve and protect rather than to promote and develop.'[15] In their influential late 1960s monograph titled *Man and Nature in the National Parks*, F. Fraser Darling and Noel D. Eichhorn declared that 'the present urgent problem is how to cope with 120 million visitors each year to the parks; there is no call for advertising the attractions' or developing new ones. The authors continued by saying that they were 'uneasy about the conception of Mission 66' because its purpose 'has been to increase visitation, making it easier to get into the National Parks and [ensuring] that the visitors should be more comfortable in various ways once they are there. Mission 66 has done comparatively little for the plants and animals.'[16]

By the late 1960s and early 1970s, the climate was right for such a 'biocentric' re-evaluation of the post-war developments in the National Parks. Preservationists had won important battles in the Grand Canyon and Dinosaur National Parks in the 1960s, and as early as 1971, people were forecasting that the 1970s would be 'the environmental decade.'[17] Certainly by the late 1960s, the terms 'environment' and 'ecology' – formerly somewhat esoteric scientific terms – had become household words.[18] Further, in the 1970s, the aesthetic environmentalism of the 1960s – characterized by urban renewal projects, historical preservation, and the highway beautification movement – developed into a more all-encompassing ecological view that 'transcended concern for the quality of life to fear of life itself.'[19]

In the late 1960s, a new influx of young white Americans from the counterculture, looking to natural landscapes for physical manifestations of their developing value systems, enlivened the wilderness movement as they adopted its rhetoric as its own. By 1970, for instance, the adjective 'wild' was widely used among those in the counterculture, who 'identified it with freedom, authenticity, spontaneity or, in the common parlance, "letting it all hang out."'[20] In a 1971 article titled 'Youth, Rebellion & the Environment,' Gilbert Stucker argued that countercultural values had originated in a response to the 'trauma' of 'progressive alienation from natural reality,' so it seemed appropriate to many that they would turn to nature to help them articulate an alternative vision. Youth were searching for a more 'authentic' alternative to the 'artificial living' that they found in cities, which to many seemed to be 'more a simulacrum of life than life – a travesty to be acted out in a milieu of plastic and asphalt, steel and concrete.' In the midst of such an environment, 'they hunger for the touch of the real – for the reality of trees and mountains and free-flowing rivers.' Stucker suggested that youths went to the wilderness 'to feel themselves flush against the raw edge of existence with recourse to nothing but their own hands and minds;' they hoped that by actively participating in wilderness landscapes, they would find more authentic experiences than were afforded in mainstream social existence. Stucker related an encounter a reporter had had with two teenage hippies in Yosemite. One told him, 'There are no real values left in society. We come here because it beautiful, it is real.' The other said, 'Here, I don't need LSD to turn me on. I can get the same feeling from seeing the beauty of the mountains and the cliffs and the trees.'[21]

The countercultural equation of wilderness with authenticity was nothing new; at least since Emerson, certain Americans had sought out an 'original relationship' with reality by immersing themselves in Nature. By the middle of the twentieth century, however, the search for authenticity had taken on new urgency as Americans found themselves surrounded more and more with artificial landscapes and had less daily contact with nature.[22] Despite the fact that tourists in the 1970s went to the National Parks for a variety of reasons, the one thing that seemed to draw all of the American subgroups along the continuum between 'wilderness purists' and 'industrial tourists' was to witness natural wonders (as opposed to cultural wonders), and this was part of the problem people had in conceptualizing appropriate uses of the park.

It is important to remember in this context that the category of 'Natural Wilderness' is not a 'found object' that exists in its own right; it is a cultural artifact *constructed* and maintained through a series of cultural acts (the same is true, of course, for the opposite category of 'Modern Urbanized America'). All landforms are transformed into 'landscapes' when we apply conceptual frameworks and meta-narratives to identify and value them *as landscapes*. As Martin Kreiger argued in his 1973 article 'What's Wrong With Plastic Trees?,'

'Paradoxically, the phenomena that the public thinks of as "natural" often require great artifice in their creation.'[23]

For example, after the passage of the Wilderness Act of 1964, the National Park Service and the National Forest Service – the two agencies responsible for maintaining the newly-designated American 'Wilderness Areas' – adopted similar plans to assure that their areas would appear to be natural to the visitors. The new wilderness management plans for both agencies showed the amount of sometimes insidious construction and management that was paradoxically necessary to make a landscape appear 'wild.' In his 1971 article 'They're Putting "Wild" Back in Wilderness,' Stephen Arno wrote that within the designated 'wildernesses,' the agencies 'put "wild" back in wilderness' by removing existing campground tables, fire grills, tourist cabins and other constructed facilities and subsequently prohibiting their construction unless they were considered to be a 'necessity for the use and protection of the resource.'[24] The new plans stressed that 'trails be built and maintained so they appear to be a natural part of the landscape – like game trails – rather than a man-made intrusion.' Wherever feasible, the agencies gave precedence to 'improvised bridges' over streams and rivers, like fallen trees or strategical-ly-placed boulders, instead of 'man-made constructions.' To further appeal to the visitor's 'powerful desire for adventure,' the agencies removed existing trail mileage markers on backcountry trails and replaced them with more accurate maps that would test the visitor's orienteering skills more directly – a test that some sought out but that others hardly wanted in an era when 'the national compass had been lost.'[25]

The underlying principle behind these distinctions was the notion that the 'natural' National Parks should be maintained in contrast to 'artificial' modern urban America. As a Park Service directive phrased it, 'natural parks today are in effect islands of (near) naturalness in a sea of civilized, man-manipulated landscape.... [C]are should be exercised to preclude the adverse and detracting influence of the modern, technological world.'[26] The process of defining the status of a landscape as a 'wilderness' was no simple 'natural' act, however. Martin Kreiger argued that the 'meanings we attach to such a piece of territory ... convert it to a wilderness' through four mechanisms: 'designating the object as rare; differentiating it from other objects of the same species; establishing its significance; and determining its position in the context of society.'[27] The process Kreiger describes is similar to the general process that anthropologist Dean MacCannell, in his ground-breaking analysis of the structure of tourism *The Tourist: A New Theory of the Leisure Class* (1976), argued is structurally necessary to 'mark' a tourist 'sight' to make it an 'attraction' which subse-quently establishes a relationship between the tourist, what he sees, how and why he sees it, and what it means to him.[28] This process of 'marking the sight' is often invisible because it is a process intrinsic to the structure of tourist attractions themselves. As MacCannell argues, 'Natural' parkscapes, defined by moderns as 'exotic' and 'anti-modern,' are necessarily antihistorical and unnatural because 'as they preserve, they automatically separate modernity from its past and from nature and elevate it above them. Nature and the past are made part of the present' by 'incorporating' them into modernity – by making them into things that function 'as revealed objects, as tourist attractions.'[29]

Generally, the vernacular landscapes that surround us in daily life often only exist for us as 'inconspicuous backgrounds' for daily life; they 'retreat from attention' unless they are 'brought forward into our awareness' by a significant change in their condition or use that renders them 'conspicuous.'[30] Tourist landscapes like National Parks, on the other hand, do not function as backdrops to daily productive work, but as landscapes intended to be consumed through aware contemplation. Therefore every effort is made (by National Park Service 'interpretive' efforts, popular cultural images of the landscapes, etc.) to make them conspicuous *as landscapes*. This does not mean that they are not 'useful,' but that their usefulness is not the same as the usefulness of, for example, the physical plant of an oil refinery. They function as liminal spaces because they are disconnected spatially and metaphorically from everyday utility value and because they are filled with people searching for ways of interacting with them as landscapes instead of interacting with them as a backdrop for daily livelihood (park personnel excluded, for the moment).

This is true for National Park landscapes particularly, but it also a characteristic of tourist endeavors in general. As Jonathan Culler wrote in his 1981 essay 'Semiotics of Tourism,' all over the world tourists are like amateur semioticians 'engaged in semiotic projects, reading cities, landscapes and cultures as sign systems.'[31] In our particular case, we can say that National Park tourists go to the National Parks *searching for* a landscape that will reveal itself to them as a sign of itself – searching for the essential quality that makes each landscape 'unique,' like the South Rim scenic overlook views of Canyon stratification which give the canyon its 'Grand Canyon-ness,' like the faces of El Capitan and Half Dome which give Yosemite its sense of 'Yosemite-ness,' and like Old Faithful which defines for many the 'Yellowstone-ness' of Yellowstone. When one sees something like Old Faithful for oneself, one sees not only Old Faithful the geological phenomenon, but Old Faithful as 'Old Faithful' – as a semiotic phenomenon.

Since this essay is essentially about the semiotic phenomenon of people encountering semiotic phenomena, semiotic analysis will be useful to us in trying to understand not only the behavior of National Park tourists in the 1970s, but also the rhetoric that surrounded it and attempted to define it as authentic/inauthentic, natural/unnatural, urbanist/wildernist, and appropriate/inappropriate. As Jonathan Culler argued, a 'semiotic perspective assists the study of tourism by preventing one from thinking of signs and sign relations as corruptions of what ought to be a direct experience of being or the natural world.' In this context, the tourist's 'quest for experience' in a National Park environment – the search for an Old Faithful America – is then better understood as a 'quest for an experience of signs' – a search for the *signs of an Old Faithful America*.[32] Wilderness purist attempts to gain unmediated contact with the wilderness 'thing itself' notwithstanding, the experience National Park tourists are chasing is only possible in those particular landscapes because they are enriched by the sign systems that give them cultural value as multi-layered resonating landscapes pregnant with significance that is simultaneously treated as a given and as a point of contention.

Central to discussions of such questions in the 1970s was the effort to understand recent developments in the context of the revered 'National Park idea.' As Alfred Runte argues in *National Parks: The American Experience*, 'the National Park idea evolved to fulfill cultural rather than environmental needs.' Those cultural needs were linked to the 'search for a distinct national identity' engendered by nineteenth century American 'cultural anxiety' – the fear that America *actually had* no culture to speak of.[33] On an even more fundamental level, however, the National Park idea not only 'fulfills cultural needs' but is *itself* a cultural artifact. The National Park idea is a category of cultural history, thus definitions of it reflect changing notions of the cultural construction of landscapes.

This is an essential point to make when we consider the discourse that surrounded the National Parks in the 1970s, because at the heart of the matter of deciding what and who the parks were for was a debate over the *meaning* of the parks in American culture. As historian Stanford Demars reminds us, the National Park idea was 'based on a cultural premise,' therefore there is always room for interpretation when we assess the role of National Parks in American culture. This is especially true of interpretations of appropriate behavior in the parks, because 'only by definition of what we want the parks to be can we determine what is an "appropriate" way to use and enjoy our national heritage.'[34] This was true from the beginning, as the National Park idea developed when Americans made Yellowstone the first 'National Park' in history. As Chris Magoc argues, Yellowstone National Park itself is fundamentally a cultural landscape, because

> Yellowstone's legal separation and cultural enshrinement in the late nineteenth century, while severing the reserve cartographically and historically from the course of environmental exploitation on the broader American landscape, nevertheless failed to disconnect Yellowstone from the culture responsible for its 'creation,' nor from the biosphere outside to which it remains irrevocably attached.[35]

Many cultural historians have linked the original founding of National Parks to cultural frameworks such as nineteenth century aesthetic Romanticism.[36] But in a broader context, the idea of preserving a portion of the natural landscape from the encroachment of modernity is itself a notion imbedded in modern American cultural discourse.

The most important National Park landscape icon of the 1970s was the Old Faithful Geyser, the primary image people associated with Yellowstone and what cultural historian Alfred Runte calls the 'enduring symbol of the National Park idea.'[37] Old Faithful was the symbolic focus of the 1970s attempt to measure contemporary developments in the parks against the heritage of the National Park idea. Many of these assessments were first seriously discussed by policy makers and critics in 1972 as Americans mobilized to celebrate the Centennial of the National Park Idea by commemorating the founding of Yellowstone National Park in 1872.[38] The general sentiment of the National Park Service officials and private preservationists alike about the Yellowstone Centennial was reflected in the statement by Verne Huser in his 1972 *National Parks and Conservation Magazine* article titled 'Yellowstone National Park: Use, Overuse & Misuse.' Huser said that the Centennial should be 'a time to do more than sing praises to the accomplishment of a good idea. It offers the opportunity to question, examine, and evaluate the direction in which Yellowstone and other National Parks are headed.'[39] Many observers were disturbed by what they saw, and were concerned that if something was not done soon to remedy 'the current National Park ills,' the parks would not even be around to celebrate a Yellowstone Bicentennial a hundred years later. The more ecologically apocalyptic among them forecast that if something was not done soon, the degradation of the parks would be the least of their worries, because life on earth itself would not make it to the Yellowstone Bicentennial either.[40]

The central official NPS document to come out of the 1972 meetings was the National Parks Centennial Commission's *Preserving a Heritage: Final Report to the President and the Congress*, published in 1973.[41] In it, the Commission discussed the major events, discussions, and recommendations that had surfaced that year (such as those in *National Parks for the Future*), and outlined the proposed official responses to them. Perhaps the most valuable thing about the book to cultural historians analyzing the discourse surrounding the National Parks in the 1970s, however, is its discussion of the Commission's 'comprehensive program to disseminate information about National Park values and the National Parks Centennial.'[42] The Commission's official medallion commemorating the National Parks Centennial Year featured an engraved representation of the erupting Old Faithful. The Commission used an image of the medallion on all of its official communications, and encouraged others to do so as well, further solidifying the Old Faithful image.[43]

The Old Faithful image was an apt choice to represent the Yellowstone Centennial, not only because by the 1970s it had become a direct representation containing all of the concepts and images associated with 'National Parks' and 'Yellowstone,' but also because of the nature of the geyser itself.

As Chris Magoc argued in a recent article, Old Faithful had become a popular icon because it was both strange *and* predictably comforting: 'Conforming to human standards of technological proficiency and theatrical showmanship, Old Faithful became the point of intellectual and emotive access between a modern industrial civilization and the capricious and alien geothermal landscape of Yellowstone.'[44] Old Faithful was an especially powerful sight in the ecologically-conscious 1970s, because the 'iconographic image of Old Faithful continuing its hourly eruption into the Yellowstone sky somehow takes the edge from our fears that the planet outside the park may be dying.'[45]

Article after article in 1972 also used Old Faithful as an ironic point of departure for analysis, juxtaposing the 'natural' wonder against its blatantly 'cultural' surroundings. In his 1972 article assessing the legacy of Yellowstone, Verne Huser included some photographs of people crowded around an erupting Old Faithful. Huser's caption to the photographs reads, 'Facilities built to help visitors "enjoy" scenic attractions in Yellowstone in some cases have made enjoyment an impossibility. ... Boardwalks, parking lots, service buildings, and the crowds themselves seem to diminish the impression of grandeur naturally created by the magnificent fountain.'[46] Huser also speculated that because they are surrounded by elements of an urbanized landscape, some people are even led to vandalize the geyser basin, because 'their sensitivities to nature [have] been dulled by the stifling atmosphere of roads and paths lined with tourists.' Huser and other preservationists looked at the context surrounding the geyser and concluded that 'the park experience has lost its true meaning' because it included too many symbolic objects imported from urban America: instead of a wilderness experience, what visitors to the Geyser Basin experienced was rather something more akin to 'a walk next to a construction site, whose protecting walls invariably are covered with graffiti by passers-by' (16-17).

Time and time again in the 1970s, park managers and preservationist writers argued for maximum physical and symbolic separation between the *style* of National Parks and urban America. Linda Graber argued in *Wilderness as Sacred Space* that this attitude was derived from the preservationist view that wildernesses were 'sacred spaces' to be protected from degradation by the secular in much the same way that believers protect churches from incongruous activities: 'purists seek a Wholly Other environment from their daily surroundings and oppose the penetration of reminders of the ordinary world into wilderness.'[47] As Edward Abbey states the case for excluding automobiles from National Parks in *Desert Solitaire*, 'We have agreed not to drive our automobiles into cathedrals, concert halls, art museums, legislative assemblies, private bedrooms and the other sanctums of our culture; we should treat our National Parks with the same deference, for they, too, are holy places.'[48] Graber argued that because purists thought the National Parks were 'holy places,' they not only judged other visitors' behavior harshly, they also took the next step by trying to *convert* the recreationists to their point of view that the only 'appropriate focus of outdoor recreation [was] undiluted contact with the natural environment':

> Purists resent the outsider's presence in sacred space because his 'inferior' mode of perception allows him to enjoy and inadvertently to desecrate the wilderness.... On the other hand, purist leaders hope that education might elevate the outsider's perception and improve his manners. Every outsider is a potential purist.[49]

Such obviously paternalistic attitudes towards the public 'outsiders' were often met in the 1970s with charges that wilderness purists were 'elitist.' To some, it seemed especially ironic that the Rangers – who were public servants – were starting to become unnecessarily hostile to the public who were 'suspected of harboring intentions of degrading the primeval wilderness or otherwise engaging in inappropriate activities.'[50] Joseph Sax rejected the term 'elitist' because it ignored the fact that the purists practiced not only judgment, but also offered methods of conversion. As he saw it, the preservationist understood that people want different recreation opportunities, but he believed that

> the parks have a distinctive function to perform that is separate from the service of conventional tourism.... The idea is not that reflective recreation should consume all our leisure time, but rather that we should develop a taste for it, and that stimulating the appetite should be a primary function of National Parks.[51]

To accommodate those wilderness purists who were searching for ways to teach other visitors how to appropriately establish an authentic relationship to Nature, the National Park Service redesigned its interpretation programs in the 1970s to 'popularize knowledge' of ecology – to 'translate [the] language of the earth' into a form understandable and useful to the urban visitor.[52] In 1972, the Conservation Foundation called for more 'relevant' interpretation programs that would not only introduce visitors to discrete park features and teach them how to behave around them, but also introduce them to general ecological processes and principles: the Park Service 'must do more than foster an environmental ethic for the parks; it must concern itself with the whole of Spaceship Earth.'[53] This idea was echoed in the National Parks Centennial Commission's *Preserving a Heritage* a year later, with a demand for more 'how-to' wilderness programs featuring more 'face-to-face interaction' between Rangers and visitors. The face-to-face interactions would serve the double purpose of offering 'wonderful opportunities for personalizing and humanizing park knowledge while advancing the understanding and practice of good park manners.'[54]

But the problem was that different people had different ideas about what constituted 'good park manners.' While many of the decade's debates over 'appropriate use' of the National Parks were couched in the language of ecology, the central issue still seems to have been about the *cultural symbolism* of the particular use being discussed. Joseph Sax argued that preservationists were 'disturbed not only – and not even most importantly – by the physical deterioration of the parks, but by a sense that the style of modern tourism is depriving the parks of their central symbolism, their message about the relationship between man and nature, and man and industrial society.'[55]

As with this example, much of Sax's criticism of 'inappropriate use' was directed at the *style of* 'modern tourism.' In his celebration of preservationists, he morally denigrated 'typical tourists' whom he thought to be satisfied with a less profound experience of the National Parks than were preservationists. But while for Sax the two entities – 'preservationist' and 'tourist' – are ontologically differentiated beings, they seem on closer analysis to differ only by a matter of degree. All visitors to the parks are by definition 'tourists,' because they are visitors and not residents of the places they are voluntarily interacting with. Nevertheless, many tourists do not like to call themselves tourists. Instead, they offer critiques of other tourists' behavior that suggest that they think that they are qualitatively different beings. But as many theorists concerned with the structure of tourism in the 1970s and early 1980s argued, moral denigration of tourists and tourism is *intrinsic to* tourism itself and not something *independent of* tourism. As Jonathan Culler observed, 'part of what is involved in being a tourist is disliking tourists (both other tourists and the fact that one is oneself a tourist). Tourists can always find someone more touristy than themselves to sneer at.'[56]

Thus it may be accurate to call wilderness purists 'anti-tourist tourists.' Anti-tourist tourists generally criticize 'typical tourists' not *because* they go sight-seeing, but for the *way* they do it. As MacCannell argued, anti-tourist tourists criticize other tourists not necessarily because tourists are tourists, but because they are 'not being tourist enough' – because they are 'satisfied with superficial experiences,' and thus fail to 'see everything the way it "ought" to be seen.'[57] Usually the distinction they made between correct and incorrect perception of the natural environment grew out of their distinction between passively consuming 'pre-formulated' spectacles on the one hand, and actively going out of their way to involve themselves in an 'unmediated' landscape on the other.

Perhaps the most insidious example of this is the cliché-ed primacy that anti-tourist tourists give to sights 'off the beaten track' that they claim are more authentic than the sights on the beaten track. The fact that most people use the same phrase to describe these places ('off the beaten track') provides a clue to their status as places framed by shared values.[58] In the case of National Parks, wilderness purists consider the 'backcountry' more authentic than the popular scenic destinations and concessions. Often anti-tourist tourists subject themselves to elaborate rituals in an attempt to ensure that their experiences will not be mediated by the sign systems framing it as 'the beaten track.' This is ironic because, as theorist Georges Van Den Abbeele puts it, 'preparation to assure the immediacy or authenticity of the experience only renders its occurrence all the more mediated and inauthentic as it has been mediated by the very preparation designed to assure its immediateness.'[59] Thus even the land beyond the beaten track is beaten, just in a slightly different way. This is what Jonathan Culler calls the inescapable 'dilemma of authenticity': 'to be experienced as authentic [the sight] must be marked as authentic, but when it is marked as authentic it is mediated, a sign of itself, and hence not authentic in the sense of unspoiled.'[60]

This dilemma seems to have escaped notice by most preservationists, however. For example, preservationists in the 1970s criticized popular scenic loop drives and scenic overlooks not only because they scarred the landscape, but because they encouraged visitors to passively experience the landscape from a distance according to someone else's program instead of actively engaging it for themselves: 'as spectators before the drama of nature rather than participants in it, park visitors can hardly be expected to come away with an adequate understanding of how we fit into the natural world.'[61] For Joseph Sax in particular, the problem with scenic overlooks and loop roads was that they did not encourage the visitor to 'penetrate the park.' Instead, they offered the visitor a self-contained 'vista with a fixed beginning and end' that left no room for 'setting one's own agenda.'[62] On a more fundamental level, however, it would be more meaningful to say that the problem with both scenic overlooks and loop roads is not so much that they *threaten* autonomy, but that they *mystify* it, by encouraging people to think that they are autonomous beings in the presence of authentic landscapes.

As Georges Van Den Abbeele argued, the 'illusion of authenticity depends upon the tourist's feeling himself to be in an immediate relationship with the sight. This immediacy is assured by the sight's presence, to which the tourist can *point*.'[63] But the physical presence of the landscape mystifies the mediations that intervene between the viewer and the thing viewed by obscuring the fact that the landscape has been certified as an authentic tourist attraction by the literal and figurative signs that surround it and present it within a sign system, such as road signs, guidebooks, post cards, interpretive facilities, etc., and the physical apparatus that 'affords' the view, whether it be the road or the scenic overlook deck. The physical closure of loop roads and scenic overlooks encourages people to think that they have 'seen all there is to see,' and further, that they 'understand' what they see, because what they have been shown purports to be a totality – a self-contained 'discrete experience' presented in such a way that it welcomes the tourist's act of appropriation which incorporates the totality into his or her own personal totalizing narrative of his or her own 'wilderness experience.'[64]

The case against loop roads and scenic overlooks was perfectly straightforward when compared to the mid-1970s debate about which sort of boat –

motor-powered or oar-powered – was appropriate for river-running on the Colorado River in the Grand Canyon. The debate centered not on resource ecology issues *per se*, but psychological and symbolic ones; it shows the subtleties at the heart of the anti-tourist preservationist drive to keep elements of the ordinary technological world out of the natural landscape and separate the style of the parks from the style of modern America. A 1976 article about the Grand Canyon motor/oars question in *National Parks and Conservation* Magazine declared that 'a heated controversy rages around the type of recreational opportunities that should be offered in the National Park. Should river trips provide an adventurous wilderness experience, or should they provide fast trips for a greater number of people?'[65] Expressed that way, and particularly expressed that way *to* the preservationist audience of *National Parks and Conservation*, it would not seem like a choice at all. By denigrating the group that opted for the motor boat experience, preservationists seemed not only to be saying that one group's behavior was more appropriate than another, but also to be claiming 'that one group would get more from a trip than another.'[66] In contrast to the motor-boat 'tours,' which were usually run by concessioner on rigid schedules that included very little time (or need) for effort from the passenger, the oar boats 'allowed for' travel at one's own pace and according to one's own stamina. They provided a 'wilderness experience' by allowing for a slow, quiet, intimate interaction with the Canyon. Such trips were celebrated as 'a source of re-creation' (as opposed to 'recreation') needed as a contrast to the everyday urban world from which the visitor came – 'a world closed in by office walls, artificial light, heating, air conditioning, and the automobile.'[67]

Joseph Sax later characterized the essential debate like this: 'the preservationist claim is simply that motors don't belong in this remote and wild place; that they betray the idea of man immersed in nature and bring industrialization to a place whose meaning inheres in its isolation from, and contrast to, life in society.'[68] In the oar-propelled boats, people open themselves up to what Sax called 'reflective recreation.'[69] For Sax, the 'purpose of reserving natural areas' like the Grand Canyon in the first place was to 'expose rather than insulate' the visitor, 'so that the peculiar character of the desert, or the alpine forest, can be distinctly felt.'[70]

In the words of another preservationist author, people who use the oar boats 'place themselves directly in the Colorado's power ... which opens them to the flow of the wilderness.'[71] Thus oar-propelled boats were all the more appropriate for wilderness use because they literally enacted a symbolic ecological ideal: in the oar boats, humans were '*going with the flow*' of the rhythms of nature versus *speeding over* them in a mechanical contraption.[72] Perhaps in the midst of such heady rhetoric it was easy for preservationists to forget that they were 'flowing with the rhythms of nature' while aboard boats that were made from rubber with human and machine labor just like the motor rafts; it was just that they did not have motors on the back of them.

When preservationists and park managers talked about the motors or oars question in the Grand Canyon, they expressed concern over the 'carrying capacity' of the river and the parks in general.[73] They borrowed the term from livestock managers, who used it to refer to the ability of a particular piece of land to withstand grazing without degrading the resource. In National Park environmental monographs, the term was used similarly to refer to the physical capacity of the parks to absorb visitation without ecological degradation. But more than physical ecological carrying capacities, preservationists and managers were concerned about the less tangible 'social-psychological' carrying capacities, such as the 'capacity of the user to sustain impacts of other users without incurring significant repugnance.'[74] Roderick Nash declared the principle most directly: 'As visitation increases there is a point at which the wilderness quality of a place disappears.'[75]

But the point is that people disagreed greatly not only about what constituted 'a wilderness experience' in the first place, but also about where to locate the precise points at which 'visitation' turned into 'crowding' and finally 'overcrowding,' because different people perceive the same environment differently. In the 1960s and 1970s social scientists concerned with the way people interpret and interact with their surroundings began to move towards models that accounted for the complexities of 'transactional interactions' between the observer and the observed instead of the two traditional models of 'object-centered' analyses on one hand, which emphasized the way features of the landscape produced certain responses in people, and 'subject-centered' analyses on the other hand, which focused on the idiosyncracies of personal perception.[76] As one 1970s landscape perception researcher characterized it, '[p]erception grows out of complex interactions between 'reality,' the human perceptual apparati, the individual aspects of environment, experience, heredity, physiology, and personality traits, as well as the effects of group values and conditioning.'[77]

Several studies of wilderness areas in the late 1960s and 1970s found wide differences of opinion among users and between users and managers regarding appropriate behavior.[78] In a study done at Dinosaur National Monument in Utah in the mid-1970s analyzing interview data in the context of current 'expectancy and discrepancy' theories, Richard Schreyer and Joseph Roggenbuck found that visitor assessments of social-psychological carrying capacities were not a universal given.[79] Instead, they depended on visitor *expectations* about crowding and subsequent perceptions of their surroundings: 'dissatisfaction in recreation due to crowding is a function of the discrepancy between the numbers of others one expects to see while participating in an activity and the numbers one actually encounters.'[80] If people both *valued* and *expected* solitude (as the wilderness purists did), but found that they were surrounded by other people, they tended to say that the area they were visiting was 'over-crowded,' whereas people who had come to the area expecting to see crowds (or even had come seeking out other people to interact with) thought the amount of people was appropriate. Schreyer and Roggenbuck's findings also showed that people who were concerned with crowding in the first place were in the minority: 'The perception of 50 per cent of all users who feel they encounter the right number of persons is considerably different from the perception of 86 per cent of High Wildernists who feel they encountered too many people in certain situations' (391). As Allan Fitzsimmons wrote in 1976, '[t]he conservationist speaks of crowds, overdevelopment, intrusion on natural landscapes, and the decline of the park experience; yet attendance figures indicate that environmental disruption has not reached unacceptable levels in the minds of most park tourists.'[81]

Despite the fact that NPS managers and wilderness activists measured park visitor behavior against the ideals they associated with the National Park idea, most visitors did not think that there was a problem, and that was itself part of the problem. Throughout the 1970s, preservationists argued that crowds compromised their ability to have a 'wilderness experience,' and reiterated that the 'Parks were meant to be spaces of scenic grandeur where people could temporarily step outside the hectic pace, material orientation, and environmental degradation of their daily settings to become immersed the natural scene.'[82] If they had bothered to ask the people in the crowds their opinion on the subject, they might have found (as many 'environment-behavior researchers' and 'leisure researchers' in the 1970s were finding) that the 'crowds' agreed with them about the *goals* of the park experience – they just used different *means* of attaining these goals than the preservationists required. Wellman, Dawson, and Roggenbuck suggested that we should think of wilderness value as a 'floating baseline' for determining the appropriateness of certain wilderness behaviors, because different wilderness users have different ideas about how to bring 'the wilderness experience' into being.[83]

Furthermore, even those visitors who *said* they valued privacy and criticized overcrowding did not always appear to practice what they preached. For example, in a 1977 study of Yosemite National Park backcountry users, Robert Lee not only interviewed backpackers and campers (as many other researchers had done), but also observed their 'greeting behavior' on trails and the extent to which campers used 'avoidance behavior' to seek out private campsites. Lee found 'no association between visitor attitudes toward crowding and observed social interaction or behavior to avoid such social interactions' in the backcountry.[84] This suggests that the perception of overcrowding was not only in the eye of the beholder, but may have also been a factor of the frequency with which it was talked about in the 1970s. As early as 1967, a writer for *National Parks Magazine* had responded ironically to a flurry of articles in the national press about National Park overcrowding with the observation that there had been so many articles on it that 'now it is knowingly referred to by almost anyone you talk to. It has even been on TV.'[85]

As a final example of the problems at the heart of the debates over carrying capacity and National Park behavior, consider the case of National Park camping. Throughout the 1970s, park managers reiterated that there were certain camping behaviors which were appropriate in the National Parks and certain ones which were not. Traditionally, campers had sought isolation from other campers (or at least other parties of campers). By the 1970s, however, as with other outdoor recreation practices, camping had become diffused into more and more levels of society, and campgrounds varied greatly in clientele and extent of development. Researchers found that many of the conflicts at campgrounds and other areas within natural recreation landscapes were derived from the fact that in general the more traditional park clientele – upper-class and middle-class Americans – were still going to the parks to find solitude, while lower classes were going to the parks to congregate with others.[86]

In such a situation, visitors with very different ideas of what was appropriate found themselves sleeping right next to each other. In their 1971 study of modern camping culture, Roger Clark, John Hendee, and Frederick Campbell suggested that a disparity in expectations among users and between users and managers 'may produce disagreements about the appropriateness of certain camping behaviors.'[87] Clark *et al.* surveyed 'recreationist' users of 'highly developed modern campgrounds' and found that even though they acted differently than traditional campers – preferring to congregate with others like themselves and to bring many of the comforts of home with them to the campgrounds – 'recreationists, at least verbally, subscribe to what we consider traditional views of camping.' When the researchers asked recreationists why they went camping, most agreed with traditionalists that the important motivations were 'teaching their children about the out-of-doors,' 'getting satisfaction from solitude and tranquility,' and 'gaining awareness of unspoiled beauty.' Clark *et al.* concluded that despite the fact that the two groups shared the same general camping values, they 'have different notions of what behavior leads to these values and different standards of judging their attainment.... Wilderness is apparently in the eye of the beholder.'[88]

The main difference these researchers and others concerned with the problem saw was that wilderness purists tended to prioritize their own means of attaining those goals and denigrate those of their fellow campers, while the recreationists apparently believed that there was room for both types of behaviors. However, as Clark *et al.* argued, the problem was that 'behaviors frowned upon by a dominant minority (managers) are considered deviant even though they may be legitimate to a majority of the users' (156, f.5). This resulted in a huge management problem in the 1970s that brought the general societal feeling of malaise into the ranks of the Park Service itself as the

Service tried to make sense of its conflicting constituencies. The fact that the minority preservationists were able to significantly influence NPS policies in the 1970s suggests that the preservationist view here *was* dominant, but the fact that the majority of visitors either openly challenged the policies or ignored them suggests that the issue was far from solved.

As we have seen, preservationists involved in the debates over natural and unnatural acts in the parks often referred to such powerful cluster concepts as 'the National Park idea,' and 'the true park experience' when trying to 'convert' the Park Service and their fellow tourists to their positions on appropriate behavior and facilities. By employing these rhetorical concepts, they were better able to formulate arguments that invested subtle details with importance. The question remains as to whether they actually converted any tourists, however. Certainly the Park Service was listening, but they were also listening to the majority of visitors, and that is what made the parks such confusing places to visit in the 1970s.

No wonder, therefore, that both tourists and anti-tourist tourists who were faced with negotiating these problems in the field, as it were, appear to have been confused about how they were supposed to act in the National Parks in the 1970s. Whether they were wilderness purists or industrial tourists (or any other Americans in the middle, for that matter) they were guaranteed to get a little dash of 'cognitive dissonance' along with their 'wilderness experience.' If they had come to the parks in search of an Old Faithful America, they invariably found that the new America they had hoped to leave at home had followed them to the parks as well. It had come with them in the form of confusing new policies designed to control their behavior, and it had literally stowed away in the form of cultural artifacts – both physical and cognitive – carried with them into the parks. If we remember that this experience of disorientation was simply a microcosm of the dominant discursive experience of American life in the 1970s, then we find that the National Parks not only were not wholly separated from the dominant trends of the day, they were also some of the most problematic places in which these trends played out.

Notes

1. Jon Nordheimer, 'Spirit of '76 in Nation and New York: Self Doubt, Hope and Pride; Americans Finding New Course is Vital,' *New York Times*, 5 July 1976, 17-18.
2. Gladwin Hill, 'Park Service Turning to Public For Help in Solving Problems,' *New York Times*, 16 May 1975, 44.
3. See Charles Reich and Douglas Carroll, III, 'After the Gold Rush,' *National Parks and Conservation Magazine*, 45:4 (1971), 4-5.
4. Philip Shabecoff, 'Park Service Takes on City Sites and City Problems; Rangers' Morale Sinking As Park System Grows,' *New York Times*, 4 August 1980, B5. For an analysis of the state of mind of the Park Service by the early 1980s, see William C. Everhart, *The National Park Service* (1973; Boulder: Westview Press, 1983). In Everhart's insider analysis of the Service (he was NPS Chief of Interpretation), he argues that the reason for the Service's 'paralysis' in the period was the 'politicization'

of the Service in the 1970s. With preservationists and pro-development forces on both sides, the Park Service had five directors in nine years in 'the most disquieting period in its history' (29). Indeed, behind the waves that Reagan's notorious first Interior Secretary James Watt made in the early 1980s was Watt's Reagan-esque attempt to counteract the conflicts of the 1970s with an authoritarian hand in policy decisions. In an early official statement, Watt made it clear which side of the preservation/use dilemma he was coming from: 'I will err on the side of public use versus preservation.' See Everhart, 141-43.

5. One problem intrinsic in an analysis of this sort is one characteristic of any cultural history project that strives for ways of concretizing popular opinion in a particular historical period. The specific problem here is trying to reconstruct the ideas, words, and behaviors of the majority of National Parks tourists who were clearly statistically important, but who – unlike preservationist activists – rarely left a personalized paper trail for us to follow. In the analysis that follows I have attempted to make up for that lack by referring instead to period social science research studies on 'environment-cognition-behavior' interactions. While social science research on both landscape behavior and preferences is inherently limited by the scope of the questions researched and the methodology employed (and could itself serve as the *subject matter of* my analysis and not only *evidence for* it), it is unfortunately the best information we have, so I have felt it necessary in my discussion of the general trends of the decade to 'bracket' these questions in the interest of brevity. For more extensive discussions of these specific kinds of research problems in the 1970s and early 1980s, see Jonathan G. Taylor, Ervin H. Zube, and James L. Sell, 'Landscape Assessment and Perception Methods,' in Robert B. Bechtol, Robert W. Maraus, and William Michelson (eds), *Methods in Environmental and Behavioral Research* (New York: Van Nostrand Reinhold, 1987); and Donald J. Ballas and Margaret J. King, 'Cultural Geography and Popular Culture: Proposal For a Creative Merger,' *Journal of Cultural Geography*, 2:1 (1981), 154-163. See also John Zeisel, *Inquiry by Design: Tools for Environment-Behavior Research* (Cambridge: Cambridge University Press, 1981); Daniel Stokols and Irwin Altman (eds), *Handbook of Environmental Psychology*, Vols. I & II (New York: John Wiley and Sons, 1987); and David Seamon and Robert Mugerauer (eds), *Dwelling, Place and Environment: Towards a Phenomenology of Person and World* (Dordecht: Martinus Nijhoff Publishers, 1985).

6. Peter Marcuse, 'Is The National Parks Movement Anti-Urban?,' *Parks and Recreation*, (July 1971), 18.

7. Joseph Sax, *Mountains Without Handrails: Reflections on the National Parks.* (Ann Arbor: Univ. of Michigan Press, 1980), 103.

8. See Freeman Tilden, 'Riches of Being: The Century Since Yellowstone,' *National Parks and Conservation*, 46:1 (1972), 4-9.

9. For an overview of these concerns, see Stanford Demars, *The Tourist in Yosemite, 1855-1985* (Salt Lake City: Univ. of Utah Press, 1991), 3. See also Doris Wilkinson, 'The Class Imperative: The "Greening" and the "Blueing" of America,' in Conservation Foundation, *National Parks for the Future* (Washington, DC: The Conservation Foundation, 1972), 243.

10. William Ellis, 'Yellowstone at 100: The Pitfalls of Success'. *National Geographic Magazine*, 141: (1972), 629.

11. Allan K. Fitzsimmons, 'National Parks: The Dilemma of Development,' *Science*, 191 (6 February 1976), 440-41.

12. Linda H. Graber, *Wilderness as Sacred Space* (Washington, DC: Association of American Geographers, 1976), 82.

13. For more extensive discussion of the post-war tourist surge in a historical context, see John A. Jakle, *The Tourist: Travel in Twentieth Century North America* (Lincoln: Univ. of Nebraska Press, 1985), especially 185-198. For an overview of how these developments played out particularly in the American West, see Earl Pomeroy, *In Search of the Golden West: The Tourist in Western America* (New York: Knopf, 1957), especially 185-232. For discussions that pertain specifically to the National Parks, see Roderick Nash, *Wilderness and the American Mind* (1967; New Haven: Yale Univ. Press, 1982), especially 317-319; Alfred Runte, *National Parks: The American Experience* (1979; Lincoln: Univ. of Nebraska Press, 1987), especially 171-173; William C. Everhart, *The National Park Service*, especially 25; and Stanford Demars, *The Tourist in Yosemite*, 122-24.

14. Everhart, *The National Park Service*, 26-7. For more information on the design and implementation of Mission 66, see Conrad Wirth's memoirs, *Parks, Politics, and the People* (Norman: Univ. of Oklahoma, 1980).

15. Demars, *The Tourist in Yosemite*, 6-7.

16. F. Fraser Darling, and Noel D. Eichhorn, 'Man and Nature in the National Parks: Reflections on Policy,' abridged reprint of *Man and Nature in the National Parks* (Washington, D.C.: The Conservation Foundation, 1967) excerpted in *National Parks Magazine*, 43:259, 17.

17. Stephen Arno, 'They're Putting "Wild" Back In Wilderness,' *National Parks and Conservation*, 45:9 (1971), 10. See also Charles Reich, *The Greening of America* (New York: Random House, 1970).

18. Nash, *Wilderness and the American Mind*, 254.

19. Nash, 254; see Paul Ehrlich, 'Overcrowding and Us: Everything We Value as the "American Way of Life" is Being Threatened by Overpopulation,' *National Parks Magazine*, 43:259 (1969), 11; and Pagan Kennedy, *Platforms: A Microwaved Cultural Chronicle of the 1970s* (New York: St. Martin's Press, 1994), 30-32; cf. Peter Blake, *God's Own Junkyard: The Planned Deterioration of America's Landscape* (New York: Holt, Rinehart & Winston, 1964).

20. Nash, *Wilderness and the American Mind*, 252.

21. Gilbert Stucker, 'Youth, Rebellion & The Environment,' *National Parks and Conservation*, 45:4 (1971), 6-9. See also Edward Stainbrook, 'Man's Psychic Need for Nature,' *National Parks and Conservation*, 47:9 (1973), 22-23; and Maitland Sharpe, 'The National Parks and Young America,' in Conservation Foundation, *National Parks for the Future* (Washington, DC: The Conservation Foundation, 1972), 197-212. For a more critical analysis of this and other 1970s 'quests for authenticity,' see Christopher Lasch, *The Culture of Narcissism: American Life in an Age of Diminishing Expectations* (New York: W.W. Norton, 1979).

22. See Peter Schmitt, *Back to Nature: The Arcadian Myth in Urban America* (New York: Oxford Univ. Press, 1969).

23. Martin Kreiger, 'What's Wrong With Plastic Trees?,' *Science*, 2 February 1973, 448.

24. Stephen Arno, 'They're Putting "Wild" Back in Wilderness,' *National Parks and Conservation*, 45:9 (1971), 10-14. See also Richard McNeil and Anne LaBastille, 'Beggars and Bums in Our National Parks and Forests: Artificial Feeding of Wildlife in Our Great Natural Areas Creates Many Unnatural Problems...and Dangers,' *National Parks and Conservation*, 48:1 (1974), 9-12.

25. Another example of the way that the National Park Service 'put wild back into

wilderness' that was much talked about in the 1960s and 1970s was the decision to let lightning-caused 'natural wildfires' in the parks 'run their courses.' The NPS had dutifully fought fires in the parks for nearly 50 years, regardless of their origin. But in the 1960s, the NPS reversed its policy – responding to the many ecologists who were arguing that fire was an important natural process in any ecosystem, especially the high-altitude forest ecosystems present in popular parks like Sequoia, Yosemite, and Yellowstone. See Arno, 'They're Putting "Wild" Back in Wilderness,' 11, and Runte, *National Parks: The American Experience*, 206. For an excellent analysis of these policies in historical context, see Stephen Pyne, *Fire in America: A Cultural History of Wildland and Rural Fire* (Princeton: Princeton Univ. Press, 1982). To the majority of park visitors who valued tangible monumental scenery more than intangible ecological principles, however, the distinction between fires of 'natural' and 'human' origin must have seemed particularly bureaucratic – especially as they watched acres of trees go up in smoke while park officials decided whether or not to fight the fire based on a determination of its naturalness or unnaturalness. A characterization of the fire policy by Alfred Runte suggests the complexity of these sorts of problems: '[t]he artificial suppression of fires had led to the problem in the first place; clearly the only way "back to nature," so to speak, was by resorting to an artificial remedy in the interest of eventually recreating the natural rhythms that had been lost' (206).

26. National Parks Centennial Commission, *Preserving a Heritage: Final Report to the President and Congress of the National Parks Centennial Commission*, 102, 116; see also The Conservation Foundation, *National Parks for the Future*, 7.

27. Kreiger, 'What's Wrong With Plastic Trees?,' 449.

28. See MacCannell, *The Tourist: A New Theory of the Leisure Class* (New York: Schocken, 1976), especially 41-45, and 109-133. MacCannell expands on his paradigm in a more recent collection of essays, titled *Empty Meeting Grounds: The Tourist Papers*, (London: Routledge, 1992). Two excellent early assessments of MacCannell's work are Georges Van Den Abbeele, 'Sightseers: The Tourist as Theorist,' *Diacritics*, 10 (December, 1980), 3-14; and Jonathan Culler, 'Semiotics of Tourism,' *American Journal of Semiotics*, 1:1-2 (1981), 127-140.

29. MacCannell, *The Tourist: A New Theory of the Leisure Class*, 82-84.

30. See David Seamon and Robert Mugerauer (eds), *Dwelling, Place and Environment: Towards a Phenomenology of Person and World* (Dordecht: Martinus Nijhoff Publishers, 1985), especially 24.

31. Culler, 'Semiotics of Tourism, 127-28.

32. *Ibid.*, 138.

33. Runte, *National Parks: The American Experience*, xx.

34. Demars, *The Tourist in Yosemite*, 5-7. For more extensive discussions of the cultural construction of landscape, see David Lowenthal, and Martyn J. Bowden (eds), *Geographies of the Mind: Essays in Historical Geosophy in Honor of John Kirtland Wright* (New York: Oxford Univ. Press, 1976), and Roger M. Downs and James T. Meyer, 'Geography and the Mind: An Exploration of Perceptual Geography,' *American Behavioral Scientist*, 22:1 (1978), 59-77.

35. Chris Magoc, 'The Ordering of Wonderland: Yellowstone National Parks and the Culture of Aestheticism, 1872-1903,' *Canon: The Journal of the Rocky Mountain American Studies Association*, 2:1 (1994), 45.

36. For a specific analysis of the initial and continuing influence of Romanticism, see Stanford E. Demars, 'Romanticism and American National Parks,' *Journal of Cultural Geography*, 11:1 (1990), 17-24. For an analysis of other cultural factors surrounding the

foundation of National Parks, see Roderick Nash, 'The American Invention of National Parks,' *American Quarterly*, 22 (Fall 1970), 726-735. For more general discussions of these concerns, see Hans Huth, *Nature and the American: Three Centuries of Changing Attitudes* (Berkeley: Univ. of California Press, 1957); Nash, *Wilderness and the American Mind*; and Runte, *National Parks: The American Experience*.

37. Runte, *National Parks: The American Experience*, 38.

38. The National Parks Centennial Symposium was held at Yosemite in April (the findings later published in The Conservation Foundation, *National Parks for the Future: An Appraisal of the National Parks as They Begin Their Second Century in a Changing America* (Washington, DC: The Conservation Foundation, 1972)); the Second World Conference on National Parks at Grand Teton National Park coincided with the neighboring Yellowstone Centennial rededication ceremonies in September. The symposium and conference provided a forum for serious reflection and reassessment of the purpose of American National Parks.

39. Verne Huser, 'Yellowstone Park: Use, Overuse & Misuse,' *National Parks and Conservation*, 46:3 (1972), 9.

40. Lawrence Merriam, 'The National Park System: Growth and Outlook,' *National Parks and Conservation*, 46:12, 12. Indeed, by the end of the decade, many preservationists had expanded their focus on park degradation to encompass problems not only inside the parks, but also problems on 'adjacent lands' like air and water pollution, energy exploration, etc. which directly influenced the parks. See the National Parks and Conservation Association's two-part study, 'NPCA Adjacent Lands Survey: No Park is an Island,' *National Parks and Conservation*, 53:3 (1979), 4-9, and 53:4 (1979), 4-7. For an excellent recent analysis of the rhetoric that surrounded such concerns, see John Freemuth, *Islands Under Siege: National Parks and the Politics of External Threats* (Lawrence, KS: University of Kansas Press, 1991).

41. National Parks Centennial Commission, *Preserving a Heritage: Final Report to the President and Congress of the National Parks Centennial Commission* (Washington, D.C.: Dept. of the Interior, National Park Service, 1973).

42. *Ibid.*, 4, 51-65.

43. One of the main components of the Commission's information program was a 'Centennial Press Kit,' which was distributed to newspapers, magazines, and television stations around the country, and featured the Old Faithful logo. The Press Kit was encased in a green vinyl envelope which paradoxically symbolized the internal contradictions of the celebration, and 1970s America in general, with its earth-toned surface and plastic composition. Most ironic in this context were the many 'corporate tie-ins' featuring the Old Faithful logo, including an Eastman Kodak 'National Parks Centennial Photo Kit,' Union Carbide-sponsored National Park photo contests, Del Monte grocery store promos and coloring books, Public Service Announcements produced and sponsored by Conoco Oil and Chevrolet, special airline package tours to Yellowstone, and even a brand of whiskey – Old Yellowstone Bourbon. See National Parks Centennial Commission, *Preserving a Heritage*, 52-63.

44. Magoc, 'The Ordering of Wonderland,' 50. For an early characterization of Old Faithful in similar terms, see also Daniel J. Boorstin, *The Image: A Guide to Pseudo-Events in America* (New York: Vintage, 1961), 111.

45. Magoc, 47.

46. Huser, 'Yellowstone Park: Use, Overuse & Misuse,' 10.

47. Graber, *Wilderness as Sacred Space*, 20.

48. Edward Abbey, *Desert Solitaire: A Season in the Wilderness* (New York: Ballantine Books, 1968), 60.

49. Graber, *Wilderness as Sacred Space*, 146, 80, 25. See also Hendee *et al.*, *Wilderness Users in the Pacific Northwest – Their Characteristics, Values, and Management Preferences*. Given the purist emphasis on education, it is perhaps ironic that purists themselves usually shun NPS educational and interpretive facilities. One explanation Graber gives for this phenomena is that wilderness purists resent such facilities because they 'involve dependence on an authority figure' and place the wilderness visitor in the position of passive consumer of information and experiences (20). Wilderness purists seem to prefer instead a personally-cultivated active involvement derived either from knowledge actively pursued by the visitor *before* the visit or brought into being by going out of their way to create an unmediated experience by eschewing official interpretations and other obvious evidence of cultural mediations between the visitor and what s/he sees. For a more extensive analysis of the uses of NPS interpretive facilities, see Tarla Rai Peterson, 'The Meek Shall Interpret the Mountains: Dramatistic Criticism of Grand Teton National Park's Interpretive Program,' *Central States Speech Journal*, 39:2 (1988), 121-133.

50. Demars, *The Tourist in Yosemite*, 148. See also Bultena and Field, 'Visitors to National Parks: A Test of the Elitism Argument,' 395-96, and Graber, *Wilderness as Sacred Space*, 80.

51. Sax, *Mountains Without Handrails*, 104, 14, 61.

52. Everhart, *The National Park Service*, 52.

53. Conservation Foundation, *National Parks for the Future*, 7-9. See also Andrew Gilman, 'In and Around the National Parks: Alternatives to the Auto,' *National Parks and Conservation*, 50:7 (1976), 6.

54. National Parks Centennial Commission, *Preserving a Heritage*, 143-5.

55. Sax, *Mountains Without Handrails*, 11.

56. Culler, 'Semiotics of Tourism,' 130. See also Van Den Abbeele, 'Sightseers: The Tourist as Theorist,' 7; and MacCannell, *The Tourist: A New Theory of the Leisure Class*, 10, 104.

57. MacCannell, 10; see also Graber, *Wilderness as Sacred Space*, 25, 78.

58. See Culler, 131-133; MacCannell, 164.

59. Van Den Abbeele, 'Sightseers: The Tourist as Theorist,' 10; see also Kimberly Dovey, 'The Quest for Authenticity and the Replication of Environmental Meaning,' in David Seamon and Robert Mugerauer (eds), *Dwelling, Place and Environment: Towards a Phenomenology of Person and World* (Dordecht: Martinus Nijhoff Publishers, 1985), 47.

60. Culler, 'Semiotics of Tourism,' 137. See also Kimberly Dovey, 33-49.

61. Lawrence Merriam, 'The National Park System: Growth and Outlook,' *National Parks and Conservation*, 46:12 (1972), 8. See also The Conservation Foundation, *National Parks for the Future*, 7.

62. Sax, *Mountains Without Handrails*, 81, 86.

63. Van Den Abbeele, 'Sightseers: The Tourist as Theorist,' 7.

64. For more on this phenomenon, see *ibid.*, 6, 10; and MacCannell, *The Tourist: A New Theory of the Leisure Class*, 68, 81.

65. Steve Martin, 'Dilemma in Grand Canyon: Motors or Oars?,' *National Parks and Conservation*, 50:10 (1976), 15. See also R. Roy Johnson, Steven W. Carothers, Robert Dolan, Bruce P. Hayden, and Alan Howard, 'Man's Impact on the Colorado River in the Grand Canyon,' *National Parks and Conservation*, 51:3 (1977), 13-16.

66. Nash, *Wilderness and the American Mind*, 339.
67. Martin, 'Dilemma in Grand Canyon,' 15.
68. Sax, *Mountains Without Handrails*, 12-13.
69. *Ibid.*, 61, 88-90; see also National Parks Centennial Commission, *Preserving a Heritage*, 116.
70. Sax, *Mountains Without Handrails*, 79.
71. Martin, 'Dilemma in Grand Canyon,' 17.
72. Sax, *Mountains Without Handrails*, 12.
73. See Nash, *Wilderness and the American Mind*, 323-5; and The Conservation Foundation, *National Parks for the Future*, 18. For an overview of the procedures involved in determining recreation area carrying capacities, see Bo Shelby and Thomas A. Heberlein, *Carrying Capacity in Recreation Settings* (Corvallis, OR: Oregon State University Press, 1986).
74. National Parks Centennial Commission, *Preserving a Heritage*, 123.
75. Nash, *Wilderness and the American Mind*, 324-5. At root, once it was identified as such, the problem of 'over-use' seemed 'intractable [because] demand is rapidly increasing for resources which are fixed in quantity.... [F]or all our productive capability, we are not able to produce another Grand Canyon, Yellowstone, or Yosemite.' See Warren Johnson, 'Over-Use of the National Parks,' 7-10. For some, the answer was to restrict use, but this was no comfortable matter, even for preservationists, especially since many of the proposed policies – such as quotas, back-country permits, campground reservations, and even back-country entrance exams – would curtail the freedom of people ostensibly coming to the wilderness to set themselves free. Again the postwar preservationist National Park idea was at the root of it: If a National Park is supposed to be wilderness, and wilderness is supposed to be something that is free from human control, then how can we even manage the wilderness, much less require permits? This argument did not get much support at the time, however, and most agreed with Roderick Nash that the 'price of the popularity that saved wilderness is intense management. The alternative to such control is a level of recreational use that would quickly deprive anyone of having even a semblance of a wilderness experience.' See Nash, *Wilderness and the American Mind*, 340-41.
76. For assessments of this trend as it was occurring, see William H. Ittelson, 'Environment Perception and Contemporary Perceptual Theory,' in W.H. Ittelson (ed), *Environment and Cognition* (New York: Seminar Press, 1973), 1-19; and Roger M. Downs & James T. Meyer, 'Geography and the Mind: An Exploration of Perceptual Geography,' *American Behavioral Scientist*, 22:1 (1978), 59-77.
77. Frank F. Cunningham, 'The Human Eye and the Landscape,' *Landscape*, 20:1 (1975), 14. While some researchers found that there was a general American preference for 'natural' vs. 'man-altered' landscapes, these preferences were by no means stable or universal. See Elwood L. Shafer, Jr., 'Perception of Natural Environments,' *Environment and Behavior*, 1:1 (1969), 71-82; Jay Appleton, *The Experience of Landscape* (London: John Wiley & Sons, 1975); E. Glenn Carls, 'The Effects of People and Man-Induced Conditions on Preferences for Outdoor Recreation Landscapes,' *Journal of Leisure Research*, 6:2 (1974), 113-124. Some important variables important for accounting for different landscape preferences here were social class, previous expectations (or 'cognitive set'), varying levels of congruity/contrast of the alterations in their larger context, and whether the wilderness visitors were generally defined as 'urbanist' or 'wildernist' in orientation. See Herbert C. Leff, L.R. Gordon, and James G. Ferguson, 'Cognitive Set and Environmental Awareness,' *Environment and Behavior*,

6:4 (1974), 395-447; Ronald W. Hodgson and Robert L. Thayer, Jr., 'Implied Human Influence Reduces Landscape Beauty' *Landscape Planning*, 7 (1980), 171-179; Joachim F. Wohlwill and Harry Heft, 'A Comparative Study of User Attitudes Towards Development and Facilities in Two Contrasting Natural Recreation Areas,' *Journal of Leisure Research*, 9:4 (1977), 264-280; Joachim F. Wohlwill and Glenn Harris, 'Response to Congruity or Contrast for Man-Made Features in Natural-Recreation Settings,' *Leisure Sciences*, 3:4 (1980), 349-365.

78. For an early site-specific study, see John C. Hendee, William R. Catton, Jr., Larry D. Marlow, and Frank C. Brockman, *Wilderness Users in the Pacific Northwest – Their Characteristics, Values, and Management Preferences*, Research Paper PNW-61 (U.S. Department of Agriculture, U.S. Forest Service, Pacific Northwest Forest and Range Experiment Station, 1968). See also John C. Hendee and Robert W. Harris, 'Foresters' Perception of Wilderness – User Attitudes and Preferences,' *Journal of Forestry*, 68:12 (1970), 759-762; Roger N. Clark, John C. Hendee, and Frederick L. Campbell, 'Values, Behavior, and Conflict in Modern Camping Culture,' *Journal of Leisure Research*, 3:3 (1971), 143-159; and Wellman *et al.*, 'Park Managers' Predictions of the Motivations of Visitors in Two Contrasting Natural Recreation Areas.'

79. Richard Schreyer and Joseph W. Roggenbuck, 'The Influence of Experience Expectations on Crowding Perceptions and Social-Psychological Carrying Capacities,' *Leisure Sciences*, 1:4 (1978), 373-394. See also B.L. Driver and Richard C. Knopf, 'Personality, Outdoor Recreation, and Expected Consequences,' *Environment and Behavior*, 9:2 (1977), 169-193; and Jerry J. Vaske, Maureen P. Donnelly, and Thomas A. Heberlein, 'Perceptions of Crowding and Resource Quality by Early and More Recent Visitors,' *Leisure Sciences*, 3:4 (1980), 367-381.

80. Schreyer and Roggenbuck, 378.

81. Fitzsimmons, 'National Parks: The Dilemma of Development,' 443.

82. J.D. Wellman, M.S. Dawson, and J.W. Roggenbuck, 'Park Managers' Predictions of the Motivations of Visitors to Two National Park Service Areas,' *Journal of Leisure Research*, 14:1 (1982), 8.

83. *Ibid.*, 11-12.

84. Robert G. Lee, 'Alone With Others: The Paradox of Privacy in Wilderness,' *Leisure Sciences*, 1:1 (1977), 11. For another study comparing stated campsite preferences with actual campsite selections, see 'H' K. Hancock, 'Recreation Preference: Its Relation to Behavior,' *Journal of Forestry*, 71:6 (1973), 336-337.

85. Warren Johnson, 'Over-Use of the National Parks,' *National Parks Magazine*, 41:241 (1967), 4.

86. Gordon L. Bultena and Donald R. Field, 'Visitors to National Parks: A Test of the Elitism Argument,' *Leisure Sciences*, 1:4 (1978), 397-99; see also Patrick C. West, 'A Status Group Dynamics Approach to Predicting Participation Rates in Regional Recreation Demand Studies,' *Land Economics*, 53 (1977), 196-211. The most problematic example of the conflicts between different ideas of appropriate camping behavior in the 1970s was the July 1970 'Stoneman Meadow Incident' in Yosemite Valley where 500 countercultural 'freaks' violently clashed for days with Park Rangers and 'Middle American' tourist campers over their right to congregate in the Meadow. Two excellent discussions of the Incident in the context of other 1970s park trends are: Robert A. Jones, 'National Parks: A Report on the Range War at Generation Gap,' *New York Times*, 25 July 1971, Sec. 10, pp. 1, 18-19, 23-24; and Edward Abbey, 'Return to Yosemite: Tree Fuzz vs. Freaks,' in E. Abbey, *The Journey Home: Some Words in Defense of the American West* (New York: Dutton, 1977), 138-145.

87. Clark *et al.*, 'Values, Behavior, and Conflict in Modern Camping Culture,' 144. See also William R. Burch, Jr., 'The Play World of Camping: Research Into the Meaning of Outdoor Recreation,' *American Journal of Sociology*, 70:5 (1965), 604-612.

88. Clark *et al.*, 'Values, Behavior, and Conflict in Modern Camping Culture,' 148.

Love and Will: Rollo May and the Seventies' Crisis of Intimacy

Robert H. Abzug

In the perceived social and spiritual desolation of the seventies, psychotherapies of all sizes, kinds, and shapes – group or individual, traditional or radical, clothed or unclothed, talking or screaming or meditating, conducted in churches, sterile offices, deserts or hot tubs – proposed to give meaning and direction to the lives of distraught souls. This burst of therapeutic energy has been satirized in such books as Cyra McFadden's *The Serial* and condemned in various pop treatises on the 'me generation.'[1] The late Christopher Lasch, among others, found in the turn to 'growth' psychotherapies a symptom of deep emptiness in the culture, a 'narcissistic' turn to a self that had been emptied of its substance.[2]

These first attempts at interpretation and satire were more interested in such events as symptoms of crisis and pathology than as expressions of broader continuity and change in culture. Without questioning the acuity of such criticism or denying the reality of bizarre, ominous, and patently comic elements in the seventies' psychotherapeutic moment, however, there can be no question that the long view concerning the psychological revolution of post-World War II America needs to be investigated more closely and less polemically. In a culture that traditionally had depended on philosophical, theological, and common sense descriptive terminologies, the startling fact that psychologies of one sort and another became leading explanatory tools is in itself a little understood phenomenon. So too is the fact that psychological language became powerful just at that moment in the seventies which was marked by challenges to virtually every social construction and personal assumption.

The crisis of the seventies, of course, devolved on every level of politics, society, and culture. Symbolic events abounded: the ungracious end of American involvement in Vietnam in 1973 and Viet Cong victory in 1975; Watergate; a skyrocketing divorce rate; even the erosion of American economic hegemony as symbolized by the Arab oil boycott and escalating energy prices. The general mood of despondency and indirection reflected itself in literature, music, art, and personal life. At the same time, for at least minorities and women, this shaking of the foundation weakened traditional assumptions concerning race and gender to a degree previously unknown.

One of the most elusive but deeply affected realms of everyday life to be transformed by this mood of collapse and new opportunity was that of intimacy – the ability of individuals to speak, act, and live with each other within a world of mutually acceptable understandings of role, language, and sexual expectation. To this crisis, psychology spoke more directly than religion. A new worldview that concentrated on issues of personal growth or analyzed problems as questions of intrapsychic confusion might well become a source of meaning when it came to intimacy. What's more, in a pluralistic society, theoretically psychology reached all. It claimed universality of meaning, no matter the social standing, ethnic or racial background, and economic state of the individual. Just as in evangelical Christianity all human beings could be saved, in most psychologies all could be analyzed and many could improve their emotional lot.

Psychology was a young language of explanation. Its influence began with the rage for Freudianism in the twenties. Soon industry employed psychologists to smooth out workplace tensions, and a reading public snapped up do-it-yourself psychology books in numbers approaching those written from a spiritual perspective. Especially during World War II, psychologists of all varieties came to be seen as essential professionals in efforts to classify individuals by personality and aptitude and to cure shell-shocked soldiers in preparation for another battle or for return to civilian life.

The postwar world witnessed the continued ascent of the profession and its language. Clinical psychologists successfully defended their right to practice psychotherapy in the face of organized psychiatry's attempts to limit the field to medical doctors. Experimental psychologists took the lead in presenting new and 'scientific' theories of human behavior, visions derived from laboratory experiments and often expressed in quantitative formulae. Their methods and theories filtered into every corner of society and economy, from advertising to military and industrial organizations.

The very success of behaviorism and other forms of experimental psychology created, in turn, a reaction from within. Psychologists, especially clinicians, who had entered the profession from more humanistic and philosophical backgrounds argued that 'experimental' and 'behaviorist' psychologists had removed the most profound questions of human existence from their vision of the human mind. By the late fifties, a small but highly visible group, including Gordon Allport, Carl Rogers, and Abraham Maslow, began to organize around existential and other approaches to psychotherapy that had as their center more philosophically humane conceptions of individual consciousness. In the early 1960s, they founded the Association for Humanistic Psychology.

Near the center of this movement was Rollo May. In the 1950s, he had established himself as a leading interpreter of personal malaise in the modern age with such books as *The Meaning of Anxiety* (1950), *Man's Search for Himself* (1953), and *Existence* (1958), which he edited and to which he contributed several essays. However, May achieved his greatest fame as the author of *Love and Will*, a best-selling psychological and philosophical jeremiad published in late 1969 that became one of the central texts of the psychological boom of the 1970s.

So great was the success of *Love and Will,* and so potent the cultural crisis in which it was published, it has had the effect of blinding posterity to the full richness of May's career and, indeed, the complexities of *Love and Will* itself. When Rollo May died in October 1994, National Public Radio devoted a special segment of its 'All Things Considered' to May's life. In an interview with the present author, Noah Adams asked whether he was correct that one could find May's *Love and Will* 'on a hippie's bookshelf alongside Robert Pirsig's *Zen and the Art of Motorcycle Maintenance* and the Castaneda books and Tolkien.'[3]

It certainly was to be found on hippie bookshelves, but *Love and Will* also won Phi Beta Kappa's Ralph Waldo Emerson Prize and gained serious notice from theologians, psychologists, and political scientists. It had resonance for a very broad public. Of the many books to make their mark on the 1970s, none is richer in history and nuance than *Love and Will*. Published in late 1969 and a national best seller for the better part of 1970, it has been in print ever since and each year still sells thousands of copies worldwide in seven or more languages.

Love and Will defined a crossroads of generations. May was sixty when the book was published, and it was a capstone to decades of philosophical and spiritual searching rather than the vision of a young upstart. Yet May assumed prophetic garb for a younger generation seeking escape from what they saw as the trap of the past. A *guru* perhaps, May reached to the deepest roots of Western rather than Eastern culture for his vision of personal and social reconstruction. He made his case using the texts of classical antiquity and the Old Testament as much as the language of psychology. In many ways, then, *Love and Will*, for a moment at least, conjoined old and new cultures in a call for personal and social renewal.

May was not the only older prophet among those read by the younger generations of the sixties and seventies. Herbert Marcuse, Erik Erikson, Abraham Maslow, Fritz Perls, and other older visionaries found audiences among the young. However, none addressed more boldly than Rollo May the confusions of intimacy and motivation, arguably the primary symptom of private life in the late 1960s and 1970s, and with less reliance on a broader socio-economic or political perspective. To accept Marcuse's *Eros and Civilization* (1955) or *One-Dimensional Man* (1964), one needed to embrace some portion of his psycho-Marxist vision of the world. To find *Gandhi's Truth* (1969) by Erik Erikson important, one had to be interested in non-violence or specifically in India, or Gandhi, or, at the very least, embrace Erikson's theory of the life-cycle.

By contrast, *Love and Will* spoke directly to a broad range of personal and social concerns of interest to middle-class Americans. It demanded no loyalty to intervening theory or ideology. For *Love and Will* to be 'relevant,' one simply had to share in an almost universal sense that events and technologies were in the saddle, that relations between the sexes were chaotic, and that too often the response of individuals to these disturbing developments was passivity, apathy, or violence.

Unlike many other books of the era, *Love and Will* went right to the heart of intimacy by exploring the individual psyche as it pressed against its social environment. May explained little about the great social and political movements of the day, at least in their outward manifestations. His lack of political sophistication or refusal to engage in detailed social analysis, a weakness in the minds of some, may well have been the source of a paradoxical strength. In Protestant, middle-class America, whose vision of society began with assessment of individual spiritual and psychological health, *Love and Will*'s viewpoint was the one most congenial to the reading public. Such a perspective also made it preeminently a book of the post-political 1970s, an era in which interior quests often replaced radical social platforms, and in which even the political became tinctured by the personal.

What *Love and Will* lacked in ideological chic it gained by speaking in congruity with the culture. Not coincidentally, Rollo May was one of the few 'prophets' of the young whose life and consciousness had been formed within the culture of Protestant Middle America. Marcuse and Erikson, for instance, were emigrés who had escaped Hitler's Germany. Maslow was the son of Jewish immigrants. Rollo May, by contrast, was born in small-town Michigan and raised in the Methodist Church. His father was a moving force in the state's YMCA movement. While much of his intellectual and professional life can be viewed as a rebellion against what he considered a narrow and shallow cultural heritage, it is nonetheless true that May's vision of the world and life deeply reflected the concerns of his family and boyhood culture.

Nor was the book's jeremiadical tone, its warning of decay, and reaffirmation of the possibility of recovery, surprising given May's own life history. This very sophisticated sermon for the times came from a man who had trained for the Protestant ministry under Reinhold Niebuhr and Paul Tillich at Union Theological Seminary and for a few years had actually shepherded a church. May left the fold because he lost his faith, and soon after found psychology a more compelling language for facing the challenges of modern

82

existence.[4] Existentialism replaced Christianity as his explanatory framework, the existentialism of Kierkegaard and Nietzsche rather than that of Sartre. May's existentialism was the Christianity of Tillich but without Christ.

Perhaps this bundle of rich contradiction allowed *Love and Will* to span the generations. Sometimes its themes of heroic individualism seemed to unfold in stark sonorities, without compromise or challenge. At other times a counter melody shone through to trouble and complicate the once simple message. Occasionally a simple sentence or phrase, much like a single note, when nuanced in some new way or read against a different texture of sound or experience, changed one's sense of the whole work.

For the seventies generation of searchers, *Love and Will* trumpeted the clarion of individualism against a discordant background of disillusion with social values – the *me* resplendent in powers of thought, feeling, and meditation. Listen again, however, and one senses countervailing yearnings for community, and condemnations of unbridled egoism, of freedom unchecked by a sense of society or the welfare of those others who inhabit the life of any individual. Dour critiques of humankind's inevitably numbed modern consciousness coexisted with almost millennial expectations for a rebirth of creativity that would rekindle authentic feelings of community. In short, *Love and Will* reflected and organized the contradictory impulses of the age and forged them into a message of dark hope.

May revealed the contrapuntal nature of the book in a short 'Foreword' that set human consciousness in relation to and against Nature. He invited the reader to imagine his summer retreat in New Hampshire, describing the world around him as it came alive each morning. A 'hallelujah' chorus of birds – the song sparrow's chirp, the goldfinch's 'obligato,' the wood thrush's unbounded warble, and the beat of a woodpecker on the beech tree. Against them all, the loons on the lake 'erupt with their plaintive and tormented daemonic.' In all, it evoked in May the 'everlasting going and coming, the eternal return, the growing and mating and dying and growing again.' Yet here May makes an exception for humankind, set off from the animals by its possession of consciousness and called to 'transcend the eternal return.' And here the note becomes plaintively heroic. 'In this transitional twentieth century,' he writes, 'when the full results of our bankruptcy of inner values is brought home to us, I believe it is especially important that we seek the source of love and will' (9-10).

The main body of *Love and Will* played itself out in musical form – dark themes, complicating variations, and cautiously hopeful resolution. The theme was an old one stated in new terms, the fate of human consciousness in an age of doubt and transition. May points his readers toward a paradox. Once the culture offered love and will as the solutions to life's problems. Now the solutions had become the problem. In 'our schizoid world,' the old sureties were gone. Love and will, instead of being integrated into the fullness of culture and relation, had become distorted through alienation. Profound love had been translated into its lowest common denominator: sex. Will had been crippled by the modern age's increasing sense of individual powerlessness.

May located authentic contemporary cultural enrichment only in the realms of modern art, music, and literature, where the very alienation and agony of the modern age had been translated into creations evocative of the age. Thus Cézanne, Van Gogh, and Picasso managed to refract their creative talents in ways that reflected the torn state of modern consciousness. So, too, W.H. Auden in his *Age of Anxiety* (1947), and Leonard Bernstein in the symphony inspired by the Auden poem, had each looked straight at modern reality.

However, for most, modernity had bred only a dull numbness, disorientation, apathy, and the impulse toward violence. Yet behind this gray surface lay a much more complicated reality. Evidence of human dilemmas revealed by patients involved in psychotherapy offered the most candid vision of our consciousness, May argued, and set as his task an intimate, psychological description of the problem of modernity that might lead to 'a new basis for the love and will which have been its chief casualties' (13-33).

What did love and will, at least in May's usage, really mean? May discussed love first, noting that there were really four types of human love: sex or *libido*, *eros*, *philia*, and *agape*. Sex simply referred to the sex drive, or *libido*. *Eros* represented the pull of love toward creation or procreation. *Philia* was brotherly love, or friendship. *Agape* stood for the love and care of human beings for others, friend or stranger, which in Christianity mirrored God's love of humankind. May proposed that authentic human love, in its fullest sense, was a 'blending' of all four. The modern age had distorted, trivialized, and alienated one manifestation of love from the other.

In five chapters, May analyzed modern love and proposed ways of reuniting and reasserting its parts in their fullness, both personally and socially. He began with sex, noting that the Victorian neurosis of repressed sexuality had been replaced by an almost oppressive openness in contemporary discussion and expectation of sex. While applauding the new sexual freedom for its honesty, he argued that *internal* anxiety and guilt had replaced older, externalized manifestations. Concentration on technique, performance, and frequency had severed sexuality's relation to feeling. Now, as before, we separated body from emotion and reason, only now body reigned supreme: 'Sin used to mean giving in to one's sexual desires; it now means not having full sexual expression. Our contemporary puritan holds that it is immoral *not* to express your libido' (45). Sex without love had replaced love without sex as a personal ideal.

May did not advocate turning back the clock. He assured his readers that he recognized the great benefits of the sexual revolution, but he worried that it ignored the goal of 'opening of our senses and imaginations to the enrichment of pleasure and passion and the meaning of love' (52). May illustrated the problem with narratives from clinical cases of four women and two men, each with some form of sexual dysfunction. The women didn't feel much during sex and the men were impotent or reported that sex lacked any 'bang.' Physical pleasure and communion had little to do with their motives for sex. Two women used it to 'hang on' to their men, another saw sex as 'something nice you give a man.' The fourth, a bit lustier, expressed both generosity and anger when she had sex. The two men mostly felt the need 'to demonstrate their masculinity' (53). All wandered in the sexual wilderness, diminishing the richness of the act itself by making it the instrument of neurotic (though culturally encouraged) behavior.

To May, this acting out in the realm of sex pointed to other underlying motives – the 'struggle to prove one's identity,' a 'hope to overcome his own solitariness,' and a related 'desperate endeavor to escape feelings of emptiness and the threat of apathy' (53-54). He recognized that these were motives and consequences of the richest normal relations. The problem was that, more and more, the culture had concentrated on physical signs of success – erection, orgasm, multiple orgasm – to the detriment of the human relationship symbolized by the sexual act. Thus one might even choose to *'feel less* in order to *perform better!'* Thus the inevitable confusion of one of May's patients, whose impotency belied his own self image as a 'screwing machine' (56). Impotency itself, and even rejection of sexual difference or sexuality itself, he argued, were the natural results of the alienation of sex from the other forms of love.

May then moved to a detailed analysis of these estrangements. In the chapter 'Eros in Conflict with Sex,' he noted that the creative urge which had once so naturally encompassed sexuality as its physiological base, now suffered from the routinization of sexuality as *simply* a physical urge to be perfected in performance and technique. In 'Love and Death,' May argued that, in an age when 'sexuality' became tied to assertions of identity and a quest for security, human beings were less likely to experience the piquant relation of sexual surrender, death, and rebirth. Indeed, he asserted that the 'obsession with sex serve[d] to cover up contemporary man's fear of death' (105-06). Death became the reality to be hidden away much as the Victorians had hidden sex.

Other aspects of modern sexual life also carried a double meaning. For instance, in addition to its liberating gifts, contraception, by separating sex from creation, also allowed human beings to repress or ignore those aspects of sexuality of which childbirth and the creation of life itself were emblematic. In short, death, tragedy, passion – all the things that once made eros a *mysterium tremendum* – had in the modern world been written out of the sexual act.

May then drew the contextual circle even wider, making eros a part of an even more elemental force – the daimonic. He quoted Plato – 'Eros is a daimon' – and explained the 'daimonic' as *'any natural function which has the power to take over the whole person.*' Whether creative or destructive, angry or ecstatic, the molten force of the daimonic lay at the root of both creation and destruction, eros and death. In this sense, the daimonic became something of a cultural Id, the engine of what Freud called eros and the wish for death. By denying the existence of such potent forces in the human psyche, we lost our sensitivity both to creation and to evil forces of destruction. We became apathetic and potentially dangerous innocents. In love, embracing the paradox of attraction and fear, of acceptance and rejection, of the edge of sanity that surrender involved, ironically made all aspects of love and life more profoundly human.

As for will, paradoxes abounded. May saw the central crisis as the inability of many to formulate some sense of wish or intention and then have the power to work toward that end. He had no great love of the nineteenth century doctrine of 'will power,' as if an uncomplicated will toward unquestioned, conscious goals, was in order or even possible. Freud's discoveries relegated the clear force of Will to the murky world of the unconscious, and, for some theorists, almost destroyed the idea of will of any sort. For them, humankind lived by unconscious and unstoppable drives.

For May, psychotherapy should have been – but only rarely was – an exercise that freed the individual to want and to will (not the reverse). This freedom was gained not by passively understanding that one's actions were controlled by invisible forces, but by learning to shape one's larger and smaller actions with an understanding of the power that the unconscious wielded. Thus will was reborn through and in service to personal understanding of one's own wishes and one's unconscious blocks to fulfilling those wishes.

Wish and will were the keys to May's vision of reconstruction. He argued that will as it once had been defined, wholly conscious and driven by the orthodox values of society, had certainly been undermined by psychology. For those values, the cultural superego, May substituted wish, the creative imagining of goals and futures appropriate to the individual in his or her healthiest state. This freeing up of the imagination, of a sense of choice, he pointed out, was almost always the implicit goal of psychotherapy even if little room existed for such choice in Freudian or behaviorist theory.

How could one, then, widen the theory to include and enrich the reality? May turned at this point to the idea of Intentionality. He defined it as 'the structure which gives meaning to experience' (223). 'Intentionality is the heart of consciousness,' he argued, '... out of which comes the awareness of our capacity to form, to mold, to change ourselves and the day in relation to each other' (224). Intentionality was thus the bridge between the objective world and the subjective inner self. It allowed individuals to move toward doing and investing meaning in actions and objects.

Through this reopening of the possibility of human assertion, May provided a means to revive will in a vision that comported not so much with the nineteenth century sense of self-reliance as with a modern refinement to psychological possibility. He sought a margin of true freedom structured within the psychological and spiritual makeup of humankind, one through which one might act as a self within the broader notion of humanity alive in the western tradition but more recently denied by the mechanistic theories of modernity. 'Intentionality,' he concluded, 'itself consisting of the deepened awareness of one's self, is our means of putting the meaning surprised by consciousness into action.' That action could in turn build a better world, one where 'in every act of love and will – and in the long run they are both present in each genuine act – we mold ourselves and our world simultaneously' (325).

Perhaps one should take for granted that the message of *Love and Will* might have some appeal to a country seemingly out of control of its institutions and destiny. In the preceding decade, Americans had experienced a crescendo of disorienting and, in some cases, tragic phenomena: a sometimes bloody struggle over civil rights, a seemingly unending string of urban riots, a frustrating and costly war, and such individual shocks as the assassinations of two Kennedys and Martin Luther King, Jr., the My Lai revelations, and the killing of students at Kent State University. Anyone who marked out a plausible road to recovery might have had some chance to engage the public mind.

Yet *Love and Will* attained its power and popularity not only for its frank admission of a cultural crisis and its spiritually uplifting solution, but also because it embraced the entirety of Western culture in doing so. Its liberal and intermixed references to Greek myth, Biblical stories, and a wide selection of philosophers defined a kind of intellectual collage, preserving tradition in the style of modernity. In fact, *Love and Will*'s references to myth, theology, and philosophy far outnumbered those to psychological theory.

'We stand on the peak of the consciousness of previous ages,' May declared on the very last page of the book, 'and their wisdom is available to us' (325). That was not necessarily the sentence or idea that captured the imagination of those who placed it on their bookshelves next to Carlos Castaneda or Robert Pirsig. One can read *Love and Will* for its insights concerning sexuality, love, and personal regeneration, concentrating on what it said to the individual, pure and simple. Yet for a fleeting moment in cultural history, its multiple levels brought together an otherwise unlikely set of readers, devotees of past, present, and future.

In this sense, *Love and Will* marked an end rather than a beginning. Soon after its publication, whether in attempts to revive lost means of intimacy or to deal with other questions related to personal relations, the field of reference narrowed precipitously. Lay culture since the middle 1970s has suffered a rapid erosion of cultural memory, the diminution of historical reference, and the condemnation of the western tradition as much out of fear of intellectual challenge as from supposed affronts to contemporary notions of gender, class, and ethnicity. Even many of those who have loudly decried the loss have done so not in the name of intellect and imagination, but rather in the cause of 'cultural literacy,' the reduction of powerful thoughts to name recognition.

The seventies, then, marked not only a crossroads of generations but a crossroads of cultural richness, the long term results of which have yet to be seen. The women's movement, the challenges of divorce to marriage and contraception to focused sex lives, and other destabilizing forces certainly disrupted traditional assumptions about the nature and meaning of intimacy, made it harder to achieve, and even masked the central human drive for such emotional completion. The decade also saw the diminution of resources from which to build some new vision of the intimate life, whether in friendships, unofficial heterosexual or homosexual sexual unions, or legally bound traditional marriages. In retrospect, we may view *Love and Will* and other, later works of Rollo May as some of the last to integrate the search for intimacy with the great themes of the pre-1970s West.[5]

Notes

1. McFadden, Cyra, *The Serial : A Year in the Life of Marin County* (New York: Alfred A. Knopf, 1977). The key article in the popular press was Peter Marin, 'The New Narcissism,' *Harper's Magazine* (October 1975).
2. See Christopher Lasch, *The Culture of Narcissism* (New York: W.W. Norton, 1979), and *The Minimal Self: Psychic Survival in Troubled Times* (New York: W.W. Norton, 1984).
3. Segment on Rollo May, 'All Things Considered,' National Public Radio, October 24, 1995. Page references in parentheses are to Rollo May, *Love and Will* (New York: W.W. Norton and Company, 1969). I refer to other sources in standard notes.
4. See my article, 'The Deconversion of Rollo May,' in a forthcoming issue of the *Review of Existential Psychology and Psychiatry*.
5. See, for instance, Rollo May, *Freedom and Destiny* (New York: W.W. Norton, 1981), for May's continued use of the western tradition, as well as May's own recognition that the cultural field was narrowing dangerously.

Jimmy Carter: Hope and Memory versus Optimism and Nostalgia

Charles Bussey

In 1977, in the preface of a slender and unfortunately little-read volume called *A Southern Baptist in the White House*, Kentucky author James Baker wrote: '[Jimmy] Carter may not be what all his interpreters have said, but he is indeed a remarkable man, and his story is just beginning. He will write the most important part of it in the coming months and years.'[1]

Those words, written just as the former Georgia Governor was about to enter the White House, were prophetic. It seems unlikely that even Baker realized how singular a man Carter was and is. To say this, however, is not to gloss over Carter's flaws, either personal or political. In fact, as the former President himself recognizes, he has his own demons. Especially pride. Nonetheless, as he approached his 70th birthday in 1994, and the 14th anniversary of leaving the White House, he had 'written' a memorable story. And it goes on.

My contention in this essay is that Jimmy Carter had a strong, and almost intuitive, sense of the distinctions between Hope/Optimism and Memory/Nostalgia. Hope and Memory reflect a distinct and positive way of looking at both the past and the future, while Optimism and Nostalgia reflect a negative way of viewing time. Hope requires hard choices and, together with Memory, demands a realistic view of the past and future. Optimism and Nostalgia, on the other hand, represent a non-realistic view of time.

America, along with much of the western world, has since the 18th-century Enlightenment taken an 'optimistic' view of the world – a view which looks upon 'progress' as meaning that more is better and which promotes the attitude that there are unlimited resources for people to exploit. This concept of optimism/progress weakens, in the words of Christopher Lasch, 'the inclination to make intelligent provision for the future.'[2] Likewise, 'nostalgia' invokes a past that 'stands outside time, frozen in unchanging perfection' (83). 'Nostalgia' disparages the present by emotionally invoking a past filled with happiness which seems impossible in the 'damned' present. 'Memory too may idealize the past, but not in order to condemn the present. It draws hope and comfort from the past in order to enrich the present and to face what comes with good cheer' (83).

The thrust of what I have to say about Carter is interpretative and is, of course, open to criticism. Despite the flood of praise he has received in the wake of his interventions in both the Korean crisis and the situation in Haiti, even there some journalists continue to view him negatively. Likewise, even though there was a monumental shift in journalistic and scholarly treatment of Carter beginning in the late 1980s, critical commentary continues to be published.[3] For example, distinguished historian Burton I. Kaufman published a scholarly work in 1993 called *The Presidency of James Earl Carter, Jr.* He wrote: 'I am persuaded ... that the earlier critics of his [Carter's] administration were justified in giving the president mediocre marks.... In my view, this contemporary image of the Carter presidency was, unfortunately, all too accurate.'[4]

There are few, however, even those who continue to view his presidency in a negative way, who argue that he has failed in his post-presidential years. When compared with living ex-presidents, he sets the standard. For example, on the September day in 1994 when he put himself in harm's way to seek a solution to the crisis in Haiti, former president Gerald Ford contented himself with tossing a coin to open a golf tournament in suburban Virginia.

As Stanley N. Katz, President of the American Council of Learned Societies, wrote in late summer 1994, 'Jimmy Carter has done more for the public service in general and for the promotion of mutual understanding among nations in particular than any American chief executive since John Quincy Adams.'[5] That is an apt comparison, for Carter and Adams shared what both called the sin of pride. And, like Adams, Carter suffered the sting of public as well as personal tragedy. Yet both emerged from what others might consider humiliating setbacks to render enormous service to both their country and the world.

What was it that enabled Carter to sustain himself and his spirit? How was he able to recover from the pain of losing the presidency to Ronald Reagan in 1980? As he wrote, 'When the voters decided to change horses in midstream, not only had they rejected us but almost 51 per cent of them had chosen a horse determined to run back as fast as possible in the opposite direction.' Yet, within just a few months, Carter was able to say to his wife Rosalynn, 'Who knows what we can do if we set our objectives high? We may even be able to do more than if we had won the election in 1980!'[6] The fact that he was able to minimize his defeat, without ignoring the pain, is striking. This story provides an example of Carter's sense of hope and memory. Rather than wallowing in the 'damned' present and yearning for a 'perfect' past, Carter *moved forward* into the uncertain future with hope.

Journalist Theodore H. White wrote in his 1982 book *America in Search of Itself* that 'Jimmy Carter was always a mystery, this man with the straw-colored hair and clear blue eyes, whose enemies came to despise him while those who would be his friends could not understand him.'[7] Perhaps at some level that is true, is true perhaps of any human being another tries to explain and understand. And yet, as even White concluded at the end of that same chapter, in recounting the difficulties President Carter had faced, 'he remained the same decent man, the same peace seeker.... He loved humankind' (224-25). My own reading of Carter is that he was remarkably consistent and tried to live his life, public and private, by a code firmly grounded in the Christian faith he first professed as an eleven-year-old boy. As James Baker insisted, Carter's growing faith, his security and inner peace, 'made him love others as he is loved by God' (67-68). Carter, as Baker described him, was a realist, who knew that 'we are sinful people being reborn' (84) who, if we 'try hard enough, create a true righteous community' (89).

Jimmy Carter, a small town Georgia boy, was inaugurated President of the United States in January 1977. In sub-zero weather, he strolled down Pennsylvania Avenue with his wife Rosalynn, and the day seemed bright with promise. The dark side of America – Vietnam and Watergate – could be pushed aside. A fresh start was possible. At least I suspect that is what many who watched that day thought.

Carter's rise to power has been chronicled by numerous writers, both journalists and scholars, and he of course has written about it himself. He was born into a rural middle-class family in Georgia in 1924 and experienced life much as any Southern boy born into those circumstances did. His father Earl was a relatively successful businessman-farmer, and his mother Lillian was a nurse. The former was a stern disciplinarian, while the latter provided a more compassionate role model for Jimmy.

Intelligent, nurtured and hard-working, Jimmy grew up with ambitions to attend the United States Naval Academy at Annapolis, a dream he realized. At Annapolis in the mid-1940s, Carter graduated in 1946 ranking 60th in a class of 822. That same year he married Rosalynn Smith, a Plains, Georgia, girl, and thus began a remarkable partnership that endured.

In 1953, after his father's death, Carter resigned his naval commission and returned home to take over the family business. Such a move made perfect sense. As one of Carter's Annapolis classmates said, the future for naval careers was not promising. 'At this time,' as he put it, 'the pay was low [and] ... promotions were exceedingly slow.'[8] In addition, Carter's brother Billy was only 16 and still in high school, while Lillian was depressed, in one of her 'black' moods, as they were characterized.

Carter's venture into the peanut business was successful, and he learned to bring Rosalynn into his life as a full partner in business as well as in private life. Such a merger carried over into Carter's political life. Rosalynn, a bright and determined woman, proved to be Carter's most influential advisor. In the mid-1950s, her prominent role in the family business appeared to irk Lillian, who commented on the limited role she had played while Earl was alive. Ten years later Carter returned to Plains, and won a disputed race for the State Senate in 1962. In that election Carter was initially the victim of 'good old boy' politics but proved his tenacity by challenging the original election result and proving his claim that the election had been stolen from him. Two years later he was unopposed for re-election.[9]

During his years in the Georgia Senate, Carter won a reputation for ability, honesty, and hard work. In 1966 he first announced his intent to run for the U.S. Congress but then switched at the last minute to a race for governor and lost. It was, as he has written and others have noted, a difficult time – Carter was a proud man and he hated to lose.

During this dark period of his life, Carter experienced a religious quickening. Whatever the objective truth of that experience, the outsider can only reflect on and record how it affected his life and actions. He became more than a 'Sunday' Christian – his religious faith became an essential part of the fabric of his life. Carter went on lay evangelism missions and committed himself to a life of service in a way unprecedented in American public life.[10] Carter's response to this difficult time in his life once again reflected his healthy sense of hope. He demonstrated his ability to recover from defeat, pick up the pieces of his life and move forward.

In 1970 Carter re-entered Georgia politics in the Democratic primary for governor opposing the incumbent Carl Sanders. Carter took the same tack that worked for him later in 1976 in his presidential bid – he ran as an outsider, a friend of the people and an opponent of the establishment. While he did not appear progressive on the race issue (Julian Bond and Hosea Williams, Georgia civil rights leaders, never forgave him), Carter never resorted to the kind of race baiting associated with other Southern governors such as Lester Maddox of Georgia, Orval Faubus of Arkansas or Mississippi's Ross Barnett. He beat Sanders and then won by a wide margin against a Republican candidate in the general election.

At this point, Carter moved in a more progressive direction. He delivered an inaugural address that left no doubt about where he stood: 'The time for racial discrimination is over. No poor rural white or black person should ever have to bear the additional burden of being deprived of the opportunity of an education, a job, or simple justice.' At this point, Carter became the 'conscience of the New South.'[11] Though he never won the allegiance of people like Bond and Williams, from this point forward Carter had the support of other black leaders such as Andrew Young and Martin Luther King, Senior.[12]

Clearly an ambitious man, Carter set his sights high, and at the mid-point of his term as governor in 1972 told his mother he intended to run for president. 'For president of what?' Lillian Carter allegedly responded.

In 1972, after the Democratic Convention, Peter Bourne wrote a ten-page memo to Carter encouraging him to run for the presidency. Bourne, a young psychiatrist who had become close friends with Rosalynn Carter during their work on a drug abuse program for Georgia, contended that Carter should simply go for the top spot. He concluded by saying, 'What is critical is the psychological and emotional decision to take the risk and to run for the Presidency to win, whatever the eventual outcome might be.'[13]

Discussion between Carter and his closest associates continued over the next several months. Hamilton Jordan, who first met Carter in 1966, produced by the end of November 1972 the long memorandum which became the 'Bible' for the campaign. Jordan took some of Bourne's ideas, added ideas from other Carter intimates, meshed them with his own and presented the results to Carter at a Thanksgiving retreat in 1972. The die was cast. Carter would run in selected state presidential primaries and would run as the outsider who would reform Washington.

In 1974, after he had determined to run for the presidency but before he made a public announcement, Carter delivered a remarkable speech. In May, Senator Edward Kennedy came to Athens, Georgia, to speak at the Law Day ceremony at the University of Georgia when a portrait of Dean Rusk was dedicated. Then-Governor Carter introduced Kennedy; but he did more. He completely upstaged the Massachusetts Senator, who delivered a lack-luster address.

Opening with a joke, he quickly turned serious. He mentioned that he was not a lawyer but said, 'I read a lot and I listen a lot.' He indicated that much of his 'understanding about the proper application of criminal justice and the system of equities is from Reinhold Niebuhr.' Further, Carter said, 'The other source of my understanding about what's right and wrong in this society is from a friend of mine, a poet named Bob Dylan.' He mentioned several of Dylan's songs and then 'railed and bitched about a system of criminal justice that allows the rich and privileged to escape punishment for their crimes and sends poor people to prison because they can't afford to bribe the judge.'[14]

Carter spoke without a text but from 'a page and a half of scrawled notes in his legal pad.' Journalist Hunter Thompson has provided the most important analysis of this particular address in *Rolling Stone Magazine*. Overwhelmed by the speech, Thompson understood correctly that it was an example of Carter's compassion and quest for justice. Clearly, Dylan's music must be understood from the Biblical perspective, Carter's frame of reference, and the direct Biblical commands to seek justice. While some writers have taken this to be merely Carter's pride in upstaging one of the most prominent figures in American politics, it was clearly more.[15]

Using unlimited energy and tenacity, and against the backdrop of Vietnam and Watergate, Carter ran a classic "outsider" campaign. The interesting thing to note is that, as Charles O. Jones clearly demonstrates in *The Trustee Presidency*, he really was an outsider, and he intended to remain one. America, as the title of this volume suggests, was lost and floundering in the mid-1970s.

The Vietnam War split America as no war other than the Civil War had, and the trauma of Watergate still hung like a dark cloud over the nation. For good reason, after the revelations of the shabby and unconstitutional antics of Richard Nixon and his team, Americans felt betrayed by public office holders. President Gerald Ford's pardon of Richard Nixon intensified the public's sense of corrupt political deals. Carter exploited the post-Watergate cynicism by his simple pledge of honesty – 'I will never lie to you.'[16]

Throughout the campaign, Carter stressed 'competence and compassion,' and he continued that theme in his inaugural address. Committed to the idea of a government of the people unbeholden to special interests, 'Carter saw it as his duty to educate the people in the realities of the new age of limits.' In the inaugural, Carter said, 'We have learned that more is not necessarily better, that even our great nation has its recognized limits, and that we can neither answer all questions nor solve all problems.' Carter extolled 'the common good' and 'exalted the good of the individual.' He was careful, however, to do so 'not in the sense of wealth-maximizing greed but in the sense of human rights.'[17]

Carter, who believed completely Reinhold Niebuhr's dictum that 'the sad duty of politics is to establish justice in a sinful world,' began in his inaugural to promote the re-education of Americans. He proposed nothing short of the rebirth of the American dream! But as Dumbrell pointed out, 'Any such rebirth ... would have to be grounded in an unequivocal acceptance of limits.' For, as Carter understood, the days of 'big spending liberalism at home' were through. A year later in his State of the Union address, he continued the educational process when he warned that government by itself could not 'eliminate poverty, provide energy [or] mandate goodness.' Only, he said, 'a true partnership between government and the people could do that.' Once again we hear echoes of Carter's strong sense of hope and memory as opposed to optimism and nostalgia.

In 1979, in the most famous speech of his administration and the one most misunderstood or misreported by the press, Carter returned to his 'competence and compassion' theme. 'In our government,' he said, 'it is a myth that we must choose between compassion and competence. Together, we build the foundation for a government that works – and that works for people.' He urged upon the American people a need to change attitude when he said, 'We cannot afford to live beyond our means.'[18] That speech, now remembered for its discussion of 'malaise,' a word which does not appear in its text, was a remarkable event.

The speech itself was the result of a ten-day retreat at Camp David at which a steady stream of scholars, ministers, thinkers, and politicians discussed in candid terms the Carter Presidency. Carter himself recalls those days as 'the most thought-provoking and satisfying of my Presidency.' Carter told the American public, 'I have been reminded again that all the legislation in the world can't fix what's wrong with America.' He proceeded to talk to America about limits, service and spirit.[19]

The speech sounds like what Southern Baptists might call a testimony with a classic organizational framework: confession of sins, reaffirmation of faith, and determination to do better. Whether one views it that way or not, the speech is extraordinary in the history of modern presidential rhetoric. As Theodore White said, 'No President since Abraham Lincoln had spoken to the American people with such sincerity about matters of the spirit' (268).

While this effort gained Carter considerable immediate support – over 65 million Americans watched it, and over sixty per cent were encouraged by it – the President shortly thereafter blundered. He called for the resignations of his entire cabinet (accepting five) and it appeared to news analysts (and perhaps the public) that the government was in disarray. 'Within days,' writes Robert Strong, 'of what might have been one of the most effective speeches in the recent history of the presidency,' Carter's 'standing in the polls resume[d] its downward drift' (647). Carter himself admitted that the cabinet changes 'could have been made in a much more effective manner.'[20]

Speaking later that year in October at the Kennedy Library in Boston, Carter continued his theme: 'We have,' he said, 'a keener appreciation of limits now.... We are struggling with a profound transition from a time of abundance to a time of growing scarcity.'[21]

In the context of his preaching about limits, but without spending an inordinate amount of time on domestic issues, some summary statements about his administration are in order. Carter, like Harry Truman before him, tackled the most difficult problems facing the nation 'rather than ducking them because the political fall-out would be damaging.' While much is made of Carter's problems with a Democratic Congress, the context of the times is important. Congress was reasserting its power after the 'imperial' presidencies of John Kennedy, Lyndon Johnson and Richard Nixon, and frankly, Congress was balky. It is also interesting to note that in the 180 years between 1800 and 1980, the executive branch dominated the Congress for approximately only 25 years. Down to Ronald Reagan, only Presidents Thomas Jefferson, Woodrow Wilson, Franklin D. Roosevelt, Dwight D. Eisenhower and Lyndon Johnson managed this feat – and none of them for the duration of their administrations.[22]

Many people, including some of Carter's own officials, have argued that he initiated too much legislation too quickly. Among those, Julius Richmond indicated that both the public and the Congress were simply overwhelmed. Richmond, Carter's Surgeon General and a liberal activist, said, 'Carter learned his lesson well. The second two years of his administration flowed more smoothly regarding bills sent to the Hill.' Former Secretary of Health, Education, and Welfare Joseph Califano, in an interview with this writer, suggested that Carter simply wasn't up to the job.[23] While the fired Secretary's comments were perhaps colored by personal feelings, Carter himself admitted in *Keeping Faith*, that 'With the advantage of hindsight, ... it would have been advisable to have introduced our legislation in much more careful phases – not in such a rush' (87).

Nonetheless, the facts do not change. Carter did send a flurry of legislation to Congress. Bills arrived on Capitol Hill to deregulate a variety of industries from oil to airlines; legislation to reorganize government arrived in 1977 and passed that same year; he put forward an energy bill which passed the House in 1977 but was bottled up in the Senate until it finally passed in 1978, though short of Carter's recommendations. It was hard to educate the Congress – and the public – about limits regarding energy. Throughout his presidency, however, Carter stressed energy conservation and was successful in winning approval of a windfall profits tax.[24]

Carter managed to secure a significant reform in the civil service, certainly the most far-reaching effort in that area since the 1883 Pendleton Act, and he improved dramatically the atmosphere regarding conservation. He signed into law the strip-mining bill which Gerald Ford had vetoed, and heightened the American consciousness about the issues revolving around conservation and environmental protection. Finally, in 1980, he signed into law the Alaska Land Act, setting aside over a million acres and protecting them from exploitative speculators. It had taken four years, and perhaps that is why the President called it 'among the most gratifying achievements in my term.'[25]

One criticism leveled at Carter was his inability to compromise. On that score, one might look at the various dam projects (the kind of pork barrel legislation the President had denounced as a candidate) which were tied to a public-works appropriation bill. In retrospect, Carter wrote that the 'compromise should have been vetoed because, despite some attractive features, it still included wasteful items.' A major regret he had was 'weakening and compromising that first year on some ... worthless dam projects.'[26]

Economic issues like inflation and energy dogged Carter for much of his term. While he failed to control inflation, other world leaders did not succeed in this either. The factors which fueled inflation were not Carter's to control. OPEC price boosts and Federal Reserve Board polices are just two examples of matters beyond the President's control. Even the *New York Times*, not noted for its pro-Carter stance, said on June 3, 1979, 'Inflation and energy are not problems of Jimmy Carter's making. The responses he has proposed have not brought notable results, in part because Congress has not let him try them. But they have been sensible. We have not yet heard from the economist or expert, let alone candidate, with better ones.'

With hindsight, it is clear that in looking at the Carter economy, most people have been (and are) guided more by image than by substance, more by what they think to be true than truth itself. For example, the most recent analysis of the economy during the Carter years, by Nebraska economist Ann Mari May, offers interesting conclusions. 'Economic growth,' she wrote, 'during the Carter years was quite strong.' Growth in real GNP, she argued, was greater during Carter's tenure than during those of Reagan, Ford or Nixon. Likewise, unemployment during Carter's presidency was lower than under either Ford or Reagan.[27]

Even more remarkable, May concluded her analysis with these words: 'A ranking of economic performance during seven postwar presidential periods on the basis of growth in output and employment, unemployment, inflation and interest rates, productivity, and capital investment shows that the Carter years outperformed the Ford, Reagan, and the Nixon years. Only in the Eisenhower years was peacetime economic performance better than during the Carter years, and only marginally so.'

One of the problems was that Carter preached a doctrine that caused pain. As he said, his policies involved 'costs.... They involve pain ... [but] with proper discipline we will prevail in our fight against inflation.' And, as May said, 'This particular sermon was not ... what the American public wanted to hear.'

Another central issue, and one which reflects Carter's sense of limits, needs to be introduced and discussed briefly: the relationship between Carter and the feminist movement. A strong supporter of the Equal Rights Amendment, Carter also demonstrated his commitment to feminism through his appointment powers. As Rosalynn pointed out in *First Lady from Plains* (1984), by the end of his term, Jimmy had appointed three of the six females to serve in presidential cabinets since the inception of the country. Additionally, he appointed numerous female undersecretaries and assistant secretaries. And as John Dumbrell wrote, 'Of the forty-six women serving on the federal bench at the end of his term, Jimmy Carter appointed forty-one.' Furthermore, the Carter Administration initiated and hosted numerous other policies and legislation to advance women's rights.[28]

Despite these impressive gains, feminist activists failed to support Carter in the 1980 election against Ronald Reagan. For example, the National Women's Political Caucus refused to choose between the two candidates, and the National Organization for Women simply issued a statement denouncing Reagan. Why? The answer is simple: Carter's position on abortion.

While criticized for waffling on the issue, he in fact never wavered. As he said in a February 1976 letter to the National Abortion League, 'I am personally opposed to abortion.' He went on to emphasize more effective family planning but was also 'opposed to a constitutional amendment' to change *Roe v Wade*. 'I am,' he wrote, 'personally opposed to government spending for abortion services. However, as President, I will be guided and bound by the courts.'[29] He held the line.

Dumbrell pointed out that, 'Carter's position was logically and constitutionally sound.' It satisfied 'his strong religious beliefs' (72). Carter was correct in his statement that abortion was an 'impossible political' issue, one which people would 'still be arguing about' five decades later. His position is strongly supported by human history: the same factions and quarrels over abortion which divide late twentieth century Americans embroiled fifth century B.C. Greece. The imbroglio will continue. Given Carter's understanding of limits, however, and the value he places on human life, his position is understandable.

In some ways, the Carter Presidency was simply ill-fated and unsuited for the late 1970s. Americans are generally unwilling to look at the long term, and they vote on the basis of the immediate circumstance. Robert Strauss, who managed Carter's 1980 presidential bid, said luck was a factor: 'Poor bastard – he used up all his luck getting here.... We've not had a single piece of good luck' since his election.[30]

In conclusion, it is appropriate to return to the Adams family for an effective analysis of the central character trait that is crucial to understanding Jimmy Carter. Former President John Adams (John Quincy's father), in *Discourses on Davila*, argued that 'the passion for distinction' is central to human motivation. In his complex argument, Adams said that most people strive for distinction 'by riches, by family records, by play, and by other frivolous personal accomplishments.' He believed that few people aimed higher but contended that a few did. 'They,' Adams wrote, 'aim at approbation as well as attention; at esteem as well as consideration; and at admiration and gratitude, as well as congratulation.' I am convinced that Jimmy Carter fits this description. And in so doing, Carter is one of those few who Adams said are of 'the tribe out of which proceed your patriots and heroes, and most of the great benefactors to mankind.'[31]

First as Governor of Georgia, then as President, and finally as a private citizen, Carter understood that 'once wealth and luxury became the principle marks of distinction, avarice would corrode even the strongest of republican structures.'[32] Carter's understanding of Christianity emphasized service to others and compassion for the weak, a concept made clear in the May 1974 Law Day Address. Distinction through service, the Adams concept, is consistent with Christianity. In St. Paul's Epistle to the Colossians, chapter 3, verses 23-24, Christians are exhorted to do their best: 'Whatever you do, work at it with all your heart, as working for the Lord, not for men.... It is the Lord Christ you are serving.' As James Baker put it, Carter took his role as 'pastor' seriously. And for Baptists, 'The pastor is their servant' (84).

Carter consistently sought what Adams called 'a public space in which actions would be visible and transparent.' He understood that 'when a public man's character and activity were open to maximum scrutiny, the public had a fair opportunity to assess his real dessert.' Integrity, Adams believed, was essential, and that meant a public man must be straightforward without exaggerating strength or concealing flaws.[33]

Although it would be wrong to argue that Christianity is the only religion or philosophy to demand of its followers a lifestyle which reflects memory and hope as opposed to nostalgia and optimism, it clearly does articulate such a worldview. Christianity, which encourages change both individually and collectively, overlays its teachings with an emphasis on limits. Additionally, I should point out that few writers today (either journalists or scholars) appear to be well-grounded in the fundamentals of Christian theology. They seem comfortable with the concept of religiosity, which is easy to condemn, but they act uncomfortable with anyone who takes faith seriously and attempts to live out that faith in a public manner. Journalists tend to make fun of public figures who openly discuss their faith. Jimmy Carter understood that. Remember, for example, the 1976 interview Carter gave to *Playboy Magazine* when he admitted to the sin of adultery because he had lusted after women in his thoughts. His comment is clearly in line with orthodox Christianity and with his understanding of sin. The pundits, however, did not know how to deal with this theology, so they merely made fun of it. In the words of James David Barber, an internationally known scholar of the American Presidency, reporters had to 'cram fast on this strange religion [Christianity], as if it were some ethnological eccentricity brought back from Pago Pago by Margaret Mead.' Barber drove his point home by saying that writers 'don't mind Christians as long as they don't really mean it.'[34]

Carter, a practicing and knowledgeable Christian, understood the limits of goodness. He clearly understood that if better stewardship of natural resources were not implemented, environmental disaster would result. One of his central problems was to foster a way of life which involved planning for the future, whereas the traditional American ideology was indifferent to the future. 'America,' according to Christopher Lasch, 'has always turned its back on history and considers herself immune to the rhythms of history.'

Carter tried to combat the traditional idea of progress in America that involved a state of mind which said that more is better. That is optimism. Rather, Carter understood that 'hope is a character trait in one's relation to the world.' It is 'a state of mind that asserts the goodness of life within limits and sees the beauty of creation in the face of all unhappiness, tragedy and injustice evident to all who have eyes to see and ears to hear.'[35]

The former President knew that. He knew too that hope is a morally demanding state of mind. Being firmly grounded morally, Carter knew, allowed one to deal with disappointment in a positive way. As he sought to teach an America lacking moral grounding, disappointment gave way to despair. Certainly Carter was not entirely successful. He lost the 1980 election to Ronald Reagan's shallow nostalgia and unrealistic optimism. Nonetheless, as anyone who professes to teach knows, the effect of the lesson often is not seen immediately. By his continued example of public service upon leaving the

Presidency, with an effort 'to establish justice in a sinful world,' Carter's impact will increase rather than diminish.

His commitment to Habitat for Humanity, a private initiative to provide decent housing for the poor internationally, has attracted much publicity. He does not simply endorse the program, he gives his time and his talent as a carpenter to it. Carter fully subscribes to the Habitat motto that decent housing is a basic human right. In addition, he stopped two potentially explosive situations in North Korea and Haiti in 1994 and in mid-December secured the promise of a cease-fire in the war-torn former Yugoslavia. Carter's approach was appropriate. As Jagoda Pericy-Anderson wrote in the Sept-Oct, 1995, *Utne Reader*, 'As long as the international community tries to negotiate peace while holding the Serbs to be monsters, no cease-fire will last.... A more effective attitude would be to view each of the groups ... as human beings with legitimate needs and fears.' Continuing, she wrote, 'Former President Jimmy Carter displayed a willingness to listen to the Bosnian Serb leadership's point of view when he negotiated a cease-fire in late 1994. Carter was ridiculed, but he was on the right track. Any successful settlement will look to the future viability of all parties' (75). The writer, born in Zagreb, is from a family emotionally touched by the conflict – her father is Serbian and her mother Croatian – and admitted that 'every day the war rages over there, it rages inside me' (74). I think her assessment of Carter's role is correct. Service. Compassion. Justice. These concepts are all central to Carter's understanding of Christianity and for Carter, everything begins there.

I do not know how history will finally rank Carter's Presidency, nor do I know how people will feel about him a hundred years from now, but it is clear to me that he was and is a man motivated to do what is right – he will act and take the consequences. My father once said, 'In American politics there are winners and losers, and sometimes it is difficult to tell which is which.' That is certainly true in Carter's case. Time will tell. I am betting that he is a winner. His life reminds me of the last chapter of Voltaire's *Candide*. There, Voltaire suggests that upon expulsion from the Garden of Eden people failed to be good stewards. He advises them to cultivate their own gardens. That is what Carter is doing; but his garden is bigger than most.

The Jimmy Carter described herein is not the mystery Theodore White described. He lives by a code and is consistent, as consistent as it is humanly possible to be. As Charles O. Jones said about Carter, 'He was not enigmatic.... Rather, his being in the White House posed an enigma for others' (207). And he will remain enigmatic for others until they come to terms with his understanding of the Christian hold on his life.

Notes

1. James T. Baker, *A Southern Baptist in the White House* (Philadelphia: 1977), 10-11.
2. Christopher Lasch, *The True and Only Heaven: Progress and Its Critics* (New York: 1991), 82.
3. While there are numerous examples of the shift, it was anticipated by Peter Jay, 'Why President Carter Had Clearly Proved his Right to a Second Term,' *The Times*, Oct. 27, 1980. Jay, British Ambassador to Washington, 1977-79, wrote: '[Carter] is ... exceptionally intelligent, ... profoundly liberal in his instincts, a democrat to his fingertips, genuinely compassionate towards the weak and the poor, ... and – though this is little recognized or deployed – capable of brilliant wit.'
4. Burton I. Kaufman, *The Presidency of James Earl Carter, Jr.* (Lawrence, Kansas: 1993), 3.
5. Stanley N. Katz, *Fulbright Association Newsletter* (Spring/Summer 1994), 1.
6. Jimmy and Rosalynn Carter, *Everything to Gain: Making the Most of the Rest of Your Life* (New York: 1987), 8.
7. Theodore H. White, *America in Search of Itself: The Making of the President 1956-1980* (New York: 1982), 197.
8. Quoted in Betty Glad, *Jimmy Carter: In Search of the Great White House* (New York: 1980), 67.
9. Accounts of this fraudulent election may be found in a variety of sources. The most interesting is in Jimmy Carter, *Turning Point: A Candidate, a State, and a Nation Come of Age* (New York: 1992). Carter's account is basically consistent with other accounts and provides an interesting personal perspective.
10. Glad, 116-19.
11. *Atlanta Constitution*, January 13, 1971.
12. Glad, 141.
13. Bourne, quoted in Glad, 210.
14. Hunter S. Thompson, *Rolling Stone*, June 3, 1976. Thompson, a uniquely American journalist, has discussed his version of the Law Day speech a number of times. While some details vary, the essence of his account is consistent. Carter's strong indictment of America's legal system and his plea for justice for the poor shocked Thompson. He confirmed this in an interview with the author when Thompson spoke at Western Kentucky University in 1987.
15. *Ibid.* See also Charles J. Bussey, 'Bob Dylan: Driven Home,' *Christianity Today*, June 26, 1981, 47-48.
16. Charles O. Jones, *The Trusteeship Presidency: Jimmy Carter and the United States Congress* (Baton Rouge, LA: 1988). Jones provides an excellent account of Carter as an outsider.
17. John Dumbrell, *The Carter Presidency: A Re-Evaluation* (New York: 1993), 2. Dumbrell, from England, is Senior Lecturer in Politics at the Metropolitan University of Manchester. His work is especially interesting, and he reaches quite different conclusions from the American scholar, Burton Kaufman, mentioned earlier.
18. See text of Carter's speech in *New York Times*, July 16, 1979.
19. Robert A. Strong, 'Recapturing Leadership: The Carter Administration and the Crisis of Confidence,' *Presidential Studies Quarterly*, 16 (Fall 1986), 636-39.
20. Carter Interview with Charles J. Bussey, January 17, 1988.
21. *Public Papers of the Presidents, Jimmy Carter*, Vol. I (Washington, DC: 1981), 481-82.
22. Reo M. Christenson, 'Carter and Truman: A Reappraisal of Both,' *Presidential Studies Quarterly*, 13 (Spring 1983), 319-20.

23. Julius B. Richmond/Califano Interviews with Charles J. Bussey, May 1987.
24. Christenson, 322-24.
25. Carter, *Keeping Faith*, 582. See also Dumbrell, 210.
26. Carter, *Keeping Faith*, 581-83.
27. Ann Marie May, 'Fiscal Policy, Monetary Policy, and the Carter Presidency,' *Presidential Studies Quarterly*, XXIII (Fall 1993), 699-711.
28. Rosalynn Carter, *First Lady from Plains* (New York: 1984), 274-75; Dumbrell, 77.
29. Letter to Karen Mulhauser as reproduced in *The Presidential Campaign 1976: Vol. I: Part I* (Washington, DC: Government Printing Office, 1978), 92-93.
30. Quoted in Hamilton Jordan, *Crisis: The Last Year of the Carter Presidency* (New York: 1982), 60.
31. As quoted in Bruce Miroff, *Icons of Democracy: American Leaders as Heroes, Aristocrats, Dissenters, and Democrats* (New York: 1993), 54.
32. Text of speech as printed in the *New York Times*, 16 July 1979.
33. Miroff, 57.
34. James David Barber, *The Presidential Character: Predicting Performance in the White House*, 3rd ed., (Englewood Cliffs, N.J.: 1985), 427-28.
35. These quotes are from the public lecture Christopher Lasch delivered at Aarhus University in April 1993, and from my discussion with him after the lecture.

The Crooked Path: Continuity and Change in American Foreign Policy, 1968-1981

*Dale Carter**

In June 1972 Republican President Richard Nixon returned from his first summit meeting with Soviet leader Leonid Brezhnev in Moscow to tell a joint session of Congress about the 'new era of mutually agreed restraint and arms limitation' between the superpowers initiated by the signing of the Strategic Arms Limitation (SALT) Treaty; by 1980, Republican presidential candidate Ronald Reagan would be calling for a comprehensive remilitarization of American foreign policy in the face of what he claimed was an unprecedented challenge from an implacably hostile Soviet Union. At the beginning of the 1970s President Nixon spoke to the American people about the 'full generation of peace' an honourable settlement of the Vietnam war would make possible; by the end of the decade candidate Reagan would be condemning his rival, incumbent Democratic President Jimmy Carter, for allowing the United States to be humiliated across the third world, from Nicaragua to Iran. During the 1970s, it appeared, détente and all its manifestations had been discredited and abandoned.[1] Yet the trajectory which led the United States (to adapt another Nixon phrase) from an era of negotiation to one of confrontation with Moscow was by no means linear, clear or even complete. Rather, during the 1970s, American foreign policy followed a crooked path: at a concrete level, in terms of its course, roots and contexts; at a more abstract level, in terms of its makers' motives and objectives. This was in one sense hardly surprising, as it was during the 1970s that American foreign policy came to terms, slowly and falteringly, with the impact of its loss of global hegemony, graphically symbolized and advanced by the debacle in Vietnam. At the same time,

* I am grateful to Kevin Quigley of the Department of History, University of Warwick, England, for his constructive comments on and suggestions for improvements of an earlier draft of this paper.

however, if the path was crooked, then, like the route described by the eternal traveller in Jorge Luis Borges' short story 'The Library of Babel', it was not without pattern. Indeed, insofar as the contours of post-Vietnam US foreign policy appear to have been shaped more by the diagnoses of Richard Nixon than those of any other recent president, this (in many ways) crooked path was distinctly repetitious. It was no accident, as Bruce Cumings noted, that after Ronald Reagan's defeat of President Carter in the 1980 presidential election, one of *Time* magazine's photographs of the victorious candidate showed him seated at a clean desk with a copy of Richard Nixon's latest book in front of him.[2]

1. The Limits of Hegemony

The era of détente is now closely associated with Richard Nixon and his chief foreign policy advisor Henry Kissinger.[3] Yet moves towards an easing of tensions between Washington and Moscow were evident well before Nixon's inauguration in January 1969, largely because the circumstances which called them forth also preceded him. As early as June 1967, Nixon's predecessor, Democrat Lyndon Johnson, had met Soviet Prime Minister Aleksei Kosygin at Glassboro, New Jersey, for talks that in retrospect (and in spite of how little they achieved) may be considered one of the first indications of what would become a sea-change in American cold war strategy.[4] Of the many subjects raised by Johnson at Glassboro, two in particular – the war in Vietnam and the strategic arms race – begin to explain why by the late 1960s Washington was seeking to revise its relationships, not only with the Soviet Union but also with the rest of the world.

By the time Johnson and Kosygin met, American inability to secure its objectives in Vietnam had created deep divisions within both the foreign policy establishment and the nation at large. Congressional hearings had already revealed deepening anxiety within the higher political echelons about the conduct of the war. Occasional journalistic accounts of the impact of the conflict on the Vietnamese were only adding to the unease. At the same time, mass demonstrations against, and public disenchantment with, US involvement in Vietnam were mounting, in part because the numbers of American troops being committed to South East Asia, as of those being killed or wounded on active duty, continued to rise without bringing victory any closer. The calculations which in 1965 had persuaded President Johnson to escalate US involvement in the war – in simple terms, that the costs of such action would be less than those of the alternatives then available – were by 1967 proving badly mistaken. The following year, in the light of further setbacks at home and in Vietnam, the President took the advice of a group of senior advisors and placed a ceiling on American troop commitments while initiating peace talks with the North Vietnamese in Paris.[5] The nation's loss of blood and treasure in South East Asia was matched by the loss or diminution of its strategic military superiority *vis-à-vis* the Soviet Union. Having determined after the 1962 Cuban missile crisis that the Americans (as one Russian official put it) would 'never be able to do that to us again,' the Soviets were by the late 1960s approaching strategic missile parity with the United States (and as a result also seeking relief from the costs of incessant military competition). Faced with an arms race that appeared not only interminable but liable to accelerate as both sides developed new weapons technologies (anti-ballistic missile systems (ABMs) and Multiple Independent Reentry Vehicles (MIRVs)), and with the prospects of the spread of nuclear weapons to other powers, Johnson at Glassboro proposed discussions about arms control and successfully promoted the Nuclear Non-Proliferation Treaty that would be signed by almost sixty nations in July 1968. At the Geneva signing ceremony, American and Soviet representatives announced that their nations intended to commence talks on strategic arms limitations in the near future.[6]

If at Glassboro the United States sought Soviet cooperation in moderating the arms race and getting Washington off the hook in South East Asia, then it was encouraged to do so by two other, closely related, developments: on the one hand, the steady diminution of its post-1945 hegemony within the NATO alliance; on the other, and more significantly, the progressive weakening of its ability to carry the economic, political and social burdens of power. By the late 1960s, the recovery of Western Europe and Japan from the ravages of World War Two had enabled both to start asserting greater independence from the United States in a variety of fields. Among the Europeans, and the West Germans in particular, a growing desire to explore the possibility of East-West trade (as well as anxiety about the destabilizing effects of the Vietnam war on relations between the superpowers) prompted efforts to remove some of the main strategic and diplomatic stumbling blocks to greater commercial relations. These climaxed between 1969 and 1971 with Bonn's signature of both the nuclear non-proliferation treaty and a non-aggression pact with Moscow, as well as its formal recognition of East Germany and Poland. There were also moves to reduce Western European dependence on American military power. In 1966, France had withdrawn from the NATO command structure (and asked American troops to leave French soil), while two years later its European allies within NATO began pressing for talks between East and West on conventional arms reductions. In one sense, the growth of West German *ostpolitik* made improvements in relations between Moscow and Washington easier and more urgent; similarly, mounting political pressures within the United States for a cut in the number of American troops in Western Europe were legitimized by the latter's desire for greater influence on military issues. At the same time, however, these developments added to American anxieties about the future of NATO. American isolation within the alliance; a drift towards Western European neutralism; attempts by Moscow to play NATO partners off against one another: all, Richard Nixon's National Security Advisor Henry Kissinger wrote in his memoirs, posed 'serious challenge[s]' to the United States.[7]

These challenges were compounded by, and closely related to, the relative decline in American global commercial and financial dominance. What for Western Europe and Japan was post-war recovery meant for the United States an erosion of its economic supremacy in international markets. Between 1948 and 1970 European exports to the United States grew four times as fast as American exports to Europe, helping reduce the American share of free world trade from 23.3 per cent to 15.3 per cent over the same period. From the mid-1960s onwards, the combined costs of the war in Vietnam and President Johnson's domestic Great Society social welfare programs fuelled inflation, further pricing American exports out of world markets. In 1971, continuing reductions in its commercial competitiveness resulted in the nation's first balance of trade deficit since the nineteenth century. Accompanied as it was by an outflow of dollars resulting from continuing military spending overseas, foreign aid and private international investment, the trade deficit only added to the nation's growing balance of payments problems and associated speculation against the dollar on foreign exchanges. Pressure had been mounting since the late 1960s for a restructuring of the post-war international monetary system established by the United States at the 1944 Bretton Woods conference. By 1971 it was clear that without some kind of action the dollar faced a crisis.[8]

Such international problems were accompanied by, and again closely related to, internal tensions. If the combined costs of the war and the Great Society fuelled domestic inflation, then they also helped erode the political, social and cultural foundations of American foreign policy. As balance of payments and inflationary problems constrained the logic of economic growth, so from 1965 onwards conflicts intensified between interest groups whose differences had since the New Deal era been accommodated by the class compromises of American liberalism. The success of the civil rights movement in wresting for black Americans various political and economic concessions from the state only deepened these conflicts: the South resenting black advances while urban ethnic and blue collar groups learned lessons from the movement and pressed their own claims for equity. As the organized labour force mobilized so the middle class, already squeezed economically by creeping inflation and rising interest rates, saw growing numbers of its younger members drawn towards the burgeoning New Left and counter-cultural movements, which were themselves being fuelled by antiwar sentiment and the struggle for racial justice. If the splintering of the Democratic New Deal coalition opened the door for the Republicans under Nixon to regain the White House in 1969, then the spectre of growing domestic divisions – and in particular of the disaffiliation of a generation of younger middle class Americans – was of great concern to the nation's political, financial and legal establishment regardless of party.[9]

2. Cutting the Price of Power

Confronted by the spiralling financial and political costs of the war in Vietnam and the arms race with Moscow, an alliance system under growing strains, a faltering and increasingly uncompetitive economy, and a society riven by social and cultural divisions, the Nixon administration in the late 1960s and early 1970s sought less to surrender power than to renegotiate its price. The objective was, in the words of David Calleo, not 'a reduced American role, but ... a less costly way to manage it.' Finding that way depended in part on a recognition that the salient features of the international system had changed since the late 1940s, and in part on an associated reevaluation of the bases of American power. As the President put it, the nation had to develop 'a new approach to foreign policy to match a new era of international relations.'[10] In a briefing to media executives in Kansas City, Missouri, in July 1971 (the so-called 'Pentagon of Power' speech), Nixon gave some pointers to this new approach by remarking that world affairs were no longer shaped by one or two military superpowers but by 'five great economic superpowers' – the United States, the Soviet Union, Japan, Western Europe and China. In the future, he went on, economic rather than military power would be 'the key to other kinds of power.' Before it could hope to reassert its leadership, these remarks implied, the United States had to temper its long-standing ideological preoccupation – anti-Communism – with a concern for other, more material, aspects of international affairs. 'The "isms",' the President reported in 1970, 'have lost their vitality.' Nixon was not seeking to abandon the Cold War entirely: as H.T. Brands has remarked, in some ways 'it had the undeniable virtue of making the planet a reasonably orderly place.' The President did, however, seek to restructure it.[11]

Sustaining American hegemony while containing its costs involved a number of initiatives. Perhaps most obviously, and in keeping with his remarks about the place of ideological factors in international affairs, President Nixon built on his predecessor's first steps by pursuing better relations with Moscow. The Soviet Union's image as a state in the service of a revolutionary ideology was dissolved; it was perceived instead as a conventional Great Power with which negotiations were possible. While the pursuit of détente was hindered by continued American involvement in Vietnam and the Soviet invasion of Czechoslovakia in 1968, the late 1960s and early 1970s saw progress on a variety of issues. The rapprochement climaxed with the May 1972 Nixon/Brezhnev summit meeting in Moscow at which a series of agreements (ten in all) were signed, including SALT and ABM accords (placing limits on numbers of intercontinental ballistic missile (ICBM) launchers and ABM sites) and a statement setting out 'Basic Principles of Mutual Relations' (establishing ground rules to minimize confrontation between the two superpowers). While each side interpreted the latter document differently, both welcomed the opportunities the weapons agreements gave for stabilizing the nuclear arms race and its attendant costs. Moreover, as Kissinger later recalled, the arms control treaties did not surrender American nuclear superiority: by freezing permissible numbers of ICBM launchers, they helped secure it.[12]

Cutting the costs of hegemony also involved a settlement of the war in Vietnam. To Nixon and Kissinger, in fact, without a withdrawal from Vietnam on satisfactory terms American authority would continue to falter. Convinced that the survival of the nation's international credibility made battlefield defeat unacceptable, but that the imposition of a 'purely military solution' would be impossible for domestic political reasons, Nixon sought between 1969 and 1973 to salvage as much as he could from the debacle without undermining the objective of US withdrawal. To this end the air wars against North Vietnam, Laos and Cambodia were expanded (and combined with armed incursions into Laos and Cambodia). At the same time, the administration pursued negotiations with the North Vietnamese while seeking assistance from Moscow and elsewhere in pushing Hanoi towards a settlement acceptable in Washington. According to the Nixon administration, the latter meant winning for South Vietnam a fair chance of long-term security following an American withdrawal; to many others it meant no more than providing for a sufficient time period – a 'decent interval' – between the withdrawal and Saigon's final collapse for Washington to claim an honourable end to its role.[13] Finally, the administration adopted a policy of 'Vietnamization,' withdrawing American troops and passing more of the human cost of the fighting on to the South Vietnamese armed forces in order to satisfy Congressional pressure and domestic public opinion. 'Changing the color of the corpses,' as one US official bluntly put it, enabled the number of American troops in Vietnam to be reduced from over 500,000 to just 3,000 between early 1969 and late 1972.[14]

In July 1969, this aspect of American policy became generalized through the so-called 'Nixon Doctrine.' In future, the President announced, while keeping its treaty commitments the United States would in most cases only furnish economic and military aid – not troops – to threatened third world nations whose security was deemed vital to American national interests. Reminiscent of parts of the 'New Look' strategy adopted when Nixon served as Dwight D. Eisenhower's vice-president in the 1950s, the Nixon Doctrine was designed not only to sanction US withdrawal from Vietnam, but also to limit its involvement in subsequent similar conflicts and to shift their physical and political burdens to American proxies. Other initiatives closely related to the Nixon Doctrine (this time adopted at the behest of Congress) were intended further to reduce the financial costs of hegemony. Those nations selected to act as American proxies, such as Iran, Saudi Arabia, Indonesia and Brazil, would henceforth be invited to *purchase* US arms rather than be given them. Between

1970 and 1974, US foreign military sales to third world countries rose in value from less than half a billion dollars to almost ten billion dollars.[15]

A third initiative involved communist China. In a significant 1967 *Foreign Affairs* article, Nixon had written that the United States could not 'afford to leave China forever outside the family of nations,' and during his first year in office the President had signalled his desire for a transformation in Sino-American relations by liberalizing US trade policy towards Beijing. Subsequent military, political, financial, cultural, legal and scientific initiatives facilitated Henry Kissinger's visits to China in July and October 1971. Confident in his own impeccable anti-communist credentials, willing to entertain what he felt were China's limited objectives, and able to hint at the prospect of international legitimacy for Beijing (as well as a partial US military withdrawal from Asia and a settlement of the Taiwan dispute), Nixon himself travelled to meet the Chinese leadership in February 1972. In addition to its recognition of reality, the opening to China served key purposes within Nixon's broader strategy. In economic terms, it promised to advance the regional stability that would enable Asia's vast economic potential – buttressed by both Sukarno's fall in Indonesia in 1965 and the internationalization of Japanese capital – to be turned to American advantage. Politically, it enabled Washington to pursue 'triangular diplomacy,' exploiting the deepening Sino-Soviet rift (the two sides had recently engaged in a number of armed border clashes) to give the United States additional leverage in its dealings with both. Insofar as it forced Moscow and Beijing to deploy military forces along their long common border, the very existence of the Sino-Soviet split helped Washington reduce the size (and therefore the cost) of its own armed forces from 3.5 million in 1968 to 2.3 million in 1973. However, building bridges to China as well as the Soviet Union promised further benefits. By raising the spectre in each communist capital of an American entente with the other, Nixon sought to gain not only Moscow's commitment to nuclear and conventional arms limitations but also the assistance of both sides in persuading Hanoi to moderate its terms for a settlement in Vietnam.[16]

In its dealings with Moscow and Beijing, the administration adopted a 'stick and carrot' strategy, offering either to advance or to withhold a range of diplomatic, material and commercial concessions depending on the behaviour of its negotiating partners in other (not necessarily related) fields. Help in securing an acceptable settlement in Vietnam or in stabilizing the arms race might yield diplomatic recognition for Beijing or technological assistance for Moscow – while failure to do so might not. However, the 'linkage' strategy was thought of in Washington not only as a means of coordinating attempts to cut the costs of hegemony; its commercial aspects were also intended to foster American economic recovery and thereby the reassertion of US international authority. Thus after the first Nixon/Brezhnev summit of May/June 1972, a credit deal was signed enabling Moscow to purchase 750 million dollars' worth of American grain over a three year period. A comprehensive trade agreement granting the Soviet Union 'most favoured nation' status followed in October 1972. Both Nixon and Kissinger emphasized that trade was primarily an instrument of diplomacy designed to control Soviet geopolitical ambitions. Yet, as Thomas McCormick has argued, détente with Moscow was in part a means of persuading the Soviet Union to open up Eastern Europe to Western capital and technology at a time when it was in precisely such areas that profit rates were highest. Nixon's opening to Beijing – and the 'great China market' it might give access to – carried with it similar prospects. Between 1971 and 1973, Soviet-American trade would triple while Sino-American trade would increase in value by almost one billion dollars. 'Containment by inclusion' to this extent meant finding new frontiers for American trade and investment.[17]

Moves to stabilize the arms race, to withdraw from Vietnam, and to open up new opportunities for American businessmen abroad went some way toward salvaging what publisher Henry Luce in 1941 had dubbed the 'American Century.' In economic terms, however, they were too little and came too late to contain the deepening commercial and monetary problems facing the country thirty years later. (Efforts to incorporate the communist world into international trade and investment networks were, in any event, as likely to benefit West German as American businessmen. Indeed it was in part the very success of Western European and Japanese commerce and industry in excluding American business from world markets that had led to the problems in the first place.) By the summer of 1971, its problems mounting, the Nixon administration felt compelled to act – and in this case to act defensively. For whereas, in its dealings with Moscow and Beijing, Washington had a number of strong bargaining chips and was dealing with economically weaker nations, in confronting its major trading partners it had rather fewer advantages. Faced, as he recalled in his memoirs, with a 'major crisis,' and under pressure from protectionist interests at home, President Nixon in August 1971 launched his New Economic Policy, imposing a ten per cent surcharge on all imports, devaluing the dollar and suspending its convertibility into gold. These moves were seen by many observers as Nixon's most illiberal, unilateralist initiatives – not surprisingly, in the light of Treasury Secretary John Connally's remark that 'foreigners are out to screw us. Our job is to screw them first.' If the import duty was inconsistent with the nation's international trade agreements, the other moves undermined the entire post-war international monetary framework. It was not simply that these initiatives acknowledged American weaknesses even as they sought to treat them; nor that they were in themselves likely less to cure the dollar's long-term instability than to fuel inflationary pressures within the economy. Taken without prior consultation, embracing protectionism and effectively forcing overseas holders of (now devalued) dollars to pay for America's economic ills, these moves bought the United States time only by adding to existing strains within its alliance system.[18]

In domestic political terms, however, growing conflicts between the United States, Western Europe and Japan were of secondary importance: the allies had no vote. In fact, as the November 1972 presidential election drew closer, Nixon saw in the nationalist dimensions of the New Economic Policy domestic political advantages extending well beyond those industrial constituencies – such as textiles and steel – which had been demanding protectionism. Much the same applied to the other dimensions of Republican foreign policy. The withdrawal of American troops from Vietnam had from the outset won popular approval; the negotiations with Hanoi enabled the President to don the mantle of peacemaker, as did the visits to Moscow and Beijing and the signing of the SALT and ABM treaties; the economic dimensions of détente, meanwhile, secured the support of important domestic constituencies, notably the American farming bloc. While Henry Kissinger in particular liked to speak in abstract terms of the grand design or 'structure of peace' he and Nixon were pursuing, the design was, as Raymond Garthoff points out, as much political as anything else. Elected to office in 1968 by exploiting the nation's cultural, social and political divisions, Nixon had by 1972 gone some way towards fashioning, if not a new consensus, then at least a new conservative electoral coalition: the so-called 'silent majority,' who saw in his moves to contain the rising costs of the Cold War abroad and of the welfare state at home a means of securing their own positions in an age of diminishing resources. Much to Nixon and Kissinger's relief, the President had also contained a dangerous drift towards isolationism amongst a public frustrated by the failures in Vietnam and weary of the burdens of power.[19]

3. The Politics of Retrenchment

President Nixon's comprehensive victory over Democratic rival George McGovern in November 1972 suggested that his efforts to restructure the Cold War had secured at least electoral endorsement. Yet to cut the nation's losses in Vietnam; deal with its long-term economic problems; control the arms race; accommodate and contain Western Europe, Japan, China and the Soviet Union within a multipolar world; and rebuild an establishment consensus, neutralize domestic radicalism and counter popular isolationism constituted an ambitious program. Even without the Watergate scandal of 1973-74, Nixon and Kissinger's approach was always likely to face opposition, not least from within the American establishment. Indeed, détente's construction and manifestations were, as Garthoff emphasizes, distinctly political in part because of Nixon's sensitivity to the environment within which his efforts would be judged. As it was, even before Watergate finally washed Nixon away in

August 1974, challenges to the grand design were being mounted from both conservative and liberal perspectives.

Ironically, given that Nixon had once used anti-communism to build a power base within the conservative wing of the Republican Party, his strategy and tactics (sustained as they were after August 1974 by President Ford's Secretary of State Henry Kissinger) were most bitterly assailed by an influential coalition of critics on the political right. Anxious about Nixon's replacement of military superiority with military sufficiency as a bench mark for national security, some conservative cold warriors contrasted what they felt was the Panglossian logic of the SALT agreements with the more realistic assumptions of NSC-68, the key strategy document which in 1950 had advocated a massive build-up of US military power in the face of an alleged Soviet threat. The June 1974 resignation of Paul Nitze from the team then negotiating the outlines of a SALT 2 agreement with Moscow was one significant expression of a growing revolt within sections of the establishment over détente. Nitze feared that, while arms control remained a worthwhile objective, the continued growth of Soviet military power was being underestimated. An extension of the SALT agreements negotiated in Moscow would, he felt, threaten American national security and destabilize the East/West military balance. Two years after his departure from government, Nitze would help found the Committee on the Present Danger (CPD), a powerful elite pressure group that characterized détente as 'one-sided disarmament.' He would also serve on the Ford administration's so-called 'Team B' intelligence review board whose conclusions would towards the end of the decade inform a growing chorus calling for a return to the logic of NSC-68.[20] A second group of critics assailed Nixon, Ford and Kissinger for their alleged failure to halt the erosion of US influence beyond the world's industrial heartlands. Mobilized in part by what they saw as growing Soviet intervention in the Middle East, and enraged by joint American/Soviet moves to prevent Israeli armed forces completing their defeat of the Egyptians in the October 1973 Yom Kippur war, these critics used influential magazines such as *Commentary* (voice of the American Jewish Committee) to call for an end to Washington's rapprochement with Moscow, whose support for the Arab cause they felt threatened Israel's survival. In attacking détente over the question of the Middle East, so-called 'neoconservative' writers like *Commentary* editor Norman Podhoretz found common ground with the cold warriors, who saw in the Arab oil embargo and price rises of late 1973 symbols of America's loss of influence and a rationale for the remilitarization of US foreign policy. To both groups, détente was at best being violated by the Soviets in the Middle East and elsewhere; at worst it was a modern form of appeasement.[21]

These views won the backing of other traditionally hawkish groups within the United States, notably organized labour in the shape of AFL-CIO leaders George Meany and Lane Kirkland. They also influenced the passage of

Congressional legislation. Articulating militarist and neoconservative critiques of détente, for example, Democratic Senator Henry Jackson and his allies between 1972 and 1975 effectively undermined détente's formal economic dimensions by extending 'linkage' to Soviet *domestic* affairs. In January 1975, in response to a series of amendments to East/West trade legislation making US commercial and financial concessions to Moscow dependent on Soviet commitments to a more liberal Jewish emigration policy, the Kremlin renounced the October 1972 Soviet/American Trade Agreement. Towards the end of the year, the anti-détente lobby was further bolstered when the Democrats in Congress refused to approve President Ford's request for additional aid for the UNITA-FNLA coalition in their military struggle against the Soviet/Cuban-backed MPLA in Angola. In the wake of the Ethiopian and Portuguese revolutions of 1974, and the victories of the Khmer Rouge in Cambodia, the Pathet Lao in Laos, and the communists in Vietnam the following year, the 'loss' of Angola was to many the final proof that, for the United States, détente was a recipe for cold war defeat. By the time of the 1976 Republican presidential nomination campaign, Gerald Ford felt compelled to substitute the phrase 'peace through strength' for 'détente' in order to contain the challenge of conservative rival Ronald Reagan.[22]

Yet if, by rejecting Nixon's 'containment by inclusion' strategy towards Moscow, militarist and neoconservative critics offered the more comprehensive challenge to Republican foreign policy, theirs were not the only dissenting voices. By the mid-1970s, a liberal critique of Nixon/Ford diplomacy had also been formulated. If only for electoral purposes, its proponents did sometimes speak the same language and address the same issues as the conservatives. During the 1976 presidential election campaign, for example, Democratic candidate Jimmy Carter defined détente as 'an opportunity [for the Soviets] to continue the process of world revolution without running the threat [sic] of nuclear war.' He also echoed militarist accusations that Secretary of State Kissinger was 'giving up too much and asking for too little' from Moscow. For the most part, however, liberal criticisms focused on procedural matters, questioning less the fundamental substance and logic of détente than the methods and standards adopted by its agents. In conceptual terms, both the shift from a bipolar to a multipolar global power structure and the primacy of economics over ideology and armaments were endorsed by Nixon's liberal critics. So too the need to contain the costs and shift the burdens of power, and to revitalize the American economy. At a more concrete level, the strategy of containment by inclusion, the process of détente as expressed through arms control and trade deals, the opening to China, the withdrawal from Vietnam, the adoption of the Nixon Doctrine, and the shift from confrontation to negotiation in the third world all accorded to some degree with the prescriptions of social democrats like George McGovern and corporate liberals like Cyrus Vance. To the extent that there were substantive differences, these involved not the Soviet Union or the arms race but US relations with, on the one hand, the European and Japanese allies and, on the other, the developing world.[23]

In both cases the differences, while significant, were less than total. Regarding America's relations with its major allies, liberal internationalist business leaders had first been worried by President Nixon's New Economic Policy of August 1971. But here criticism was levelled as much at the execution of Republican foreign policy as at its logic. The New Economic Policy's uncompromising introduction and harsh financial and commercial effects, it was felt, not only alienated both the Europeans and the Japanese but as a result also threatened to provoke counter measures that would undermine the ability of US multinationals and banks to trade and invest freely across the world. Liberal business and political elites had been further disturbed by the impact on Japan of Nixon's opening to China in 1972 (again, Tokyo had neither been informed nor consulted), and by the bitter war of words launched by Nixon and Kissinger when the 1973 Yom Kippur war and the accompanying oil embargo, price rises and US military alert led the Europeans to distance themselves from Washington. (Kissinger's 'I don't care what happens to NATO' was, in this regard, only a marginal improvement on Nixon's alleged 'I don't give a shit about the Italian lira.') Nixon's New Economic Policy prompted international banker David Rockefeller to begin the moves that would in July 1973 lead to the formal establishment of the Trilateral Commission, bringing American, European and Japanese leaders from the worlds of business, politics and academia together to lobby for a coordinated approach to relations between the major capitalist powers. Those selfsame leaders acknowledged, however, that the New Economic Policy was not the ultimate problem. Rather than seeking to rescind it entirely, indeed, they came quickly to accept – and even appreciate – the new order of floating exchange rates, while concentrating on the need to manage their causes and consequences.[24]

In the case of American relations with the developing world, criticism was addressed less at the motives behind Republican policy than at its unreliable means and limited ends. According to liberal critics, the Nixon doctrine's reliance upon military aid and regional policemen instead of Vietnam-style interventionism was a partial solution to the challenge of third world revolution. It certainly reduced one set of risks. By committing the United States to the support of authoritarian regimes on the periphery, however, it magnified others. Like the 'New Look' strategy of the 1950s, it left Washington hostage to the fortunes of governments whose survival could never be guaranteed. Moreover, by backing dictatorships and repression – when shipping arms to a Pakistani regime engaged in mass killing during the Bangla Desh crisis in 1971, for example, or when helping depose the popularly-elected socialist government of Salvador Allende Gossens in Chile in 1973 – the

114

Nixon administration did nothing to improve the tarnished image the United States had acquired in Vietnam. Responding to mounting third world calls for a New International Economic Order through indirect violations of human rights meant, in addition, that Washington was ignoring opportunities to accommodate and translate those calls into a new – and, for American business, profitable – international division of labour. Finally, even when it cost fewer American lives and dollars in the short term, the continuing commitment to reaction and corruption abroad infected the nation's own institutions and values, as the congressional Church Committee investigation into the CIA revealed in 1975. According to liberal critics, indeed, an amoral foreign policy was in this sense just one symptom of the broader, cynical commitment to secrecy, corruption and centralization of power that would ultimately bring the Nixon presidency to its knees in 1974.[25]

4. Trilateral Thinking

The failure of successive Republican administrations to resolve the nation's persistent economic shortcomings during the 1970s probably played the key role in the process. At least in part, however, it was to Watergate and its aftermath (in particular President Ford's decision to pardon his predecessor for any criminal actions in relation to the scandal) that Jimmy Carter owed his election to the presidency in November 1976. The Democrats' emphasis upon their candidate's personal honesty, integrity, openness and distance from Washington, as well as Carter's call for a foreign policy invested with a moral dimension, certainly indicated a desire to distinguish a prospective Democratic administration from the corruption and disgrace of Watergate and the debacle of Vietnam. Similarly, Carter's appeal for a consensus based on faith in common values contrasted strongly with the vaguely sinister undertones of Richard Nixon's celebration of the silent majority. Yet the relationship between the Carter administration and its predecessors was marked more by continuity than change. Articulating the liberal – and more specifically the Trilateral – critique of Republican foreign policy, Carter sought less to demolish Nixon's grand design than to stabilize, modify and in some cases extend it; to translate what had to some degree been a series of *ad hoc* and politically-motivated responses to crisis into a more coherent structure for the management of change.[26]

It would be an exaggeration and simplification to equate the Carter administration and the Trilateral Commission. If the latter clearly selected, promoted and sought to influence the Georgia governor from 1971 onwards, then the exigencies of political power meant that Carter was unable (even had he so desired) to translate Trilateral designs directly into public policy once elected. Some critics have even suggested that Carter used the financial, media and personal support his membership of the Commission provided to win election, subsequently abandoning its prescriptions as public and Congressional demands necessitated. From another perspective, experience indicated that from the outset the Carter administration harboured competing groups rather than just one. It is, nonetheless, difficult to ignore the close association – in terms of personnel, concepts and proposals – between the two. President Carter, Vice-President Mondale, Secretary of State Vance, National Security Advisor Brzezinski, Treasury Secretary Blumenthal, Defence Secretary Brown, Federal Reserve Board Chairman Volcker, chief arms control negotiator Warnke, and UN Ambassador Young were all Trilateralists, as were almost twenty other top-level Carter appointees.[27] Articulating the views of the leading international corporate financiers, lawyers, business and insurance men (known variously as the 'eastern establishment,' 'traders' or 'managers') who established the Trilateral Commission, these public officials shared Trilateralist assumptions and pursued what was to a considerable degree a Trilateralist agenda. The assumptions, illustrating the continuities with the Nixon era, included the primacy of economic power, the obsolescence of bipolarity, the value of détente and arms control, the need to contain Moscow and Beijing by inclusion and the need to cut the costs of hegemony. The agenda, in general terms, included attempts to extend the scope and improve the functioning of both the international commercial and financial system (and of the United States' place within it) and the political and administrative institutions and relationships that sustained it; what some have called 'world order politics.' At a more specific level, it addressed a variety of established and new items, ranging from arms control via the North/South divide to human rights.[28]

Having been alarmed in 1971 by the effects of Nixon's New Economic Policy on international business and relations with Western Europe and Japan, those who advised and staffed the Carter administration six years later advocated cooperation rather than confrontation in dealings with the major allies. The objective was, in the words of Bruce Cumings, to 'work toward common policies, transnational economic planning and general solidarity that would eliminate the threat of anarchy in the world monetary system [and] protectionism in world trade.' Encouraged by the 1976-77 economic recovery from the 1974-75 recession, and assisted by a still-depreciating dollar, the Carter administration inherited and committed itself to a controlled reflationary policy at home, hoping to win the support of the other major capitalist powers for coordinated action via the Organization for Economic Cooperation and Development and regular international meetings, notably the annual 'group of seven' summits. The ability of the United States to enjoy the commercial and financial benefits of economic growth rather than its costs – rising inflation and trade deficits – would be enhanced, the administration hoped, through state-sponsored domestic economic restructuring. Tax reforms, spending cuts and other measures would reduce labour costs and social overheads, facilitate the modernization of the nation's aging plant and machinery, and thus enable the United States to compete more effectively in world markets.[29]

The international business system would further be enhanced, and the United States' place within it strengthened, by a series of initiatives designed to reduce and redistribute the military costs of containment. Prior to his election, Carter claimed that his administration would cut US defence spending by up to seven billion dollars. In June 1977, as part of what he called 'a freeze on further modernization and production of weapons,' he cancelled the B-1 bomber project and suspended Minuteman III ICBM production. During his first year in office, he also proposed the removal of American troops from South Korea, a comprehensive nuclear test ban treaty, a ban on chemical warfare, and cuts in US military sales and aid programs (the latter extending the financial more than the strategic logic of the Nixon Doctrine). Within the broader strategy of policy coordination, the President also sought – with some success – to shift the burdens of military spending from the United States to the NATO allies. Finally, Carter pursued further arms control with Moscow. Seeking initially to move beyond the SALT framework established in 1972 and extended at the 1974 Vladivostok summit between Ford and Brezhnev, the President called in March 1977 for reductions in, rather than limits to, strategic arms levels (a proposal shaped in part to appeal to liberals and conservatives inside and outside the administration). Following Moscow's rejection of his initiative, he sought to revive the SALT 2 agreement that had been near completion before the 1976 election. Carter and Brezhnev would sign a SALT 2 treaty – limiting the use of MIRVs and extending existing limits on strategic missiles – in Vienna in June 1979.[30]

These initiatives were in turn related to what was perhaps the most significant item drawn from the Trilateralist agenda by the Carter administration: economic relations with peripheral regions of the international business system. Here the objective was to improve the system by revising in part the global division of labour between the advanced capitalist, third world and eastern bloc countries. Anxious about the more radical implications of calls for a new international economic order as symbolized by the OPEC oil price rises of 1973-74, yet also aware of the growing contribution of (highly-profitable) investment in these regions to aggregate US corporate balances, leading public and private officials advocated their modernization and integration into the international structure of trade and investment. In effect, the United States hoped to promote an extension of the Nixon Doctrine's economic dimensions, adding to the primarily political and military roles previously assigned to selected third world 'regional policemen' more active commercial ones. Such an initiative would, it was hoped, enable the United States (and the industrialized world in general) to accommodate and contain the challenge of elites within the developing world, sustain first world hegemony, and secure both future profits and strategic raw materials, notably (though not exclusively) oil. It would, in short, preserve the global liberal economic order and defend the American position within it.[31]

Policy initiatives designed to implement these objectives were extensive. At the general level, the Carter administration's emphasis on North/South issues and human rights – 'a fundamental tenet of our foreign policy' – was intended, amongst other things, to persuade the third world that the United States had more to offer than napalm and carpet bombing. Its less interventionist approach towards disorder and revolution in the third world – in Angola, Ethiopia, Cambodia, Zaire, Nicaragua and elsewhere – had the advantage of demonstrating that Washington was not opposed to all change around the world *per se*. The appointment of black former civil rights activist Andrew Young as Ambassador to the United Nations was designed in part to appeal to those African nations whose raw materials were considered vital to future US industrial prosperity.[32] At the more specific level, the Carter administration saw in the passage of the Panama Canal treaties in June 1977 a key expression of its desire, in Cyrus Vance's words, 'to forge a new and more constructive relationship with the nations of the Western hemisphere and the third world.' In Africa, the administration sought to win friends among the black majority – particularly oil-rich nations like Nigeria – by endorsing the 'Sullivan principles' on apartheid, not violating a UN Security Council mandatory arms embargo on South Africa, and backing British attempts to end formal white rule in Rhodesia. In Eastern Europe and the wider communist bloc, Washington supported efforts to draw Poland and Yugoslavia further into the western financial system while making diplomatic moves to improve relations with Cuba and Vietnam, amongst others. Meanwhile, the administration sought to build on President Nixon's earlier initiatives by considering both a normalization of relations with Beijing and a revival of the Soviet/American Trade Agreement that had been in abeyance since 1975.[33]

5. Something to Worry About

Had the Carter administration been able to execute the Trilateral program within a domestic and international political vacuum; had it not been obliged to contend with the exigencies of economic, social and military change; had the program itself been fully coherent and its drafters united; had the Trilateral map, in short, been powerful enough to make the historical territory fall into place – then its designs might not have proven so elusive. As it was, from almost its first day in office, difficulties beset the new administration. Over the next four years these would undermine the liberal vision from within and without, paving the way for the return of those conservative and neoconservative forces whose criticisms of the Nixon/Kissinger grand design had been but briefly repressed (and then only in presidential terms) by the traumas of Watergate and Vietnam.

The ambiguities, tensions and contradictions that would transform and eventually bring down the Carter administration were evident even before it took office. As Fred Halliday notes, during the 1976 campaign Jimmy Carter had been both conciliatory and belligerent, denouncing militarism and détente at the same time. This ambivalence, or political opportunism, was reproduced from the outset within the Executive branch. While Trilateralists occupied many of the top posts, particularly within the State Department, their influence was balanced by officials who embraced more conservative, cold warrior attitudes, such as Energy Secretary James Schlesinger. Even some Trilateralists, notably National Security Advisor Zbigniew Brzezinski and Defence Secretary Harold Brown, were (in part because of their bureaucratic affiliations) hawkish regarding important aspects of Soviet/American relations. It was hardly surprising that the administration accommodated these divisions: political logic and circumstance encouraged such a balancing of forces. But the political circumstances within which President Carter appointed his staff over the winter of 1976-77 made it clear that the Trilateral agenda would not go unchallenged either inside or outside government circles. Indeed, even as Trilateralism articulated the views of East Coast liberal internationalists, so it found itself confronted in Washington and elsewhere by a powerful alliance of so-called 'sunbelt' industrialists, land and real estate developers, oil producers and military-industrial firms: an alliance with vested interests in a nationalist and militarist agenda whose views were articulated by neoconservative and cold warrior lobby groups like the American Security Council. These interests were bolstered by other conservative fractions mobilized around a variety of social and cultural issues, notably the so-called Moral Majority and other radical right groups.[34]

The accusations with which this conservative coalition had attacked Nixon, Ford and Kissinger were now turned against Jimmy Carter, the inheritor and guardian of key elements of Republican foreign policy. Warning of a mounting Soviet military and political threat, and increasingly preoccupied with an alleged loss of American willpower, critics like Ronald Reagan, Paul Nitze and Jessie Helms placed the East/West conflict at the top of their agenda. They called for an end to 'one-sided détente' (with its trade deals and technology transfers to Moscow), a much tougher approach to arms control negotiations, comprehensive US rearmament, a return to the strategy of containment as embodied in NSC-68, and a reassertion of American authority whether in relation to the communists, the NATO allies or the developing world. This powerful blend of military Keynesianism, anti-communism, resurgent nationalism, and what Jerry Sanders has dubbed 'containment militarism' had first been clearly articulated by President Ford's 'Team B' intelligence review board in 1976. It also informed Ronald Reagan's unsuccessful campaign to secure the Republican presidential nomination that same year. It would be drawn upon by conservative pressure groups the following year in their attempts to prevent the appointment of Paul Warnke as Arms Control and Disarmament Agency Director and passage of the Panama Canal treaties.[35]

Both the Trilateral Commission and the Committee on the Present Danger aimed primarily to influence decision-makers and opinion-formers. But whereas the Trilateral Commission sought to contain and reduce the general public's influence on decision-making, the CPD and other such groups combined their elite lobbying with much greater large-scale mass media and direct mail initiatives designed to shape public attitudes and foment popular pressure on Washington. As Alan Wolfe emphasizes, these activities were facilitated by the fact that, in a nation devoid of powerful leftist political parties or trades unions, 'popular majorities ... tend to be strongly supportive of ... hostility toward communism, support for the defense budget, and the promotion of US chauvinism.' With public opinion polls in 1977 indicating for the first time since the late 1960s that more people felt the US was spending too little on defence than felt it was spending too much, the initiative in the late 1970s lay with the opponents of détente. As Norman Podhoretz put it in 1977: 'Common sense tells you there must be something to worry about. That is where our reservoir of public support lies.' Such trends became all the more pronounced as the long-term domestic and international costs of Nixon's New Economic Policy finally began to outweigh its short-term benefits, and as the Carter administration then sought belatedly to pursue the domestic economic restructuring and modernization programs its influential supporters had been advocating since the early 1970s. In October 1979 Federal Reserve Bank Chairman Paul Volcker had bluntly announced that 'the standard [of living] of the average American has to decline.' The raw economic statistics suggested that just such a reduction was indeed being imposed: as President Carter sought a second term in office in late 1980, blue collar unemployment at almost eleven per cent was greater than when he had been elected four years earlier, while inflation was no less than five per cent higher. But calling upon the American public, and in particular the American labour force, for sacrifice in the name of progress proved highly counterproductive. It gave the American worker something all too concrete to worry about. Oriented towards and reluctant to compromise their high mass consumption lifestyles, Americans rejected such appeals (most obviously in connection with Carter's 1977 energy proposals). By the end of the decade, Nixon's silent majority would be turning vocal and rallying in ever greater numbers to the confident, conservative populism of Ronald Reagan.[36]

If the administration found itself constrained by pressure groups and public opinion when trying to move forward on East/West issues, then its attempts to improve US relations with its major allies also faced difficulties. In the political realm, West Germany refused to follow American policy towards the Soviet Union in the wake of the latter's invasion of Afghanistan in 1979 and the Polish crisis of 1980; and there were also trans-Atlantic arguments over policy towards Iran during the hostage crisis of 1979-81. Disagreements between Washington and Bonn also arose over theatre nuclear weapons deployment in Europe during 1977 (German Chancellor Helmut Schmidt subsequently described President Carter as a man who 'knew everything but understood nothing'). In the economic realm, tensions between Washington, Bonn and Tokyo resulted when West Germany and Japan proved reluctant to pursue the reflationary economic policies Washington advocated in 1977 and 1978. These differences were compounded by disagreements over the Japanese trade surplus with the United States and the decline in the value of the dollar. The Carter administration's own violations of its commitment to free trade in response to domestic political pressure (regarding steel imports, for example) further damaged Trilateral economic relations. In short, even though the so-called Tokyo round of multilateral trade negotiations did insure against a broader slide towards protectionism in 1979, the late 1970s did not see the kind of political, economic and military coordination Trilateral theory anticipated. Underlying contradictions in the relationship between the world's three leading capitalist areas – at once partners and competitors – meant that, at a time of economic volatility, Trilateralism made progress only fitfully if at all. By contrast, economic nationalism became increasingly popular, in Congress and elsewhere.[37]

Developments in East/West relations added more fuel to the nationalist fire. Already constrained by the influential anti-SALT lobby, the White House found its room for manoeuvre further reduced during the course of 1977 and 1978 as Moscow lost confidence in the President's reliability and credibility. Kremlin leaders had already been angered by what they saw as the Carter administration's unacceptable interference in Soviet internal affairs regarding human rights. They also took a sceptical view of what to them was Washington's continual tendency to define détente as involving limitations upon the projection of Soviet, but *not* American, power abroad. Moscow was further alienated by Carter's own crowning achievement – the September 1978 Camp David accords – which by freezing the Russians out of the Middle East peace negotiations rendered null and void an earlier agreement on joint Soviet/American mediation in the region. Indeed, by starting to deploy SS-20 medium range ballistic nuclear missiles in October 1977, Moscow may already have signalled the abandonment of its hopes for substantive agreements with Carter in light of the prevalent political trends in Washington at the time. The cooling of relations between Washington and Moscow accelerated during 1978 as a sequence of coups in Ethiopia, South Yemen and Afghanistan produced Marxist governments backed by Moscow. While the roots of these developments did not all lead back to the Kremlin, Soviet support for the new governments may have been a response to its exclusion from the Middle East peace process. The Soviet moves certainly played into the hands of those critics of the SALT process who believed that the United States should suspend current arms negotiations with Moscow and instead draw a line in the sand. In short, just as the Trilateral logic of inter-allied cooperation was proving tenuous, so too by 1978 was the Trilateral concept of containment by inclusion. Neither the allies nor the Soviets, it seemed, would cooperate.[38]

Nor, for that matter, would the developing nations. On the contrary, the succession of coups that in 1978 had led Zbigniew Brzezinski to speak of an 'arc of crisis' leading from Afghanistan to the Horn of Africa were but a prelude to a further series of upheavals across the globe the following year. In January 1979 came the Iranian revolution, the fall of the Shah and the elevation of the Ayatollah Ruhollah Khomeini. Six months later the Sandinista revolution deposed long-time US ally Anastasio Somoza in Nicaragua. In August, the presence of a Soviet combat brigade in Cuba prompted a brief scare in Washington. Three months later Iranian students and revolutionary guards stormed the American Embassy in Tehran, taking fifty-eight embassy staff hostage, while a few days after that Islamic rebels seized the Holy Mosque in Mecca, Saudi Arabia. Finally, in December, Soviet troops launched a massive armed invasion of neighbouring Afghanistan, carried out a military coup, and imposed on Kabul a government acceptable to Moscow. These developments not only confirmed the shortcomings of the original Nixon Doctrine (the Shah of Iran had been supported by successive administrations as the United States' policeman in the Gulf region); they also exposed the limitations of Trilateral plans for the developing world: it was difficult to imagine modifications in the international division of labour being sufficient to prevent the kinds of revolutionary upheaval Khomeini and his followers represented.[39]

6. Circling the Wagons

With Trilateralism proving easier to conceive than to implement, the Carter administration found itself during 1978 and 1979 under growing pressure from conservative critics inside and outside the executive branch. As strains showed in Washington's relations with its allies and the Soviet Union, and as disorder and revolution swept the developing world, so the strategy of containment by inclusion fell victim to both political opposition and internal contradiction. The attempt to reduce the costs of, but not abolish, the cold war lay Carter open to charges that he was fighting with only one hand, not sure who the enemy was, and in any case losing the struggle by default. If this was truly a fight, the militarists implied, then it was better to fight using both hands. But was the United States seeking to defeat the Soviet Union or to help it modernize? Was it trying to prevent third world revolutions or to facilitate them? Questions were also raised about specific aspects of Carter's foreign policy. If the United States was pursuing détente with Moscow, why then alienate the Soviet leadership by its human rights crusade? If it believed in human rights, why then apply double standards, promoting them in Latin America while ignoring them in the Shah's Iran? Having attempted from the outset to bridge gaps between liberals and conservatives, whether over arms negotiations or human rights, the administration by 1979 found itself caught in a no-man's-land and internally divided: on the one hand, Vance and the State Department liberals; on the other, the more hawkish staff working for Brzezinski at the National Security Council and Brown at the Pentagon.[40]

Given the prevailing political winds and the administration's own evaluation of changing strategic, military and diplomatic circumstances, Carter's move away from a Trilateral stance towards a more traditional conservative one was perhaps to be expected. His would not, however, be just a move to the right. Rather, from 1978 onwards the President took Trilateral initiatives to secure bilateral objectives. Having sustained a balance in relations with Moscow and Beijing during his first year in office, for example, Carter responded to Soviet SS-20 missile deployments and the political upheavals in Africa and Asia by tilting towards China. In May 1978, against Vance's advice, he despatched Zbigniew Brzezinski to visit Beijing. The trip resulted in agreements on the transfer to China of dual-use (civilian/military) US computer technology then being denied the Soviets. Normalization of relations between the two countries was completed in December 1978 and a triumphant visit to Washington by Chinese vice-premier Deng Xiao-Ping took place the following January and February. China, one of the multipolar points in Nixon's 'Pentagon of Power,' found itself being drawn (much to Moscow's concern) into the bipolar anti-Soviet alliance system. Carter used Trilateral instruments, in other words, to play a cold war song.[41]

A second presidential initiative again showed the growing synthesis of Trilateral and conventional cold war thinking. In March 1978, Carter gave a major foreign policy speech at Wake Forest College in which he promised to match any Soviet military build-up (and more specifically its SS-20 missile deployment) step by step. Two months later, the President won NATO commitment to a force modernization and expansion program, and its agreement in principle to deploy Pershing II and ground-launched cruise missiles in Western Europe in late 1979. These steps were to take place alongside a long-term increase in US military procurement from 1978 onwards. Remilitarization was in one sense fully in keeping with the long post-war history of the East/West arms race. In another sense, however, it too reflected some of the strategic revisions of the Nixon and Trilateral eras. For the modernization of forces that the Carter administration pursued placed much greater emphasis upon advanced technology and cost-effectiveness than on men. (Cancellation of the B-1 bomber in June 1977, for example, made room for the less expensive and less vulnerable Cruise missile as well as the more advanced 'stealth' bomber.) It also focused more upon the need for third world rapid deployment forces designed to protect the nation's growing stakes in the periphery. Shaped in part by the adoption of the Nixon Doctrine, the end of the draft in 1973, the development of advanced and increasingly computerized weapons (cruise and 'MX' missiles, the 'stealth' bomber, 'smart' and neutron bombs) and the introduction of new military strategies and directives (notably 'counterforce' in nuclear targeting and 'PD-18' for third world intervention), the US armed forces of the 1980s were intended to carry 'more bang for the buck' than ever before. So that, while the administration returned to more traditional cold war refrains from 1978 onwards, its instruments were again modern.[42]

By the time the Soviet Union sent its troops into Afghanistan in December 1979, the White House was increasingly attuned to the cold war chorus rising from both inside and outside the administration's walls. Moreover, in the wake of the events of 1978, the fall of the Shah in early 1979 and the beginnings of the Tehran hostage crisis, it had also orchestrated a good deal of its response in advance, again bringing together a variety of instruments, new and old, for the purpose. To demonstrate American condemnation of the Soviet invasion, the SALT 2 treaty, signed by Carter and Brezhnev in Vienna the previous June, was withdrawn from the process of ratification in the Senate. Embargoes on grain and high technology exports to Moscow and a ban on American participation in the 1980 Moscow Olympics were imposed; scientific and cultural links with Moscow were cut and Aeroflot landing privileges in the United States restricted. Soviet diplomats in the United States were sent home, the American Ambassador in Moscow was recalled for consultations, and a broad diplomatic offensive was launched in order to build a global anti-Soviet coalition. While Moscow was isolated, relations with Beijing were strengthened through the granting of 'most favoured nation' trading status and (again over Vance's opposition) an effective transfer to China of US grain and technology shipments originally destined for the Soviet Union. Washington and Beijing began shipping aid to the Afghan rebels while a Chinese military mission travelled to the United States for talks with Defence Department officials. At the strategic and military level, the President in his January 1980 State of the Union address proclaimed the 'Carter Doctrine,' extending containment militarism to the Persian Gulf region, a move backed up by the despatch of additional US naval forces to the area. Finally, the President committed the administration to a real annual increase in military spending of five per cent per year for the coming five years. (In spite of his campaign pledges, between 1977 and 1980 the US military budget rose from 108 billion dollars to 142 billion dollars. Likewise, the policy of troop withdrawals from South Korea was abandoned in June 1979, while US arms sales remained at a high level – over ten billion dollars per annum – throughout the Carter presidency.)[43]

'Afghanistan,' Raymond Garthoff wrote, 'provided a focus and crystallized the consensus that the United States must do something.' And so, in many ways, it did. In the case of President Carter's commitment to an increase in military spending, however, something else appeared to have done Afghanistan's work already, as Carter made his commitment on 12 December 1979, two weeks *before* the major Soviet intervention. In this sense, there was a similarity between the Soviet invasion of Afghanistan in 1979 and the North Korean invasion of South Korea in 1950, the attack which in the words of former US Secretary of State Dean Acheson, 'came along and saved us' by providing a justification for the enormous increase in military spending called for in advance of the North Korean invasion by NSC-68. If scholars remain divided over the relative influence of economic, military and political factors in explaining the birth of NSC-68, Thomas McCormick, at least, is in little doubt about the role of the 1979-1980 recession in tipping the administration's scales towards what he terms 'the remilitarization of American society.' By 1979, he argues, a deepening third world debt trap was making it impossible for returns from semi-peripheral investments to sustain aggregate US profit rates. In response, he claims, the administration turned towards military Keynesianism to stimulate and modernize the economy via high technology military spending, the resultant hardware being used 'to protect and expand America's share of global economic opportunities.' The recession made rearmament 'not merely useful strategically and psychologically but imperative economically.'[44]

However persuasive or otherwise McCormick's argument may be, this latest boost in weapons production, combined as it was with a return to the ideology of anti-communism and the strategy of containment militarism, certainly gave comfort to those industrial, commercial, military and bureaucratic interests who depended on the cold war for their financial and political well-being. Significantly, moreover, since there remained a good deal of common ground between the two sides, the short term victory of the militarist coalition within the American establishment did not spell disaster for the Trilateralists, many of whom had important ties to the arms industries or the areas in which they were based. This was of little consolation to President Carter who, unlike some of the Trilateralists, found it impossible to pursue détente and confrontation simultaneously. In spite of his adoption of an increasingly hard-line approach towards Moscow, in the 1980 presidential election Carter fought a losing battle against the standard bearer of the traditionalist forces, Republican Ronald Reagan. As Bruce Cumings put it, the choice presented to the American electorate between Carter and Reagan that year amounted to this: 'do you want the MX missile, the Trident sub, the Rapid Deployment Force, the "stealth" bomber, the cruise missile, counterforce targeting strategy leading to a first-strike capability, the China card, containment in the "arc of crisis," and a 5 percent increase in defense spending; or do you want all the above plus the neutron bomb, the B-1 bomber, antiballistic missile systems, civil defense capability, and a 8 percent increase in defense spending?' Those who voted, it seemed, wanted the latter.[45]

President Carter might be forgiven for lamenting that in November 1980 he became a fall guy for Trilateralism: rejected by the voters for imposing the economic sacrifice deemed necessary for industrial modernization at home and for allowing national defeat and disgrace abroad in the name of what Commission author Richard Cooper called a 'renovated international system.' While such an interpretation would probably overstate the influence of the Trilateralists at the expense of many other factors, domestic and international, it might also be seen as a less than generous reading of events: Carter, after all, owed his elevation to high office in large part to the Commission. It might, that is, be more accurate to agree with David Calleo that there was 'a certain rough justice in his fate. Carter came to office as the beneficiary of Nixon's mistakes at home; he left it as the scapegoat for Nixon's mistakes abroad.' In any event, in spite of the Republican victory in 1980, and of the new president's explicitly nationalist and confrontational rhetoric, Trilateralism itself was far from finished. Reagan's vice-president, George Bush, had been a Commission member, while both his Secretary of Defence Caspar Weinberger and subsequent Secretary of State George Schultz still were. Reagan's circle of advisors during the transitional period between the election and the inauguration included the founder of the Trilateral Commission, David Rockefeller himself. In broader terms, during the early 1980s, as in the early 1970s, Washington would blend guns and butter in its relations with the rest of the world, even as it revised the balance. Just as President Nixon's triumphant June 1972 summit meeting with Soviet leader Leonid Brezhnev was accompanied, and put at some risk by, the American mining of Haiphong harbour and a major escalation of US bombing across North Vietnam, so President Reagan's calls in the early 1980s for a new American militarism would be tempered by other, less hostile, demands. Within a few years of the Great Communicator's election, indeed, the crooked path of American foreign policy would turn full circle: there would be not only Colonel Sanders in Beijing but McDonald's in Moscow, adding commercially (if not gastronomically) to the Soviet Pepsi concession won by Nixon a decade and more earlier. As Bruce Cumings remarked when the new President entered office in 1981, 'the real meaning of Reagan's foreign policy ... has been obscured' by the rhetoric of conflict. In truth, and as many of Reagan's key advisors and appointments would illustrate, it was 'Nixonism recrudescent.' In this sense, at least, while the cold warriors prevailed in the short term, in the long term the traders would win.[46]

Notes

1. President Nixon's remarks on the SALT treaty, made on 5 June 1972, are quoted in Raymond L. Garthoff, *Détente and Confrontation: American-Soviet Relations From*

Nixon to Reagan (Washington: Brookings Institute, 1985), 193. The President used variations of the 'full generation of peace' phrase on a number of occasions, particularly between 1970 and 1972. See Richard A. Melanson, *Reconstructing Consensus: American Foreign Policy since the Vietnam War* (New York: St. Martin's Press, 1991), 66. For a summary of Reagan's charges against the Carter administration, see Melanson, 138-46. Nixon spoke about moving from 'an era of confrontation to an era of negotiation' in his first presidential speech on Vietnam policy in May 1969. See *Public Papers of the President, 1969* (Washington: US Government Printing Office, 1970), 370.

2. 'The Library of Babel,' in Jorge Luis Borges, *Labyrinths. Selected Stories and Other Writings*, ed.Donald Yates and James Irby (1964; Harmondsworth: Penguin, 1970), 85-6; Bruce Cumings, 'Chinatown: Foreign Policy and Elite Realignment,' in Thomas Ferguson and Joel Rogers (eds), *The Hidden Election* (New York: Pantheon, 1981), 228. President Nixon used the phrase 'era of negotiation' in his January 1969 Inaugural Address.

3. Kissinger served as President Nixon's National Security Advisor from January 1969 to August 1974. In August 1973 he added to this status the position of Secretary of State, replacing the previous incumbent William Rogers. Kissinger would retain his post as Secretary of State between August 1974 and January 1977 during the presidency of Gerald Ford.

4. On the Glassboro talks, see Lyndon Baines Johnson, *The Vantage Point: Perspectives on the Presidency, 1963-1969* (New York: Popular Press, 1974), 479-86.

5. A good survey of the impact of the war on the United States between 1965 and 1967 is given in Marilyn Blatt Young, *The Vietnam Wars, 1945-1990* (New York: Harper and Row, 1991), 192-209. On the decision-making process in 1965, see Larry Berman, *Planning a Tragedy: The Americanization of the War in Vietnam* (New York: Norton, 1982).

6. Walter LaFeber, *The American Age: United States Foreign Policy at Home and Abroad, 1750 to the Present*, 2nd ed. (New York: Norton, 1994), 622-3; Walter LaFeber, *America, Russia and the Cold War, 1945-1992*, 7th ed. (New York: McGraw Hill, 1993), 256-7. Soviet-American moves towards a non-proliferation treaty were driven in part by the continuing growth of the number of members of the nuclear club. France exploded its first atomic bomb in 1960, and China in 1964. A Chinese hydrogen bomb was tested in 1967.

7. Richard Stevenson, *The Rise and Fall of Détente* (London: Macmillan, 1985), 148-51; Thomas McCormick, *America's Half Century* (Baltimore: Johns Hopkins University Press, 1989), 173-4; Henry Kissinger, *White House Years* (Boston: Little, Brown, 1979), 403, 408-10, 529-30; David Calleo, *Beyond American Hegemony* (Brighton: Harvester, 1987), 54. On the development of West German relations with the Soviet Union, see Angela Stent, *From Embargo to Ostpolitik* (Cambridge: Cambridge University Press, 1981).

8. David Calleo and Benjamin Rowland, *America and the World Political Economy* (Bloomington: Indiana University Press, 1973), 147-51. A fine summary of the deepening international commercial and financial problems of the United States is provided by McCormick, 161-5. For further discussion of monetary issues, see Herman Van Der Wee, *Prosperity and Upheaval: The World Economy, 1945-1980* (1986; Harmondsworth: Penguin, 1987), 454-78. US balance of payments figures are given in Calleo, 241-2.

9. See Jonathan Rieder, 'The Rise of the "Silent Majority,"' in Steve Fraser and Gary

Gerstle (eds), *The Rise and Fall of the New Deal Order* (Princeton: Princeton University Press, 1989), 243-68; Irving Horowitz, 'The Revolution of Falling Expectations,' in Irving Horowitz, *Ideology and Utopia in the United States, 1956-1976* (New York: Oxford University Press, 1977). On the concept of an American 'establishment' see Godfrey Hodgson, 'The Establishment,' *Foreign Policy*, 10 (1973), 3-41.

10. Calleo, 57; *US Foreign Policy for the 1970s: A New Strategy for Peace*, Report to the Congress by Richard Nixon, 18 February 1970 (Washington: US Government Printing Office, 1970), 1.

11. *Public Papers of the President, 1971* (Washington: US Government Printing Office, 1972), 806-7; *US Foreign Policy for the 1970s*, 2; H.T. Brands, *The Devil We Knew: Americans and the Cold War* (New York: Oxford University Press, 1993), 130-31. On the Nixon administration's reconceptualization of the international system, see Robert S. Litwak, *Détente and the Nixon Doctrine* (Cambridge: Cambridge University Press, 1984), 73-79.

12. Garthoff, 289-300; Stevenson, 144-48, 179-80; Henry Kissinger, *Years of Upheaval* (London: Weidenfeld and Nicolson and Michael Joseph, 1982), 256-60. Changes in American perceptions of the Soviet Union were not new. On earlier shifts, see Daniel Yergin, *Shattered Peace: The Origins of the Cold War and the National Security State* (1977; Harmondsworth: Penguin, 1980).

13. As Walter Isaacson has argued, Kissinger himself embraced the 'decent interval' interpretation as long as responsibility for any future collapse in South Vietnam could be placed at the doors of the Saigon government. See Walter Isaacson, *Kissinger. A Biography* (London: Faber and Faber, 1992), 485.

14. Seymour Hersh, *The Price of Power: Kissinger in the Nixon White House* (New York: Summit Books, 1983), 50-51; Richard Nixon, *RN: The Memoirs of Richard Nixon* (London: Book Club Associates, 1978), 347-8; Frank Snepp, *Decent Interval* (New York: Vintage, 1978); LaFeber, *America, Russia and the Cold War*, 264. On the broad contours of administration policy regarding Vietnam, see Young, 232-299.

15. Litwak, 117-50; Michael Klare, *Supplying Repression: US Support for Authoritarian Regimes Abroad* (Washington: Institute for Policy Studies, 1977), 12-13, 39-40. Figures for arms sales are in current dollars.

16. Richard Nixon, 'Asia After Vietnam,' *Foreign Affairs*, 46 (1967/68), 121; Stevenson, 147-8, 155-6; Nixon, *RN*, 544-580; Kissinger, *White House Years*, 167-82, 684-787, 1049-1096; McCormick, 170; Young, 266-68.

17. Garthoff, 249, 254-5; Kissinger, *White House Years*, 144-5, 152-5; Brands, 128-9; Stevenson, 152-5, 158-9; McCormick, 165-9. On the use of economic relations as a means of containing the Soviet Union, see Angela Stent, 'Economic Containment,' in Terry Deibel and John Lewis Gaddis (eds), *Containing the Soviet Union* (London: Pergamon, 1987), 63-5.

18. Miles Kahler, 'The United States and the World Economy,' in Robert Gray and Stanley Michalak, Jr. (eds), *American Foreign Policy Since Détente* (New York: Harper and Row, 1984), 199-202; Nixon, *RN*, 518. Defenders of Nixon's moves argued that they were in effect forced upon Washington by its allies in Western Europe and Japan, who refused to revalue their currencies or to pay their fair share of the costs of their defence. See Calleo, 90-92. The relationship between Nixon's New Economic Policy and the NATO alliance is discussed in Seyom Brown, *The Crises of Power* (New York: Columbia University Press, 1979), 112-117.

19. Hersh, 334-5, 343-8; Brown, *Crises of Power*, 7-15; Garthoff, 127, 135, 149-50, 184-5,

191-2; Kissinger, *White House Years*, 65-66; Nixon, *RN*. On Nixon's domestic political appeal, see Melanson 35-43; Rieder, 260-63.

20. Nixon, *RN*, 415; Samuel Wells, 'Sounding the Tocsin: NSC-68 and the Soviet Threat,' *International Security*, 4:2 (Fall, 1979), 116-58; Strobe Talbott, *The Master of the Game: Paul Nitze and the Nuclear Peace* (New York: Alfred Knopf, 1988), 114-41; Jerry Sanders, *Peddlers of Crisis: The Committee on the Present Danger and the Politics of Containment* (London: Pluto Press, 1983), 150-54, 197-204; Stevenson, 169-74; Melanson, 70-71; Garthoff, 538-52. The militarist critique of détente is exemplified by Paul Nitze, 'Assuring Strategic Stability in an Era of Détente,' *Foreign Affairs*, 54 (1975/76), 207-32. Recognizing the likelihood of a conservative challenge to détente, Nixon had included a number of potential critics *within* his administration to assuage the right, including both Nitze and Defence Secretary James Schlesinger. In retrospect, this tactic appears less to have neutralized his critics than to have provided them with better sources of intelligence.

21. Garthoff, 405-408; Brands, 149-52; McCormick, 179-80; Michael Klare, *Beyond the Vietnam Syndrome* (Washington: Institute for Policy Studies, 1981), 41-44; Theodore Draper, 'The United States and Israel,' *Commentary*, 59:4 (April, 1975), 29-45; Robert Tucker, 'Oil: The Issue of American Intervention,' *Commentary*, 59:1 (January, 1975), 21-31; Miles Ignotus, 'Seizing Arab Oil,' *Harper's* (March, 1975), 45-62; Sanders, 211-2. For examples of the neoconservative critique of détente, see Theodore Draper, 'Détente,' *Commentary*, 58:5 (June, 1974), 23-47; Norman Podhoretz, 'Making the World Safe for Communism,' *Commentary*, 60:4 (April, 1976), 31-41; Norman Podhoretz, 'The Culture of Appeasement,' *Harper's* (October, 1977), 25-32. Neoconservatives were so called because their party affiliations often were or had once been Democratic.

22. Fred Halliday, *The Making of the Second Cold War* (London: Verso, 1983), 86-92, 117-8; Sanders, 211-12; Garthoff, 453-63, 502-37, 548; Brands, 135-8, 149-50; Stevenson, 161-4, 181-2. Though untouched by the Soviet rejection of the 1972 Trade Agreement, the 1972 wheat deal had within a year of its signing been redubbed 'the great grain robbery' as it became clear that Moscow had persuaded the US Department of Agriculture to contract the sale at heavily subsidized prices. The news did little to endear détente to American consumers who had to pay higher prices as a result (see Stevenson, 163-4; Garthoff, 305-7; Kissinger, *White House Years*, 1269-73). A variety of public opinion polls indicated that calls for remilitarization found growing support among the American public between 1973 and 1976 (see Sanders, 193-4; Kissinger, *Years of Upheaval*, 984-98).

23. Robert Gray, 'The United States and the Soviet Union,' in Gray and Michalak (eds), 4; Alan Wolfe, 'Reflections on Trilateralism and the Carter Administration: Changed World Realities vs. Vested Interests,' in Holly Sklar (ed), *Trilateralism* (Boston: South End Press, 1980), 534-5; Brown, *Crises of Power*, 146; Stent in Deibel and Gaddis (eds), 64-5; Cyrus Vance, *Hard Choices: Critical Years in America's Foreign Policy* (New York: Simon and Schuster, 1983), 24-5.

24. Sanders, 174-6; Brown, *Crises of Power*, 114-9; Stevenson, 166-7; Brands, 123; Kahler, 203, 205; Stephen Gill, *American Hegemony and the Trilateral Commission* (Cambridge: Cambridge University Press, 1990), 132-42; Calleo, 89-91; Holly Sklar, 'Founding the Trilateral Commission: Chronology, 1970-77,' in Sklar (ed), 76-9; Jeff Frieden, 'The Trilateral Commission: Economics and Politics in the 1970s,' in Sklar (ed), 66-9. A good example of the initially harsh liberal internationalist critique of Nixon's New Economic Policy is C. Fred Bergsten, 'The New Economics and US

Foreign Policy,' *Foreign Affairs*, 50 (1971/72), 199-222. Bergsten wrote that Nixon's moves encouraged an 'isolationist trend' which 'court[ed] disaster for US global interests.' One benefit international business reaped from the end to fixed exchange rates was the loosening of capital controls, which had been called for by Washington's attempts to defend the inflated dollar's parity. See Calleo, 90.

25. Sanders, 174-5; Brown, *Crises of Power*, 125-9; Brands, 131-3, 136-42. For an example of the Ford administration's hostility towards calls for a new international economic order, see Daniel Patrick Moynihan, 'The United States in Opposition,' *Commentary*, 59:3 (March, 1975), 31-44. For the liberal – in this case Trilateral Commission – critique, see John Pinder, Takashi Hosemi and William Diebold, *Industrial Policy and the International Economy* (New York: Trilateral Commission, 1979).

26. On distinctions in style and ethos, see Melanson, 97, 101-2. It is possible to identify a number of links between the Ford and Carter administrations. If the latter was characterized by its reliance upon the Trilateral Commission for members, then Ford's 19 August 1974 appointment of Nelson Rockefeller to replace him as vice-president indicated that Trilateral views quickly obtained representation in the highest echelons of government following Nixon's resignation. In policy terms, it is also interesting to note the shift (in 1976) in the Ford administration's attitude towards Africa in general, and South Africa in particular, and to compare its revised views to those of the Trilateral Commission regarding Africa. See Richard Ullman, 'Trilateralism: Partnership For What?' *Foreign Affairs*, 55 (1976/77), 1-19, esp. 11; Frieden, 69; Brown, *Crises of Power*, 129-39; Carolyn Brown, 'Apartheid and Trilateralism: Partners in Southern Africa,' in Sklar (ed), 374-6.

27. Laurence Shoup, 'Jimmy Carter and the Trilateralists: Presidential Roots,' in Sklar (ed), 199-211; Fred Block, 'Trilateralism and Inter-Capitalist Conflict,' in Sklar (ed), 519-31; Holly Sklar, 'Trilateralism: Managing Dependence and Democracy,' in Sklar (ed), 2; Sanders, 180-82. A third notable element in this connection is the journal *Foreign Policy*, established in 1970, which functioned as a prominent forum for debates advancing Trilateral thinking. As Jerry Sanders points out, *Foreign Policy* was to Trilateralism what *Foreign Affairs* was to the Council on Foreign Relations. See Sanders, 172, 189.

28. Klare, *Beyond the Vietnam Syndrome*, 5-8; Cumings, 204-5; McCormick, 195, 200; Sklar, 'Trilateralism: Managing Dependence and Democracy,' 21-22; Melanson, 90-91, 102; Brands, 143-4.

29. Cumings, 204; Kahler, 205; Halliday, *Making of the Second Cold War*, 215; Jeremiah Novak, 'Trilateralism and the Summits,' in Sklar (ed), 190-96; Calleo, 93-96; William Tabb, 'The Trilateral Imprint on Domestic Economics,' in Sklar (ed), 212-37; William Tabb, 'Social Democracy and Authoritarianism: Two Faces of Trilateralism Toward Labor,' in Sklar (ed), 308-322. The first of what are now called the G7 summits was held in Rambouillet, France, in December 1975.

30. Sanders, 236; McCormick, 202-3; Brands, 143, 145; Melanson, 96, 106-7; Garthoff, 442-53, 728-40, 791, 801-22; Robert Bresler, 'The United States and Arms Control,' in Gray and Michalak (eds), 18-34. Between 1969 and 1979, the European share of NATO expenditure rose from 22.7 per cent to 41.6 per cent. See Halliday, *Making of the Second Cold War*, 184. Something of the thinking behind the Carter administration's initiatives in arms control may be found in Paul Warnke, 'Apes on a Treadmill,' *Foreign Policy*, 18 (1975), 18-29. Warnke served as President Carter's chief SALT negotiator and Director of the Arms Control and Disarmament Agency (ACDA).

31. Sklar 'Trilateralism: Managing Dependence and Democracy,' 24-29; Vance, 428-30; Kai

Bird, 'Co-opting the Third World Elites: Trilateralism and Saudi Arabia,' in Sklar (ed), 341-51; Klare, *Beyond the Vietnam Syndrome*, 56-7; Sklar, 'Trilateralism and the Management of Contradictions,' in Sklar (ed), 558-9, 563-4; Halliday, *Making of the Second Cold War*, 191-8. For a brief but informed theoretical discussion of the concepts of periphery and semi-periphery, see Gill, 38-41. On the theory and practice of the new international economic order, see Alain Lipietz, *Mirages and Miracles: The Crises of Global Fordism* (London: Verso, 1987); Van Der Wee, 380-420; Norman Girvan, 'Economic Nationalists vs. Multinational Corporations: Revolutionary or Evolutionary Change?' in Sklar (ed), 437-67. The emerging Trilateral viewpoint is developed in Richard Cooper, 'A New International Economic Order for Mutual Gain,' *Foreign Policy*, 26 (Spring, 1977), 66-120; Tom Farer, 'The United States and the Third World: A Basis for Accommodation,' *Foreign Affairs*, 54 (1975/76), 79-97; C. Fred Bergsten, 'The Threat From the Third World,' *Foreign Policy*, 11 (Summer, 1973), 102-24.

32. Brands, 145-6; Brown in Sklar (ed), 374-5. The human rights policy was also intended to counter Soviet charges concerning American foreign policy, to highlight Soviet human rights abuses, and (within the United States) to contain isolationist tendencies and unite liberal and conservative factions around a common initiative. See Melanson, 95-6, Halliday, *Making of the Second Cold War*, 217-8. For evaluations of Carter's human rights policy, see Michael Klare and Cynthia Arnson, *Supplying Repression: US Support for Authoritarian Regimes Abroad*, 2nd ed. (Washington: Institute for Policy Studies, 1981); Lars Schoultz, *Human Rights and US Policy Towards Latin America* (Princeton: Princeton University Press, 1987).

33. McCormick, 200-2; Vance, 156; Walter LaFeber, *The Panama Canal: The Crisis in Historical Perspective* (New York: Oxford University Press, 1978), 202-16; Prexy Nesbitt, 'Trilateralism and the Rhodesian Problem,' in Sklar (ed), 379-402; Sklar, 'Trilateralism: Managing Dependence and Democracy,' 32-35; Stent in Deibel and Gaddis (eds), 64-5. For surveys of US policy towards Africa in this period, see Leon Gordenker, 'The United States and Sub-Saharan Africa,' in Gray and Michalak (eds), 149-67; Henry Bienen, 'US Foreign Policy in a Changing Africa,' *Political Science Quarterly*, 93 (Fall, 1978), 443-64.

34. Halliday, *Making of the Second Cold War*, 112-8, 214; McCormick, 199-200; Michael Klare et al., 'Resurgent Militarism,' in Sklar (ed), 286-88; Sanders, 178-86, 213-217; Calleo, 94-95.

35. Sanders, 197-210. Key criticisms of the SALT 2 negotiations which Carter would inherit are set out in Paul Nitze, 'Assuring Strategic Stability in an Era of Détente,' and Paul Nitze, 'Deterring Our Deterrent,' *Foreign Policy*, 25 (Winter, 1976-77), 202-221. See also Brands, 152-6; Talbott, 144-7.

36. Sanders, 264-5, 268; Wolfe, 'Reflections on Trilateralism,' 536-41; Sklar, 'Trilateralism and the Management of Contradictions,' 560-62; *New York Times*, 18 October 1979; Brands, 146-9; Garthoff, 794; Gerald Epstein, 'Domestic Stagflation and Monetary Policy: The Federal Reserve and the Hidden Election,' in Ferguson and Rogers (eds), 173-4. For the Trilateral Commission and democracy, see Michael Crozier et al., *The Crisis of Democracy* (New York: New York University Press, 1975); Calleo, 96; Alan Wolfe, 'Capitalism Shows Its Face: Giving Up on Democracy,' in Sklar (ed), 295-307.

37. Fred Block, 'Trilateralism and Inter-Capitalist Conflict,' in Sklar (ed), 519-32; Halliday, *Making of the Second Cold War*, 182, 217, 219; Kahler, 208-11; Calleo, 68-71, 96; Sklar, 'Trilateralism and the Management of Contradictions,' 568-72.

38. Halliday, *Making of the Second Cold War*, 220-224; McCormick, 203-5.

39. McCormick, 207-12; Garthoff, 622-89, 828-47, 887-965; Klare, *Beyond the Vietnam*

Syndrome, 24. On Soviet policy in the region, see Fred Halliday, *Soviet Policy in the Arc of Crisis* (Washington: Institute for Policy Studies, 1981).

40. Thomas Hughes, 'Carter and the Management of Contradictions,' *Foreign Policy*, 31 (Summer, 1978), 34-55; Walter LaFeber, 'From Détente to the Gulf,' in Gordon Martel (ed), *American Foreign Relations Reconsidered, 1890-1993* (London: Routledge, 1994), 152-4; Sklar, 'Trilateralism and the Management of Contradictions,' 563-65; Sanders, 241-7. Perhaps the best known of the militarist criticisms of Carter's foreign policy is Jeane Kirkpatrick, 'Dictatorships and Double Standards,' *Commentary*, 68, 5 (November, 1979), 34-45. Kirkpatrick subsequently served as President Reagan's Ambassador to the United Nations.

41. Halliday, *Making of the Second Cold War*, 224-5, 229-30; Vance, 114-9; Cumings, 210-11.

42. Sanders, 250-53; McCormick, 206-7; Klare *et al.*, 276-85; Halliday, *Making of the Second Cold War*, 123-24, 216-17, Klare, *Beyond the Vietnam Syndrome*, 67-82; Sanders, 244-7. The militarization process prompted the resignation of Paul Warnke as ACDA Director in October 1978. Warnke was replaced by General George Seignious, a member of the hardline Coalition for Peace Through Strength and former member of the equally militarist American Security Council. Warnke's replacement as chief SALT negotiator was Ralph Earle, a protégé of Paul Nitze. See Klare *et al.*, 281; Sanders, 261-2; Talbott, 150, 156. For the shifting balance of expenditures from men towards machinery, see Calleo, 239, note 22.

43. Garthoff, 938-990; McCormick, 209-210; Halliday, *Making of the Second Cold War*, 227-9; Brands, 159-61; Sanders, 236-7; Vance, 390-91; Jimmy Carter, *Keeping Faith. Memoirs of a President* (New York: Bantam, 1982), 471-83; Cumings, 210-13; Klare *et al.*, 284; Noam Chomsky, *Towards a New Cold War* (London: Sinclair Browne, 1982), 422. Calleo (p. 246) indicates that the military budget rose from $98 billion in 1977 to $136 billion in 1980.

44. Garthoff, 946; Sanders, 236; McCormick, 212-5. For the debate over NSC-68, see Fred Block, 'Economic Instability and Military Strength: The Paradoxes of the 1950 Rearmament Decision,' *Politics and Society*, 10 (1980), 35-58; Wells, 138-141. On comparisons between the Korea and Afghanistan crises, see Cumings, 215-6.

45. Wolfe, 'Reflections on Trilateralism,' 541-46; Klare *et al.*, 288; Cumings, 196-7.

46. Richard Cooper *et al.*, *Towards a Renovated International System* (New York: Trilateral Commission, 1977); Gill, 173-79; Sklar, 'Trilateralism and the Management of Contradictions,' 572-76; Cumings, 218; Young, 271; Thomas Ferguson and Joel Rogers, 'The Reagan Victory: Corporate Coalitions in the 1980 Campaign,' in Ferguson and Rogers (eds), 49-52; Calleo, 71; Cumings, 224-8.

Sixties Activism in the 'Me Decade'

Douglas T. Miller

On July 4, 1976, nearly two years after President Richard Nixon's resignation and more than one year since Saigon fell to the North Vietnamese, Americans celebrated their Bicentennial. 'Happy Birthday America,' proclaimed a Bloomingdale's ad, 'for a free people all things are possible.' This message, and thousands like it, reverberated throughout the land. From coast to coast, more than 64,000 public festivities commemorated the nation's past and extolled its future. Communities held old-fashioned, nostalgic events such as pie-eating contests and hog-calling competitions. In Greenville, Ohio, celebrants attempted to shinny up a greased pole; the city of El Paso, Texas, staged a Pony Express ride. Other events included art fairs, balloon races, a longhorn-cattle drive, and 20 teams of horse-drawn covered wagons that wheeled from Washington D.C. to ceremonies at Valley Forge. More than 2,000 bicyclists pedaled a 4,250 mile historic cross-country course in what sponsors billed as 'Bikecentennial '76.'

The most massive and spectacular celebrations took place in the nation's larger cities. San Francisco held a week-long jubilee in commemoration of both the nation's and the city's founding. New Orleans put on parties, parades, dances, and concerts from July 4 to Bastille Day, July 14, when officials crowned 'Miss Bastille.' In the nation's capital, more than half a million gathered to watch a parade, a space show, and to see President Gerald Ford open a time capsule that had been locked in a safe and placed in the Capitol building on July 4, 1876; it contained a temperance book, some old photos, and the complete federal payroll list for 1876, fewer than one hundred thousand people as opposed to almost three million in 1976.

The largest celebration of all took place in New York City. Although barely bailed out from near bankruptcy by the federal government the previous year, New York on July 4 appeared in rare splendor. An armada as varied and magnificent as any ever assembled filled the harbor. Spectators gazed at naval vessels from 32 nations, an estimated 30,000 pleasure boats, and 225 high-masted sailing ships. Covered by the three national television networks, New York's triumphant observances climaxed that night with a massive fireworks display synchronized and choreographed by Walt Disney Attractions, accompanied by the music of the Boston Pops, and paid for by Macy's department store. Millions of Americans watched with patriotic pride as thirteen giant sky searchlights arced their beams to form a crown of lights above the Statue of Liberty, while from three harbor islands and three special barges came explosions of red, white, and blue pyrotechnics and a torrent of gold and silver.

Anxious to forget the traumas of Vietnam and Watergate, inflation and recession, Americans welcomed the patriotic diversion. The colors red, white, and blue appeared everywhere – on sidewalks, fire hydrants, cars, and houses. Commercial interests cashed in on the nationalistic outpouring. One could buy everything from red, white, and blue baby blankets and teddy bears to hats, beer cans, and bikinis. One manufacturer featured a red, white, and blue commemorative coffin, while in Nebraska a company offered a Bicentennial special of seven quarts of frozen bull semen for the price of six.

No one better exemplified America's self-congratulatory, patriotic mood than President Ford. Over the Fourth of July weekend, he delivered six separate speeches at as many different sites. Reminiscing about the home-made ice cream and fireworks of his boyhood Independence Days in Grand Rapids, Michigan, he eulogized American virtue ('We are a happy people because we are a free people'), and claimed that the Bicentennial would rekindle the American spirit.

Nevertheless, some minor dissident notes sounded on that commemorative day. Black farmer Raymond Lane pushed an old lawnmower frame laden with watermelon 750 miles from Statesboro, Georgia, to Philadelphia as a protest against the plight of black farmers in the South. Nationwide, many African-Americans, just as during slavery days, refused to participate in Fourth of July festivities lest it appear that they condoned continuing racial injustice and inequalities. Other minorities also dissented. During San Francisco's week of celebrations, nearly 100,000 people joined in a Gay Freedom Day parade. One San Francisco group calling itself 'The Rich Off Our Backs July Fourth Coalition' held demonstrations protesting the self-satisfied nature of official celebrations. An ad in the *New York Times* signed by a number of writers, scholars, politicians, and civic leaders read: 'It is with profound regret that on this Bicentennial Fourth of July we, the undersigned citizens of the United States of America proclaim one truth to be self-evident: The inalienable rights of life, liberty and the pursuit of happiness have yet to become a reality for the majority of Americans.' Even a *Times* editorial that day contrasted the words of the Declaration of Independence with present-day realities, lamenting 'the gaping holes and strident deficiencies of our society.'

On Bicentennial Day 1976, such voices of criticism were scarcely heard over the national chorus of 'America the Beautiful.' But as time passed, the euphoric unity generated by the nation's 200th birthday quickly faded. The malaise induced by the legacies of Vietnam and Watergate, continuing inflation and recession, and the decline of order at home and authority abroad proved difficult to shake. In retrospect, the mid-seventies popularity of Hollywood disaster movies proved a better indicator of the national mood than did the bicentennial hoopla. The most notable of these films, *Jaws* (1975), also focuses on the nation's birthday. Because of a shark scare, the fictional seaside tourist town of Amity has closed its beaches, throwing people out of work, forcing shops to shut, and leaving rental properties unoccupied. Finally, town officials, more fearful of financial ruin than swimmers' safety, reopen the beaches for the Fourth of July weekend. All is joyous – until the giant killer shark returns and transforms a tranquil afternoon at the beach into a nightmare of horror and death. The phenomenal box-office success of *Jaws* gave rise to a host of films treating such threats as a killer whale, killer bees, crashing meteors, and, of course, *Jaws 2*. Clearly, millions of Americans found in such disaster movies a certain relief from the more mundane crises of daily life.

On the surface the mid- to late-seventies appeared relatively stable, and certainly in contrast to the preceding volatile decade they were so. Yet beneath this calm facade seethed much frustration and anger. The surprise hit of the 1976 television season was a bizarre show entitled *Mary Hartman, Mary Hartman*. A late-night spoof of daytime soap operas produced by Norman Lear, *Mary Hartman* depicted in comic fashion a hopeless world of moral chaos with characters such as an alcoholic, philandering minister, an incompetent doctor, a shady lawyer, a geriatric exhibitionist, an impotent husband, and an unfulfilled, unfaithful wife. 'The whole world,' stated lead character Mary Hartman, 'is becoming just like a bad connection.'

In the world of *Mary Hartman,* traditional figures of authority were demystified and debunked. Many Americans shared this skeptical outlook. Sixty-nine percent of respondents to a 1975 national opinion survey agreed that 'over the last ten years, this country's leaders have consistently lied to the people.' Other polls revealed declining confidence in such figures as doctors, lawyers, corporate leaders, and advertisers. Public trust in the medical profession, for instance, fell from 73 to 42 percent between 1966 and 1976; by the latter date, faith in the legal profession had plummeted to a mere 12 percent, and this at a time when more and more Americans vented their frustrations through litigation. 'Hardly more than a quarter-century after Henry Luce proclaimed "the American century,"' wrote historian Christopher Lasch,

American confidence has fallen to a low ebb. Those who recently dreamed of world power now despair of governing the city of New York. Defeat in Vietnam, economic stagnation, and the impending exhaustion of natural resources have produced a mood of pessimism in higher circles, which spreads through the rest of society as people lose faith in their leaders.[1]

Indeed, by the mid-seventies, the traumas of the sixties, defeat in Vietnam, the scandal of Watergate, and continuing economic troubles appeared to have sapped the public's passion for social commitment. The political pendulum swung to the right as a conservative reaction set in, and for many Americans, possibilities seemed to contract. People who had always believed in the gospel of progress began for the first time to see the future as a threat. Time and resources looked to be running out.

One reflection of this national exhaustion was the great nostalgia expressed in the seventies for an earlier America, especially the 1950s. As the sixties and early seventies receded in violence, repression, anguish, and disillusionment, the fifties loomed as a blank screen on which people could project fantasies of a better America. Television shows such as *Happy Days* and *Laverne and Shirley* and movies like *American Graffiti* and *Grease* re-created an idyllic world of youth and innocence. Excessive, sentimental nostalgia generally occurs during times of perceived crisis; such was the case in the seventies. The rise of enthusiasm for the fifties coincided with widespread disillusionment and a growing conservatism. For many people, the 1950s came to symbolize a golden age of happiness and simplicity, an era supposedly unruffled by riots, racial violence, Vietnam, Watergate, and assassinations. People numbed by the traumas of the sixties and early seventies yearned for a quieter, happier time.[2]

In addition to becoming more retrospective, millions of Americans also grew more introspective. The seventies witnessed a widespread retreat from the public world to purely personal preoccupations. 'The 1970s,' wrote social chronicler Tom Wolfe in an influential article, 'will come to be known as the Me Decade.'[3] 'The new alchemical dream,' claimed Wolfe, 'is: changing one's personality – remaking, remodelling, elevating, and polishing one's very *self* ... and observing, studying, and doting on it (Me!)'(32). One indication of this personal preoccupation was Robert Ringer's best-seller *Looking Out for No. 1*, a book that spawned a small library of self-respect volumes.

A host of self-awareness disciplines also competed for the privilege of putting people in touch with their true selves. Transcendental Meditation, a yogic discipline, drew nearly half a million adherents to its more than two hundred teaching centers; EST (Erhard Seminars Training) self-discovery programs grossed $10 million a year by 1975. On a beautiful cliffside overlooking the Pacific at Big Sur, California, the Esalen Institute, which Wolfe described as 'the Harvard of the Me Decade,'(33), helped people to learn about themselves through such techniques as encounter sessions, massage, and group touching. Such psychic therapies, or what came to be called the 'human potential movement,' taught that one could determine one's fate. Interest in things outside the self diminished.

While many Americans insulated themselves from the larger world through therapeutic self-absorption, others made moral sense of their lives through religion. A 1977 survey reported that seventy million Americans identified themselves as 'born-again' Christians. This statistic constituted more than one of every three adults and, in addition to President Jimmy Carter, included such figures as former Watergate criminals Charles Colson and Jeb Magruder, ex-Black Panther militant Eldridge Cleaver, football hero Roger Staubach, and singers Pat Boone, Johnny Cash, and Bob Dylan. Spurred by a number of TV and radio revival programs and stations, evangelical, fundamentalist Christianity, once believed by sophisticated Americans to be part of a dying, superstitious past, grew spectacularly from the late sixties through the early eighties.

Most of the search for spiritual solace took place within the framework of organized Christian churches. But this quest also spawned various new sects and cults, generally headed by charismatic leaders. Buffeted by international and domestic crises, alarmed at apparent social and moral chaos, some Americans surrendered their personal wills to spiritual masters. The Reverend Sun Myung Moon, Korean founder of the Unification Church, converted thousands of young Americans to his religion, a blend of Christian faith and anti-communism that worshipped the Reverend Moon as the new Messiah. Others became disciples of the Maharaj Ji, the young 'perfect master' from India who established the Divine Light Mission. Zen Buddhism and other Eastern religions and practices also enlisted enthusiastic followers.

Whereas millions of Americans sought spiritual or psychic well-being in the seventies, millions more devoted themselves to perfecting their physical bodies. 'I hear America puffing,' exclaimed *Newsweek* in a May 23, 1977 cover story on the national exercise craze. Concern for physical fitness became a major factor in American culture in the seventies and has remained so. Millions of hitherto sedentary citizens took to running, hiking, biking, swimming, and cross-country skiing. Health, tennis, and racquetball clubs flourished. 'We are discovering,' claimed George Leonard, author of *The Ultimate Athlete*, 'that every human being has a God-given right to move efficiently, gracefully and joyfully.'[4] To the prophets of the new athleticism, competition seemed less significant than the physical and spiritual benefits of exercise. 'Sports,' asserted Leonard, 'may open the door to infinite realms of perception and being'(241-258).

Concern for physical fitness also brought about a new awareness of the importance of diet. Although the vast increase in the consumption of fast foods such as hamburgers, fried chicken, and tacos belied this trend, millions of Americans nevertheless grew much more conscious of what they ate. Realizing that bad eating habits contributed to heart disease and cancer, health-conscious consumers chose to limit the amounts of fat, sugar, and salt in their diets. 'Natural' foods without preservatives or excessive processing became popular. Americans also changed their drinking habits. Per-capita consumption of hard liquor and regular beer dropped, and sales of low-calorie 'light' beer and wine 'coolers' soared.

To what purpose were Americans leading more healthful and 'spiritual' lives? Commenting on the proliferation of therapeutic, religious, and fitness fads, social critics such as Tom Wolfe and Christopher Lasch expressed alarm at what Lasch labelled 'the culture of narcissism.' 'To live for the moment,' complained Lasch, 'is the prevailing passion – to live for yourself, not for your predecessors or posterity. We are fast losing the sense of historic continuity, the sense of belonging to a succession of generations originating in the past and stretching into the future.'[5] America, such critics contended, had turned into a fragmented nation of fractious individualists. To Irving Louis Horowitz America had 'become a Hobbesian rather than a Marxian nation, a place where the war against all is conducted with a ferocity that makes nineteenth-century class warfare seem tame in comparison.'[6]

Critics who saw the seventies as a decade of solipsistic selfishness contrasted this era with the activist political concerns of the Vietnam years. Lasch claimed that

> After the political turmoil of the sixties Americans have retreated to purely personal preoccupations. Having no hope of improving their lives in any of the ways that matter, people have convinced themselves that what matters is psychic self-improvement: getting in touch with their feelings, eating health food, ... immersing themselves in the wisdom of the East, jogging, learning how to 'relate,' overcoming the 'fear of pleasure.'(29)

All of this, Lasch concluded, signified 'a retreat from politics and a repudiation of the recent past'(30).

Such criticisms of the new consciousness were not without merit. Certainly much that took place in the seventies was banal, selfish, excessively hedonistic, apolitical, and often downright silly. Wolfe, for instance, related the story of a woman who, when asked at an EST seminar what one thing she would most like to eliminate from her life, blurted out 'hemorrhoids' (26). Yet such an interpretation of seventies America contains serious problems. For one thing, the dichotomy that Lasch and others made between a politicized sixties and a personalized seventies fails to hold up under close scrutiny. What historian Peter Clecak (1983) described as 'the quest for the ideal self' was not unique to the seventies but grew quite naturally from the sixties counterculture.[7] Indeed, the counterculture stressed personal liberation as a basic aim. Aided by drugs, music, meditation, organic foods, and communal living, thousands of radical youths of the sixties had sought greater psychic and spiritual awareness and physical well-being. In this respect, the main difference between the decades was that, by the seventies, people pursued personal fulfillment with more intensity and on a far wider scale than they had in the sixties. During the seventies, virtually every sector of American society came to be affected by the human potential movement to some degree.

Nor was the consciousness revolution of the seventies as solipsistic and selfish as critics claimed. Lasch insisted that 'narcissism holds the key to the consciousness movement and to the moral climate of contemporary society' (71-103). Yet as Theodore Roszak, a proponent of the new consciousness, noted, the critics tended to generalize on the basis of the movement's 'worst excesses of silly self-indulgence and commercial opportunism.'[8] In *Person Planet* (1978), Roszak claimed that Americans searched not merely for personal salvation but 'for a new reality principle to replace the waning authority of science and industrial necessity'(xxi). To Clecak, Americans were making a 'quest for personal fulfillment,' but one conducted 'within a small community (or several communities) of significant others' (7-9). The search for meaningful community, for an end to separation, segmentation, and alienation, formed a basic part of seventies culture.

A final fault of the Wolfe/Lasch schema of the seventies is that political activism in fact did not end with the Vietnam War. Although the political pursuit of change became less vociferous and less well-publicized in the post-Vietnam, post-Watergate years, it nevertheless remained an important feature of American life. Throughout the seventies, the environmental, feminist, gay-rights, antinuclear, and peace movements flourished. Thousands of communes, women's centers, free schools, alternative publishers, food cooperatives, and various other counter-institutions proliferated. However, disillusionment with national politics and the inadequacies of past federal programs increasingly led seventies activists to concentrate on the community or state as more effective arenas for change. As Milton Kotler, director of a coalition of community groups, claimed, 'There's a new recognition that the country's not going to be saved by experts and bureaucrats. It's going to be saved by some moral vision and some moral hope coming from the grass-roots and the neighborhoods.'[9]

By the end of the seventies, an estimated twenty million Americans had participated in various community-action programs working for social betterment. In hundreds of cities, groups toiled to restore older urban neighborhoods, choosing to rebuild existing buildings rather than follow the traditional bulldozing patterns of urban renewal. Besides neighborhood restoration, various grass-roots groups supported such tasks as improving public spaces, experimenting with alternative energy, creating crisis-intervention centers, establishing abortion and birth-control clinics, and promoting consumer advocacy. 'The media is selling us on this notion of apathy and paralysis in the country,' criticized former antiwar activist Sam Lovejoy.[10] 'The movement did not die. It did the most intelligent thing it could do; it went to find a home. It went into the community. It's working, unnoticed, in the neighborhood. They're starting to blossom and make alliances, connections.'

As Lovejoy's statement implies, sixties activists continued to play important roles in the social movements of the seventies and more recent times. Scholars who debunk the sixties and find few lasting legacies of the Movement frequently sight the post-sixties experiences of a few well-known activists who 'sold out' to join the establishment. Most frequently presented as evidence of the ephemeral nature of sixties activism is the career of Yippie leader Jerry Rubin. After becoming a New Left media celebrity through such antics as wearing revolutionary battle dress into an House UnAmerican Activities Committee hearing, trying to levitate the Pentagon, throwing money onto the floor of the New York stock exchange, and nominating a pig for president, Rubin immersed himself in the human potential movement. In his autobiography *Growing (Up) at 37*, he confessed: 'In five years, from 1971 to 1975, I directly experienced EST, Gestalt therapy, bioenergetics, Rolfing, massage, jogging, health foods, tai chi, Esalen, hypnotism, modern dance, meditation, Silva Mind Control, Arica, acupuncture, sex therapy, Reichian therapy, and More House.'[11] After all this, he settled down and became a Wall Street stockbroker.

Others who gave up the radical quest for social justice included Black Panther Eldridge Cleaver who, in addition to becoming a born-again Christian, attempted to join the capitalist system by marketing men's pants with polyester codpieces. Panther Bobby Seale, after an unsuccessful run for mayor of Oakland, authored a cookbook, *Barbecuing with Bobby*. Rennie Davis, an early Students for a Democratic Society (SDS) leader and one of the Chicago Eight, became a follower of the guru Maharaj Ji. Radical *Ramparts* writers Peter Collier and David Horowitz reemerged as Reagan supporters and wrote a scathing attack on the sixties as the 'Destructive Generation.'[12]

Historian Joseph Conlin, whose book *The Troubles* is an unrelenting diatribe against the Movement, presents the story of Charles C. 'Chip' Marshall III as representative. An organizer for SDS and one of the 'Seattle Eight' jailed for conspiring to destroy federal property, by 1980 Marshall had become the director of a major private housing development company. In a *Time* story that Conlin quotes, Marshall claimed that 'liberal economics just doesn't work. ... Self-reliance, productivity and independence are important. ... Business interests me.' Conlin concludes, 'Now there is how a chap named Chip ought to talk! Just like fellows with names like Jerry Rubin.'[13]

There were, of course, hundreds of Marshalls and Rubins – socially conscious youths who became conservative capitalists and consumers in subsequent decades. However, this is not an accurate group portrait of what became of the generation of sixties activists. The Movement left an indelible imprint on most members. Like the nineteenth-century transcendentalist Henry David Thoreau, Movement participants had acted as moral witnesses against what they perceived as an unjust society. Their individual rebellions led innumerable activists to a higher level of consciousness, a democratic vision that would remain with them. Not surprisingly, a great many of them have continued to work for social justice in more recent years. Although, as one would expect, most of the youthful rebels eventually settled down and chose careers, they did so less to make money than to serve society and to find self-fulfillment. Studies of Mississippi Freedom Summer volunteers, for instance, indicate that whereas only 7 percent entered the business world, about half went into helping professions, with teaching, social service, law, and medicine being the most popular.[14] They often worked with the poor in inner cities. They taught African-American and women's history, ran legal aid and medical clinics, and established housing and job-training programs. Many found employment as social workers, counsellors, and planners in the various government agencies established by the Economic Opportunity Act. Summarizing the findings of research on the post-sixties careers of participants in the civil-rights, antiwar, and Free Speech movements, sociologist Joseph R. DeMartini concluded that 'former activists' current political beliefs are consonant with those held by activists during the 1960s.'[15] Thus, unlike the Old Left of the thirties, which witnessed many dramatic deconversions when that group reached middle age in the postwar years, members of the New Left remained remarkably true to their early ideals.

Moreover, many New Leftists returned to school, earned Ph.D.s, and became university professors, bringing a radical perspective to such fields as history, sociology, and African-American and women's studies. Three early SDS leaders, Bob Ross, Todd Gitlin, and Richard Flacks, became professors at major universities. Ross's work has focused on creating a model for a more humanistic international capitalism. Gitlin and Flacks have written well-received books about the Movement. Bernice Johnson Reagon, who joined the sixties crusade for racial justice in Albany, Georgia, became director of the Black American Culture program at the Smithsonian Institute. Student Nonviolent Coordinating Committee activist Joyce Ladner today is a well-known sociologist at Howard University specializing in race relations. Indeed, at colleges and universities across the country, former Movement people, both leaders and rank-and-file, can be found in disproportionate numbers in the liberal-arts and social-science disciplines.

Other sixties activists settled into careers as authors, investigative reporters, documentary film makers, high school teachers, clergy, labor organizers, urban planners, health and child-care workers, and various social-service professions. Some have chosen physical labor, such as carpentry or farming. Students for a Democratic Society founder Al Haber, for example, works as a cabinet-maker. He lives in Berkeley and remains involved in radical organizing and protest.

A number of black leaders entered politics. Southern Christian Leadership Conference staffers Jesse Jackson and Andrew Young came to play important national roles. Jackson is recognized today as one of the leading voices for African-Americans within the Democratic party. Young has twice served as mayor of Atlanta, has been a congressman, and was Jimmy Carter's ambassador to the United Nations. The Student Nonviolent Coordinating Committee's first chairman Marion Barry went on to be elected Mayor of Washington,

D.C., though later he became tainted by cocaine and corruption. SNCC leaders John Lewis and Julian Bond have had more illustrious careers. Bond served for many years as a Georgia state senator and more recently as a visiting professor at Harvard; Lewis today is a respected member of the U.S. House of Representatives.

Although fewer white New Leftists entered politics, Tom Hayden did. Elected to the California state legislature, he has led the Campaign for Economic Democracy (later renamed Campaign California), a network of grass-roots citizen-action groups that have taken up such measures as rent control, energy conservation, clean air, and opposition to environmentally destructive development. Still evoking the ideals of participatory democracy, Hayden recently wrote that 'the process of trying to find a consensus rather than going ahead with a slim majority still strikes me as key.'[16] Although scarcely a movement leader of Hayden's stature, Bill Clinton, an antiwar activist and casual marijuana smoker in the sixties, is the first member of the Movement generation to have won election to the presidency.

In addition to picking helping professions, many sixties activists have continued to volunteer their services in environmental, feminist, antinuclear, consumer, and community service movements. Even most of those no longer active in progressive organizations have absorbed sixties values and lead lives in which they remain conscious of environmental and equal-rights issues. They recycle, share in household tasks, and strive to raise nonprejudicial children.

Although it would be presumptuous to pick the post-sixties career of any single individual as representative of the Movement generation, certainly one could do better than Chip Marshall or Jerry Rubin. Heather Tobis Booth makes an excellent choice. In 1964 Heather Tobis, a student at the University of Chicago, joined other northern volunteers and traveled to Mississippi for Freedom Summer. Back in Chicago, she joined SDS and took an active role in the antiwar movement, feminism, and various local issues. She married Paul Booth, a former SDS national secretary and in more recent years a union organizer. In 1973 she founded the Midwest Academy in Chicago, which became the training center for Citizen Action, a national federation of grass-roots citizen organizations.

Over the years, Booth's Midwest Academy has trained thousands of community activists in organizing, in raising funds, in establishing networks, and in holding public hearings, demonstrations, and petition drives. Former SDS leader Steve Max has served as the academy's curriculum director for years, helping to stimulate what Max calls 'resurgent populism.' Academy-trained activists have played an important role in aiding the causes of environmentalists, feminists, the poor, trade unionists, small businessmen, tenants, and peace groups. Citizen Action has furthered the sixties goals of social change and personal empowerment, but this time with the necessary organizational clout to win more lasting victories.

As the post-sixties careers of people such as Heather Booth, Tom Hayden, John Lewis, Richard Flacks, and Bill Clinton would indicate, numerous Movement veterans have persevered in attempting to implement the values of the sixties. With maturity, their objectives have become less grandiose and their tactics more pragmatic, but the goals of achieving social justice and real democracy remain strong. Aquarian dreams have been tempered, not abandoned.

Notes

1. Christopher Lasch, *The Culture of Narcissism: American Life in an Age of Diminishing Expectations* (New York: Warner Books, 1979), 17.
2. Douglas T. Miller and Marion Nowak, *The Fifties: The Way We Really Were* (Garden City, New York: Doubleday, 1977), 3-6.
3. Tom Wolfe, 'The "Me" Decade and the Third Great Awakening,' *New York,* August 23, 1976, 29.
4. George Leonard, *The Ultimate Athlete* (New York: Viking Press, 1975), 3-29.
5. Lasch, 30.
6. Irving Louis Horowitz, *Ideology and Utopia in the United States, 1956-1976* (New York: Oxford University Press, 1977), 6-7.
7. Peter Clecak, *America's Quest for the Ideal Self* (New York: Oxford University Press, 1983).
8. Theodore Roszak, 'Expanding on the New Consciousness,' *San Francisco Bay Guardian,* January 20, 1977, 7-8.
9. James V. Cunningham and Milton Kotler, *Building Neighborhood Organizations* (Notre Dame, Indiana: University of Notre Dame Press, 1983), 1-15.
10. Peter N. Carroll, *It Seemed Like Nothing Happened: The Tragedy and Promise of America in the 1970s* (New York: Holt, Rinehart and Winston, 1982), 321.
11. Jerry Rubin, *Growing (Up) at Thirty-Seven* (New York: M. Evans, 1976), 19.
12. Peter Collier and David Horowitz, *Destructive Generation* (New York: Summit Books, 1989).
13. Joseph Conlin, *The Troubles: A Jaundiced Glance Back at the Movement of the Sixties* (New York: Franklin Watts, 1982), 356-357.
14. Doug McAdam, *Freedom Summer* (New York: Oxford University Press, 1988), 199-232.
15. Joseph R. DeMartini, 'Social Movement Participation: Political Socialization, Generational Consciousness, and Lasting Effects', *Youth and Society,* 15:2 (1983), 195-223.
16. Tom Hayden, *Reunion: A Memoir* (New York: Random House, 1988), 502-507.

'Power to the People' through Television: Community Access in a Commercial System

*Nancy Graham Holm**

In April of 1970, President Richard Nixon ordered the invasion of Cambodia. Within days, demonstrations against the escalation of the war erupted throughout the nation as increasing numbers of Americans fell into the ranks of the angry and disillusioned. On May 4, 1970, at Ohio's Kent State University, National Guardsmen killed three students and wounded nine more. The entire nation watched it on television.

Also in 1970, Federal Communications Commissioner Nicholas Johnson published *How to Talk Back to Your Television*.[1] In retrospect, it is now abundantly clear that for many citizens, especially in California, the link between Kent State and Johnson's irreverent document was firmly established.

The years 1970 to 1987 saw the development of public access television broadcasting in America. Public access was defined as the right of non-station personnel to influence program ideas and 'get on TV.'

It was understood that requests for air time must originate within community-based groups with identifiable constituencies whose suggestions for programming reflected the public interest. Although it was not a national phenomenon, it was sufficiently significant to influence broadcasters throughout the nation who feared a license challenge if they did not demonstrate a sensitivity to the trend.[2] It continued until 1987 when Reagan's deregulation of broadcasting removed the Fairness Doctrine, thus taking the clout out of the Federal Communication Commission rules which made it possible. After Reagan, stations continued to do 'public service' programming,

* This paper is undocumented history and could not have been written without the cooperation of Betty Ann Bruno, Ian Zellick and Roger Rice. I am indebted to them for their patience and collective memories. I accept full responsibility, however, for any errors which may result from misunderstanding.

but at a bleak minimum, using it primarily as a marketing device to promote station identification and specific on-air presenters.[3] The Golden Years of public access, 1974-1986, was a window in time, not to be repeated.

Stations which agreed to give up commercially sponsored program time to community affairs journalism were located in densely urban areas within the major markets. Most notable were stations in Los Angeles and the San Francisco Bay Area. Boston, in particular, contributed to the concept but it was mainly California which started the people's TV revolution.

1. Why California? Why Television?

It is not a coincidence that California experienced more public access than other parts of the nation. Historically, California has always been on the cutting edge of change and social activism, and California in the seventies was no exception.

Social trends and political activism, however, had two different faces in the 1970s. One was a type to promote life enhancement such as *est,* transcendental meditation and gestalt therapy, collectively called the Human Potential Movement. The other type was strictly political, attempting – as the catch-phrase said – to *access process;* jockeying to win power in order to influence public policy. This latter group – certainly the biggest – represented every major trend in American society, including the emerging presence of racial and ethnic minorities. Women, environmentalists, peace activists, gays, prisoners and the handicapped competed for attention with Mexican-Americans, Blacks and Asians.

What these groups had in common was a fundamental belief that satisfaction was an entitlement. Their efforts characterized what historian Christopher Lasch calls 'the legitimacy of immediate gratification.'[4] It was not unusual for some groups to march into the lobby of a TV station and literally demand to see the manager, sitting down and refusing to leave until they were heard. Some more militant groups even marched into recording studios and disrupted programs in progress until they were received by station management. Most groups seeking access to TV did not use 'Mau-Mauing' tactics, however.[5] Instead, they made their presence felt by threatening to challenge a station's license to broadcast. Regardless of tactics or the constituency they represented, each group proceeded with the belief that they were entitled to win, and they chose television as a means to this end.

Television was the obvious choice. It had by the early 1970s demonstrated its power to influence behavior and correct evils. Americans had watched the girl at Kent State wailing over the body of a fellow student, and by May 1971, sixty per cent of all Americans were opposed to the war in Vietnam.[6] In 1973, they witnessed John Dean III take his oath on television to tell the truth about

Watergate. In August 1974, Americans watched Richard Milhouse Nixon resign as President of the United States. In 1975, television news dramatized the bitter, brutal end of the Vietnam War. In 1977, Americans watched CBS journalist Walter Cronkite serve as the link between President Anwar Sadat and Premier Menachem Begin, preparing the path for Jimmy Carter's Camp David Accords. Television was the way to be heard and effect change. And change is what California was all about.

No other State in America experienced as much turmoil in the 1970s. While the nation as a whole was affected by social and political movements, California served as a prism through which every new idea was intensified. '"Tumultuous" might be a label for such a wildly varied time,' wrote *Life* Managing Editor Philip B. Kunhardt, Jr. in December 1979 in the introduction to the special issue, *The 70's*. '"Or Roller Coaster." Or "Dangerous." Or even "Astounding," for surely no one would have predicted much that happened in these years.'

It was in California that the Symbionese Liberation Army kidnapped millionaire heiress Patty Hearst in 1974. One year later, two attempts to assassinate President Gerald Ford occurred in two California cities, by Lynette 'Squeaky' Fromme in Sacramento and Sara Jane Moore in San Francisco. The Human Potential revolution found a home in California with The Esalen Institute, Silva Mind Control, gestalt therapy, bioenergetics, Arica training, *est* and transcendental meditation. Body work gained legitimacy as an alternative to traditional psychotherapy as middle class professionals experienced 're-birthing' and Rolfing to exorcise childhood traumas. Homosexual civil rights gained local public support, largely as a result of the 1978 assassinations of San Francisco Mayor George Moscone and Supervisor Harvey Milk.[7] It was in the California seventies that the Rev. Jim Jones started his People's Temple, moving his apocalyptic congregation from San Francisco to the Northern California farming community of Ukiah and eventually to their death in Guyana in 1978.

The Women's Movement – although national in scope – was a major force in 1970s California. Women's health collectives legitimized a woman's need for reclaiming control of her body from male physicians. Women's Groups intensified their work of the sixties, some in mainstream politics and others in separatist organizations.[8] In many cities, some women started orgasm therapy and sexual fulfillment went public as a human right.[9]

Other movements developed, each demanding 'rights' and claiming legitimacy. Berkeley's handicapped became the Disabled Movement, showing citizens for the first time wheelchair activists 'out of the nursing homes and into the streets.'[10] Telegraph Avenue became the power center and home for The Center for Independent Living, serving as both a national and international model.[11] California was also a center for significant prison reform as both criminologists and the incarcerated lobbied for community based correctional programs. Most prominent of all were racial and ethnic minorities. The so-called Black Power decade is usually looked upon as the years 1965 to 1975. It was in the California seventies that the Black Panthers became 'legitimate' with breakfast programs, elementary schools and free health clinics. It was in Oakland – birthplace of the Panthers – that the party became *the* in-your-face organization.[12] Lionel Wilson, the city's first Black mayor, would not have been elected without the Panthers' efforts. Eventually, the party influenced other officials and agencies. It was in 1976 that Elaine Brown, a party leader, attended the Democratic convention as a delegate for Governor Jerry Brown. Later, Elaine Brown was appointed to the Oakland Council for Economic Development, a group of key business leaders who controlled thousands of job opportunities.

Taking their cue from the Black Power movement, other racial and ethnic minorities organized to gain political influence. The San Francisco Bay Area and greater Los Angeles saw Asian-Americans and Hispanics form a wide variety of organizations to gain influence. Some agencies focused on single issues such as The Narcotics Education League in Oakland, started by a former 'Chicano' junkie who wanted to serve his community. Other Hispanic groups started *ad hoc* committees to pressure school boards to develop bi-lingual education in the elementary schools, hoping that it would give Mexican-American, Spanish-speaking children an equal opportunity for learning.[13]

The 1968 and 1972 elections demonstrated another growing constituency within California. Socialists and others on America's left had until that time been relegated to the fringe. In both 1968 and 1972, this changed as a coalition of leftist activists formed California's Peace and Freedom Party, gaining enough signatures to qualify for the ballot and to send delegates to a convention. Their presence was felt throughout the seventies as they organized politically on local, regional and state levels. There would never be enough members, however, for them to become a national force.

Finally, there were spectacular achievements of science and technology in the 1970s and they, too, influenced activist movements. Space exploration and human cell engineering were not sufficiently impressive to reverse a growing feeling among many Americans that Mother Earth was suffering from abuse. The environmental movement coalesced in 1970 with the first Earth Day and by the end of the decade California was a leading force among Americans who wished to give modern technology a conscience. Governor Jerry Brown was the first American governor to establish an office of alternative technologies in a State capital, asking taxpayers to fund research in solar energy and wind technology. Californians started movements to ride bicycles, warning each other about America's dependence on oil. From this concern grew other movements to push for better land use so that people could afford to buy homes close to their places of work. No one died in Three Mile Island's accident, but the future of nuclear power became a citizen's issue.[14]

Political and social activism was not limited to the powerless and marginalized, however. It was also in California that middle-class taxpayers went public with their list of injustices. One result was the passing of California's 1978 Proposition 13, cutting property tax by fifty per cent.

Parallel to this was the birth of organizations such as Citizens for Law and Order who reacted to a perception of *society running amok*. Backlash politics gained legitimacy when Caucasian pre-med student Allan Bakke charged reverse discrimination and challenged in court the very premise of affirmative action and quotas.[15]

Most of these trends have been studied and recorded by historians and journalists alike. Tom Wolfe's essays 'Radical Chic and Mau-Mauing the Flak Catchers' and 'The "Me" Decade and the Third Great Awakening' describe the paradox of individual narcissism and spiritual re-evaluation.[16] For some, California's Governor Jerry Brown was a symbol of America's search for its soul. Moving like a latter-day prophet through California's capital, the Governor, who refused to live in the Governor's Mansion, interpreted socio-political trends and warned Californians about excessive gratification and possible limits to political answers.

'There is a limit to the good things we have in this county,' Brown wrote.

> We're coming up against those limits. It's really a very salutary exercise to learn to live without them. Everybody looks for politicians to come up with the solutions to the society's problems. It really is a rather totalitarian urge if you analyze it. Maybe the answer is the Ten Commandments.[17]

Jerry Brown was nicknamed 'Governor Moonbeam' by his critics, who saw him as a New Age visionary, out of touch with the common citizen. In retrospect, however, it can be argued that he signaled an impulse that was rapidly gaining ground among some California intellectuals. The sixties had been a decade of awakening, unity and optimism. The seventies gave way to disillusionment about the ability of traditional institutions to deliver a fair and just society. Citizens began to find ways to 'do it!' themselves.

They collected signatures in order to put major issues on local and state ballots, claiming that legislators were weak and excessively partisan. Counter-culture California lawyers formed a publishing house to print 'Do It Yourself' guides to everything from forming a company to divorce. Women's health collectives started teaching women how to examine their own vaginas. Community colleges started video workshops so that television could be 'demystified.' In fact, *demystification* became a buzz-word in the seventies as 'the people' attempted to take back 'power.' The impulse behind community access television was just another trend in the spirit of the times.

148

2. KTVU, Channel 2, Oakland-San Francisco

KTVU-TV, licenced in both Oakland and San Francisco, was an independent station owned by Cox Broadcasting in Atlanta. From the late sixties until the deregulation of broadcasting under the Reagan administration in 1987, KTVU served America as a model for community access programming.[18] At its peak, (1973-1986), KTVU broadcast as many as five hours of non-commercial, informational programming a week to its viewing public with two of the programs scheduled in coveted commercial time slots. In order to appreciate the significance of this fact, it should be noted that during the same years, the News Department was programming five to six hours a week. As an independent station, i.e. a non-affiliate of any of the three networks, CBS, ABC and NBC, KTVU was free to act locally without network constraints.[19]

It is also significant that KTVU was physically located in Oakland. Oakland's political forces were unified in ways that were impossible across the Bay in its big sister city, San Francisco. The Black Panthers were in Oakland and a municipal chapter of the League of Women Voters was there too. Unlikely partners that they were, both pressured KTVU in similar ways.[20]

3. Public Access Meant Community Affairs

Public access meant that non-professionals could get on TV. It also meant, of course, that non-journalists could influence programming decisions made by the station's staff producers. 'Public' meant *the community*. Community was interpreted as self selected groups that could demonstrate a constituency, a sphere of influence and a desire to inform the public about issues which they considered important. Public access, therefore, became *community affairs.* Because most of the programming was non-sponsored, it was considered a gift to the community, otherwise known as public service.[21]

In the beginning, it was rather low key. As early as 1967, Oakland's League of Women Voters contacted KTVU and asked politely for air time to cover issues which were not being covered in the regularly scheduled informational programs, i.e., daily newscasts. Having done their homework, these primarily middle-class, university educated women demonstrated a lack of coverage by offering statistics from amateur analysis of program types. Quite simply, League members would sit at home and watch TV, writing down what they saw and what they didn't see. The League wanted more attention to Oakland's economic development and California ballot propositions.[22] When KTVU said they couldn't get it, some League members, acting as individuals, joined forces with other groups to apply political pressure. The station feared a license challenge, although it never developed that far. In the sixties, a coalition of community groups had, in fact, challenged KTVU's license, and although they lost, it had cost the station hundreds of thousands of dollars to defend itself. There was an important lesson to be learned from this experience. It was reinforced in 1971 when a Mexican-American group, La Raza Media Coalition, filed a complaint against KTVU and the other three principal stations in the San Francisco Bay Area. Once again, it cost KTVU thousands of dollars to defend itself.

4. In the Public Interest: The FCC and Its Role in Meeting the Community's Demands

Prior to the 1970s, most Americans assumed that TV broadcasting was just another type of Big Business and because television in America was almost exclusively commercial in nature, it was commonly believed that only commercial sponsors and station administrators could control what was transmitted. This belief was shaken in the seventies when concerned citizens began to examine the language in the Federal Communication Commission's regulations. Nicholas Johnson, author of *How to Talk Back to Your Television Set*, was a Lyndon Johnson appointee to the Commission from 1966 to 1973 and influenced a significant number of middle-class intellectuals. Many other publications appeared in the seventies from academics and journalists who offered guides to community groups, wishing to influence public affairs programming by accessing the TV airwaves.[23]

For the first time in American broadcasting history, average citizens began to think about the FCC's regulations and licensing process.[24] According to the Commission, every TV station owner in the United States must act as a trustee for viewers. The broadcaster is permitted to use the airwaves only in 'the public interest.'

Under the American commercial TV system, a broadcast license is issued to a business, granting a certain position on the electromagnetic spectrum. Each frequency can accommodate only one broadcast signal at a time, otherwise interference garbles the transmission and nothing intelligible can be seen or heard. To prevent interference, the US government evolved a regulatory system which granted a particular frequency to one broadcaster in an area, denying the channel to all others. In effect, the broadcaster was given a federally protected monopoly over a valuable piece of public property since, in theory at least, the airwaves belong to all citizens. In return for this protected right to broadcast, therefore, broadcasters were required to act not just in their private interests, but in 'the public interest.' Stations who were not acting in the public interest could have their licenses challenged before the FCC.

At the heart of a license challenge was the little known FCC tenet, the Fairness Doctrine. This established a set of principles for broadcasters to follow, giving them vital responsibilities, legally known as 'affirmative obligations.' If these obligations went unfulfilled, citizens had the right to protest to the station and ultimately to the FCC, forcing the station to serve the public interest in a demonstrable fashion.

The Fairness Doctrine asked stations to do two things: to provide programming which addressed controversial issues of public importance *and* to ensure that, overall, such programming was balanced, providing a reasonable opportunity for the presentation of contrasting views. More specifically, it asked stations *to seek out* these controversial issues, a directive which departs from traditional news reporting. In effect, the Fairness Doctrine gave the citizen the right to expect serious, open coverage of important public questions, no matter how controversial they were and no matter how obscure. It also gave the citizen the right to expect to hear all sides of an issue, preventing one-sided presentation. Thus, the Fairness Doctrine effectively forbade a broadcast station from operating as a powerful propaganda outlet for a particular point of view.[25]

Television stations are required to apply for license renewal at regular intervals and the paperwork for this application is crucial. In each document they have to 'promise' that they will deliver a designated number of minutes per week to public service. If they fail to deliver their 'promise,' they become vulnerable to a license challenge. Stations seldom lose on a challenge to their licenses, but it has happened. The clout in a challenge threat is that defending the allegations costs the station hundreds of thousands of dollars.

Once these concepts were understood, community groups began to mobilize in order to talk back to their televisions. Some saw it as a means to an end. Others were motivated by a profound feeling of indignation. The League of Women Voters was motivated by both. As watchdogs of America's political system, they saw public access as a guarantee for open forum and free debate, essential ingredients for the exercise of Americans' First Amendment rights.[26] They also saw public access as a right, carefully concealed in ordinary conversations with station management.

5. Three People Who Made a Difference

As a regional independent station in the San Francisco Bay Area, KTVU developed public access programming because it was locally administered without affiliate interference. It also happened as a result of three individuals who happened to meet at the right time. It was, in effect, a result of personal chemistry between the Vice-President and General Manager, Roger Rice; a set designer, Ian Zellick; and a social activist from the Oakland branch of the League of Women Voters, Betty Ann Bruno. Rice was a man with vision, pragmatic and intelligent enough to see the wisdom in listening to the community. Zellick was an intellectual and artistic iconoclast with a mischievous sense of irony and a big appetite for variety. Bruno was a Stanford University graduate; an earnest liberal Democrat whose ideals included a sincere belief in an informed electorate. Without this cast of characters, many believe that KTVU would never have developed the scope and depth of community affairs programming that it did. Rice, Zellick and Bruno took the task seriously and made KTVU's community affairs programming the national model.

Betty Ann Bruno came to KTVU as a member of the Oakland League of Women Voters. They were members of a coalition who had started lobbying the station as early as 1967, asking for better informational programming in the 'public interest.' The League had joined forces with the Council of Churches, COPE (Committee on Political Education) and the Black Caucus. Not until Roger Rice became Vice-President and General Manager in 1969, however, were their complaints taken seriously. Rice knew that license challenges were expensive to fight and he recruited Ian Zellick to manage the community's demands. Zellick was the perfect choice. On the payroll but temporarily without a specific job, Rice believed that Zellick was the only person at KTVU who could talk to *anyone* about *anything.* Interpreting his new position as a 'green light,' programs and staff evolved throughout the seventies until Zellick had a department of four full-time paid journalists, a variety of part-time producers and countless interns. At the beginning, however, everyone was a volunteer.

6. Free Labor, Free Broadcasts

KTVU's Department of Community Affairs started out by borrowing people from the League of Women Voters to help produce Community Affairs programs. These volunteers were not trained journalists but educated women who came to the station with university degrees, exceptionally informed minds about current affairs and a passion for local politics. They worked primarily in research, and on specific occasions, as production assistants. The first television program was *Head On* in 1969. Hosted by KTVU's news anchor, it aired on Sunday evening and offered a half hour of unedited confrontational studio interviews. In 1970, the first big production occurred in KTVU's studios when the Oakland League helped to produce a three hour live special on the general election.

Bandwagon was the creation of Ian Zellick, but without the volunteered labor of over thirty members from the Oakland League, it never would have happened. Formatting the three hours was Zellick's responsibility. Adhering to the format became the work of the volunteer production assistants, each of whom was assigned to one candidate from either local, State or Federal races. All questions to the candidates were researched by the League members as well as the pro and con arguments on the ballot propositions. The studio was elaborately decorated in red, white and blue and a live Dixieland Band played music while 800 people wandered around on and off camera, eating hotdogs and waving placards. Starting at eight o'clock on the Sunday evening before the Tuesday election, the program continued for three uninterrupted hours without commercial sponsorship. Although KTVU was willing to forfeit sales revenue from the highly desirable three Sunday evening hours, they never would have produced the program without volunteer labor. It simply would have been too expensive. *Bandwagon* was repeated in 1971 and 1972.

7. Lunch with the Black Panthers

Concurrent with the political programs, Roger Rice and Ian Zellick instituted community affairs ascertainment luncheons. These occurred three to four times a week and were compulsory for the News Director, Program Director and other department heads. Each lunch was hosted at the station's expense and designed to introduce key programming personnel to various community leaders. The assumption behind the luncheons was that broadcasters needed to keep *informed*, an agenda not infrequently insulting to the News Department. From 1969 until Roger Rice's sudden and unexpected departure from the station in 1974, KTVU's department heads ate lunch and participated in discussions with community leaders from segments of society they probably would never have met otherwise. These included the alienated, the angry and the pro-active: former drug addicts, ex-offenders, women's groups, Blacks, Hispanics and Asians.

In 1971, Betty Ann Bruno was hired as a staff producer. She and Zellick started a Community Advisory Board to help produce programs. The meeting occurred on the first Monday of the month and included a wide spectrum of political activism: the League of Women Voters, the Black Caucus, peace coalitions, drug abuse prevention agencies, community based rehabilitation organizations and representatives from the same ethnic and racial minorities who had come to lunch.

This Board continued to exist throughout the seventies and into the early eighties. Membership was open to anyone, providing he or she represented a viable constituency. The Board's profile changed dramatically over the years as groups splintered and fought one another for legitimacy. A typical board in the late seventies would have included both conservative and radical groups within each racial and ethnic community; activists for gay and lesbian rights; Native Americans; prisoner reform advocates; environmentalists; a wide variety of women's groups, including health collectives and shelters for battered women; representatives from both the physically and mentally handicapped; bilingual education advocates; community based drug rehabilitation programs;

153

and Planned Parenthood. Conservative community activists such as Citizens for Law and Order also attended the meetings. Throughout the entire period, members of the Oakland League of Women Voters remained active and strongly involved with KTVU's Community Advisory Board.

8. The Department Develops

From 1972 to 1976 many other television programs came into existence. In 1972, a Spanish language talk show went on the air once a week, produced by someone recommended from the Community Advisory Board and hosted by a community leader who was recruited directly from one of the lunches. *Revista de la Semana* eventually became *Aqui y Ahora* and aired early on Sunday mornings. Next came a weekly Asian program designed to communicate with the four principal demographic groups of Asian-Americans. The first Sunday of *Asians Now* was in Chinese; the second in Japanese; the third in Korean and the last in Tagalog. The producers were recruited by advertising in local Asian language newspapers.

Roger Rice had entrusted Ian Zellick with the task of satisfying the community's substantive demands. He and Betty Ann Bruno often emerged from Community Advisory Board meetings with a new idea for yet another new program. In 1972, the League of Women Voters wanted a half-hour program to replace *Head On*, broadening the base of participation by allowing citizens to phone in questions to invited guests, the majority of whom were to be politicians and public policy makers. Thus *Open Line* was created, produced by KTVU but once again researched and staffed by telephone volunteers from the Oakland League. *Open Line* continued throughout the seventies and well into the eighties, eventually paying the Oakland League for its services.

In 1973, a one hour community billboard program was developed to inform Oakland residents about their city. *On the Square* was the brainchild of Ian Zellick, who named it after KTVU's location in Jack London Square. Betty Ann Bruno produced and hosted it every Sunday at noon. *On the Square* changed producers and hosts over the next ten years, but while Bruno was in charge, it served as a hard facts vehicle with six different segments to inform the audience about local politics and Bay Area cultural events. During the time that Bruno did *On the Square*, some people claim she was the most informed person at KTVU about the San Francisco East Bay. Parallel to these regularly scheduled programs, Betty Ann Bruno produced several five part specials on the subjects of drugs, crime and juvenile justice. She remained the key player in the Department of Community Affairs until she left to join the News Department in 1976.

In 1973, *All the People* was created to create a mirror opposite of *On the Square*. While *Square* was segmented to allow for six different topics, *All the*

People was restricted to one topic for one hour, focusing on life style and multi-culturalism in the Bay Area and allowing for in-depth interviews with one or several guests. Ian Zellick produced and hosted the program until the late seventies, when the focus of the program began to change to include mainstream public affairs topics.

In 1974, I went to KTVU with a film I had made while teaching radio and video at the women's state prison at Frontera, California. In it were 'messages' to the public from the women about their life inside a maximum security institution. KTVU agreed to extract some of these messages and broadcast them as public service messages.[27] During my negotiations with Zellick and Bruno, I took the opportunity to criticize them for not having *women's programming* at a time when women's issues were prominent in Bay Area journalism. By the end of lunch, they had hired me as a freelancer to produce *A Woman's Choice.* It went on the air for the first time in the autumn of 1974 and lasted until June of 1976. It was a thirty minute studio discussion program devoted to women who were making conscious choices about their lives. Over the same two years, I wrote and produced two one-hour film documentaries for programs which Bruno anchored from the studio. One was on the 'New Erotic Cinema;' the other on 'The Future of Marriage,' both offering new interpretations of women's rights.

In the autumn of 1976 I was hired as a full-time staff producer to replace Betty Ann Bruno. I was expected to produce a fifteen-minute mini-documentary once a month for a studio 'wrap around' discussion originally called *Mosaic,* later changed to *Montage.* The half-interhour program aired every Saturday evening at 10:30, eventually and finally changing its name to *The Saturday Night Special.* Because I was also a member of the League of Women Voters, I was asked to host *On the Square.*

Other producers were now on board, each managing one of the other three Saturday slots for *The Saturday Night Special.* Tomas Roman was a Puerto Rican-American with a theater background who came to KTVU from a local Hispanic advocacy organization. Johnny Barnes Selvin was a Black high school French teacher. Rosy Chu was a Chinese-American who had started at KTVU as a secretary, in spite of a college degree in broadcasting. We were four full-time paid staff and our labor was eventually supplemented by two other part-time producers: Serena Chen who produced and eventually hosted *Asians Now* and Laura Rodriguez who co-produced and co-hosted *Revista.* Chen was a social worker. Rodriguez was a trained historian from Madrid who had come to California from Oxford University in England.

By the mid-seventies, the six producers were links to the community. Our job was to listen, interpret and design a treatment whereby a particular issue could be communicated. *Whenever possible and when appropriate, we would put the community source 'on TV' and allow the person to speak for himself.*

During these years, we gave a voice to lesbian mothers who were about to lose custody of their children; Catholic families who chose to defy the Pope on birth control; normal children who spoke only Spanish but who had been labeled mentally retarded by school authorities; drug addicts who were human guinea pigs on Methadone; poverty income-level residents of public housing who hated living with rats; criminals who were living in community based correctional facilities; Vietnam veterans who had been contaminated with Agent Orange; battered wives; middle class housewives who were addicted to Valium; fathers who sexually molested their own children; advocates for and opponents of interracial adoption; run-away wives from Islamic countries; and social workers and community leaders in the Black, Chinese, Japanese, Cambodian, Thai, Vietnamese, Philippine, Korean, Chicano, Nicaraguan, Salvadorean, Cuban and Native American communities.[28] The department also gave a voice to homeless families; political organizers for Earth Day, advocates of regional government, organizers of solid waste management (called 'recycling') and citizen committees for clean water. We gave airtime to the 'boring but important' subjects such as insurance reform, nuclear waste, tax reform and campaign financing, none of which the News Department would touch without a hard news angle.

Montage, later *The Saturday Night Special*, became the high profile program within the department, probably because it had higher production values than the programs limited to studio discussions. The film (later videotape) segments to establish background and facilitate studio discussion were, in fact, self-contained documentaries.

There were other formats, however, which gave the public access to the airwaves. A San Jose State University professor had aggressively lobbied the station to create Free Speech Messages on the air. Indignant at his style, the station resisted until he was defeated. Zellick, however, liked the concept and reversed the station's original position, providing that the FSMs followed KTVU's rules, which Zellick himself would write. Thus, KTVU was the first station in the United States to create electronic 'letters to the editor.' An FSM was sixty seconds in length and a 'spot' to be inserted – just as commercials are – between programs. It was sixty seconds of pure opinion that could be rebutted by another citizen.

Besides FSMs, KTVU used the other kind of 'spot' to support public access. Public Service Announcements – or PSAs – were used to promote community organizations and to give publicity to nonprofit fund raising events. PSAs could be ten, twenty, thirty or sixty seconds in length. They were 'promised' in the license renewal and counted as a form of Community Affairs programs.[29]

Between 1976 and 1986, the four principal producers developed into serious journalists, writing and producing significant reports on nearly every conceivable subject relevant to Northern California society: medicine, law, crime, civil rights, drugs, sexuality, agriculture, senior citizens, insurance reform, capital punishment, the military, California's economy, handicapped rights, etc. It would be hard to think of topics on which the Department of Community Affairs did not produce programs. We were a staff of four full-time and two part-time journalists, producing five hours of programming a week. In contrast, the News Department had a staff of fifty to produce six hours a week.

As ever, the producers often used members from the Oakland League of Women Voters as volunteer research assistants. Their reliable research skills and impeccably high ethics made them the most valuable researchers a TV journalist could have. Most significant in my memory are four documentaries I wrote and produced with the League's research assistance: California water politics in *Agribusiness and Its Secret Subsidy* ; the hidden costs of living in a technological world in *The High Costs of High Tech;* the oil lobby and the absence of research into alternative energies in *The Politics of Solar Energy;* and the catastrophic problems of toxic chemicals in *Information Is the Best Defense.*[30]

The department's staff worked together for the better part of ten years, until Reagan's deregulation killed The Fairness Doctrine.[31] This resulted in a slow demise of the department's budget, since the station's management no longer needed such elaborate license protection. As of 1995, only Rosy Chu is left as the single producer in her own department.

9. Advocacy Journalism

The most common type of informational programming is a newscast. Community affairs was different in three ways from ordinary news. The first is that by its very definition, community affairs journalism departed from the traditional model of detached reporting which reacts to a specific event. Community affairs journalism was not *reactive*, but *proactive*. It was committed, and the commitment was a form of social activism. Until the phenomenon of public access, people without power were seldom heard from unless they committed crimes or staged public demonstrations, i.e., *until they became a news story*. Community Affairs journalists were different and unapologetic about their advocacy position. They saw themselves as a voice for the marginalized populations of the community.[32]

It should come as no surprise, therefore, that KTVU's News Department saw this type of programming as unprofessional. Indeed, throughout the entire period of 1969-1987, the News Department was less than friendly to the department's efforts. It was always with poorly disguised embarrassment that they would ask to use the department's journalistic sources. It was even more embarrassing for them to borrow film or videotape footage.

157

It must be said, however, that advocacy journalism did not mean *one-sided* treatments. Indeed, the management of KTVU depended on the Community Affairs journalists for balanced presentations and ethical treatments of the subjects covered. Studio discussions about American foreign policy in El Salvador, for example, always included the full spectrum of opinion. The same can be said for programs about such issues as capital punishment, welfare reform, neo-Nazism, bilingual education, reapportionment, campaign financing, nuclear waste, US-USSR arms control, California water politics, the military draft, Vietnam veterans or community based correctional institutions for juvenile offenders. Unbalanced and biased presentations could have threatened the station's license just as much as an absence of the programming itself.

If the News Department didn't or wouldn't recognize the high quality of journalism in Community Affairs programs, there were sectors of the public who did. Critical viewers wrote supportive letters and community leaders often acknowledged the various producers for their work. And always, of course, the viewing audience included members of the League of Women Voters, who were the watchdogs for accuracy and the Department's most severe critics.

It cannot be denied that the programs were information intensive, requiring committed attention on the part of the viewer. One favorite criticism from the News Department was that a Community Affairs program on any subject taught the viewer far more than he ever wanted to know! One General Manager used to say that he used the late Sunday night talk show *All the People* as a cure for insomnia. 'Elitist' is how the department was often described. Needless to say, this only managed to extend the debate further about the growing superficiality of American television news as a genre compared to serious informational programming which dug deep into a subject. The News Department asserted that Community Affairs programming was limited to a small audience. *Television,* they liked to remind us, *was a form of mass communication for the masses and the masses don't care about fringe politics and boring subjects, no matter how important.*[33]

Part of Community Affairs' 'elitist' reputation with its intensely infor-mational style was due to the leadership of Ian Zellick. Coming to television from theater, he arrived at commercial television with sensibilities and idiosyncratic behavior fundamentally out of sync with a sales-oriented management. His capacity for general knowledge was gargantuan and his repertoire of educated and refined conversation exceeded that of any other station employee. People who knew him well often wondered why he had never defected to PBS (Public Broadcasting System), the intellectual-cultural network. In fact, his general orientation to life was far removed from street fighting and the mundane policy issues of the inner city. Zellick's life outside the station was filled with a wide variety of esoteric hobbies such as Egyptian hieroglyphics and the construction of elaborate dollhouses. He often engaged his department staff in long animated conversations about opera, ballet, gourmet cooking, archeological digs and the latest issue of *Smithsonian Magazine* while they were desperately trying to study disability issues of Vietnam veterans or research charges of police brutality in East Oakland. Zellick was an eccentric genius in a pool of ordinary people, and it is a grand irony that he inspired a stable of streetwise journalists into putting ordinary people on television. It was no secret that his position at the station was up for re-evaluation every time a new General Manager was appointed from Atlanta. One likes to think that it was his unparalleled ability to out-talk his adversaries which saved both him and the department.

The second difference between Community Affairs journalism and traditional news was in the 'production values' of the programs. In brief, it is fair to say that there were no production values in the majority of the shows. Some critics might even suggest that it was not really 'television' at all but a picture form of radio in which one could see the face of the 'talking head.'[34] *Montage* and *The Saturday Night Special* used documentaries to add value, but in the absence of formal training, the journalists' technical efforts were often sub-standard. Rosy Chu and I were the only ones in the department who came to KTVU with any formal education about television, and this had been a training that was far more theoretical than practical. What we learned we learned by doing and by listening to our editors. By 1986 we knew a great deal about picture-sound story telling.[35]

The third way in which Community Affairs journalism differed from news was in its non-commercial status. KTVU could have sold sponsorships for the airtime but they chose not to. They could have used the promotion department to give on-air advance publicity – just as they did to 'hype' news specials – but they did not. Their reluctance to go commercial was no secret. The contents of the programs were often controversial and made the sales department nervous about the possibility of offending sponsors. The low viewership of most of the programs was another problem. Commercials could not be sold for large sums of money, which meant small commissions. In brief, it just wasn't worth a salesperson's time to try and sell programs from Community Affairs.[36] The rationalization for this attitude, however, was expressed as a desire to remain 'pure' in order to demonstrate an unambiguous type of true public service.

This rather spurious attitude tainted the department's reputation for ten years. Community Affairs was perceived as consumers of station revenue who did not pay their share of expenses. One cynical interpretation has maintained that the management's decision not to sell time on the programs was designed to keep Community Affairs in a second class position. After Roger Rice, top administrators perceived Ian Zellick's department as a necessary nuisance, required to protect the station's license.

None of these facts discouraged the Community Affairs journalists. They saw their role as crusaders against Big Business broadcasting and were only too happy to have the airwaves serve as a link between the voices and people's living-rooms. One rating point represented 20,000 viewers. If a Community Affairs program managed to get even a 1 rating, the producers knew that the program was reaching far more people than an organized rally in a local town hall.[37]

10. What Did It All Mean?

If one uses public awareness with attendant changes in public policy as a measurement of effectiveness, it is impossible to say whether any of the programs made a difference. Both Zellick and Bruno think it did. So do I but we can't prove it. Only students in mass communication studies with time and resources could come close to saying anything conclusively. It is, indeed, a compelling field of study, inviting investigation from public policy scholars.

If one considers KTVU's Golden Years of Community Affairs Programming as an example of *public access*, however, then it must be declared an unmitigated success. It was an exercise in democracy; an electronic soap-box. And it worked.

It was also a decade of unparalleled intensity for those of us who worked in it. Now, some twenty years later, Ian Zellick remembers KTVU as

a period of chaos, politically, intellectually and sometimes physically. It was a period of tightrope walking with the station caught between the FCC, private interest groups who wanted more and radicals who wanted everything. There were blackmailers who tried to get money and jobs and new regulations every other month from the FCC. All this when in fact the stations were private corporations with stockholders and traditional management. The whole thing was like a wild soup being made in a badly equipped washing machine, reaching stages of demented hysteria. It was exhilarating, maddening. And sometimes even worth it.[38]

In the end, however, the News Department was correct. Most people are just folks and folks in America are the ones who watch TV. They want their informational programming short and sweet, without excessive detail. At its best, Community Affairs programming never reached more than a hundred thousand people in a market of five million.

In the final analysis, Community Affairs programming was a grand irony. Ordinary people used an elite medium to communicate with an elite audience of policy makers, politicians and public opinion makers. It was an elaborate reversal of the norm and a grand experiment.

Notes
1. Nicholas Johnson, *How to Talk Back to Your Television Set* (New York: Atlantic Monthly Press, 1970).

160

2. Eventually, a national organization of Community Affairs Directors was established, representing a majority of the commercial stations in the country. Most stations, however, limited the 'department' to one person without a production staff.

3. The concept of public service broadcasting is just the opposite of what the concept has historically meant in the traditional European model. Public service in Europe means tax-supported broadcasting, an anathema in America because it is considered undemocratic and elitist. In seventies America, public service came to mean 'giving up' and 'giving away' airtime that could have been purchased by commercial sponsors.

4. Christopher Lasch, 'Voices,' *Life*, December 1979, 87. For a fuller discussion of Lasch's ideas, see *The Culture of Narcissism* (New York: W.W. Norton, 1979).

5. I am borrowing this phrase from Tom Wolfe, *Radical Chic and Mau-Mauing the Flak Catchers* (New York: Farrar, Straus and Giroux, 1970). Using this expression was acceptable in the seventies, but in terms of today's sensitivity to political correctness, it is not. Mau Maus were Kenyan Kikuyu tribesmen who fought ferociously and often viciously against white rule forty years ago.

6. Harris Poll, quoted in *Life*, December 1979, 37.

7. Historians are likely to say that the gay revolution started in New York City in 1970 with the Stonewall riots. In San Francisco, however, it was greatly accelerated by the murder of gay city official Harvey Milk in 1978. *Life* stated, 'This public declaration of homosexual solidarity was one of the decade's more dramatic social changes. In 10 years the number of gay groups increased from 20 to 2,500. They include airline pilots, nurses, athletes, psychiatrists, clerics and business people' (82).

8. California feminists in the 1970s fell into two camps: the heterosexual group called 'straight' and the lesbian faction which more than often became separatist, refusing to deal with men on any level. Straight or gay, women formed support groups and collectives, generically calling them Women's Groups.

9. California drivers use bumper stickers to express a wide variety of opinions and communicate messages. In the 1970s one said: 'Honk if you're horny!' *Life*: 'Sexual taboos burst out of the brown-paper wrapper: there was mate swapping in suburbia and incest on primetime television' (75).

10. 'Out of the Nursing Homes, Into the Streets!' was a slogan often heard at demonstrations by the wheelchaired handicapped. I used this as a title for a TV documentary I wrote in 1979.

11. Telegraph Avenue in Berkeley, California was the heart of the counter-culture movement. It is a main street running north and south from the University's Sather Gate.

12. I am indebted to Bob Blauner for this description of the Black Panther Party. See 'The Outlaw Huey Newton,' book review of *The Shadow of the Panther* by High Pearson, *The New York Times Book Review*, July 10, 1994, 1.

13. The seventies in California saw new language develop as Mexican-Americans chose to call themselves *Chicanos;* the handicapped became *the disabled;* and the press became *the media.*

14. Radioactive emissions from the nuclear power plant at Three Mile Island near Harrisburg, Pennsylvania, occurred in 1979. The incident threw the entire future of the nuclear industry into question.

15. Allan Bakke was refused admission into medical school and challenged the decision, claiming reverse racial discrimination due to a quota system in the name of *affirmative action.* His case was reviewed on three levels, eventually reaching the US Supreme Court, which upheld the California Supreme Court's decision in favor of Bakke by a 5 to 4 vote in 1978.

16. See note 6.
17. Jerry Brown, *Thoughts* (New York: Time-Life, 1976).
18. It was the Federal Communication Commission itself that marked KTVU as a national model. It offered the station's paper application for license renewal as an example to other stations who were trying to ward off license challenges or looking for viable models of public service programming.
19. At the time there were five VHF (very high frequency) stations in the Oakland-San Francisco market: the three network affiliates, KPIX (CBS), KGO (ABC), KRON (NBC); the one independent, KTVU; and the PBS station, KQED. There were also several UHF stations (ultra high frequency) as well a few cable stations. The VHF stations had a signal range of about five million viewers which were divided almost equally between them. The single exception to this was KQED, channel 9, which never received more than 8% of the potential viewing audience. This PBS station (Public Broadcasting System), supported in part by tax money, was also funded by viewer subscriptions and considered the 'intellectual' TV channel, since it did not enjoy popular support.
20. The League of Women Voters is an organization designed to enhance the democratic process. Originally organized in 1920, it has 1,100 national, state, regional and local branches and has done more than any other American institution to help citizens exercise their right to vote in an informed and responsible manner. Outside America it is best known for its sponsorship of the televised Presidential debates in 1976, 1980 and 1984. The League enjoys a reputation for outstanding non-partisan research on initiatives and referenda which appear on ballots as propositions. Although membership is open to everyone, including men, most members are middle-class women, university educated and white. The League celebrated its 75th anniversary in 1995.
21. See note 4.
22. Ballot propositions can be either a referendum or an initiative. Both ask the voters to say 'yes' or 'no' on items that could become law or which are already law and could be rescinded. Not all States in the USA have the practice, but California is well known for using both referenda and initiatives as ways of creating or rescinding laws outside the State legislature.
23. Other authors who encouraged 'talking back' include: Jerome A. Barron, *Freedom of the Press for Whom? The Right of Access to the Mass Media* (Bloomington: Indiana University Press, 1973); Les Brown, *Television ... The Business Behind the Box* (New York: Harcourt Brace Jovanovich, 1971); Barry Cole and Mel Oettinger, *The Reluctant Regulators: The FCC and the Broadcast Audience* (Reading: Addison-Wesley Publishing Company, 1978); Fred W. Friendly, *The Good Guys, the Bad Guys and the First Amendment ... Free Speech vs. Fairness in Broadcasting* (New York: Random House, 1975); Benno C.S Schmidt, Jr., *Freedom of the Press vs. Public Access*, sponsored by the Aspen Institute Program on Communications and Society and the National News Council (New York: Praeger, 1976); Tony Schwartz, *The Responsive Chord* (Garden City, New York: Anchor Press/Doubleday, 1973); Andrew O. Shapiro, *Media Access: Your Rights to Express Your Views on Radio and Television* (Boston: Little, Brown and Company, 1976).
24. I am indebted to the Public Media Center in San Francisco for their research and public policy publications. A special thankyou to Executive Director Herb Chao Gunther for his discussions on the Fairness Doctrine. For further information, see *Talking Back* (San Francisco: Public Media Center, 1983).
25. The ascertainment process is part of the FCC's requirements for license renewal. This means that middle management station personnel must conduct face-to-face interviews

with identified leaders of the community. It is the Public Affairs Director's responsibility to identify leaders from all sectors of the community and assign these interviews. Categories include health, culture, government, education, military, women and racial and ethnic minorities, etc. An interview may be with someone from an established institution or from a grassroots agency. Stations in major markets are required to complete 400 or more interviews a year. By ascertaining the community, the station actively *seeks out* significant issues. Records and license renewal applications are kept in a Public Inspection File.
26. The First Amendment to the US Constitution guarantees Americans freedom of speech. It is one of the most fiercely protected of the many freedoms stated in the Bill of Rights. Therefore, all records pertaining to a license renewal application and 'promise' are kept in a Public Inspection File at every station and must be available to the public on demand.
27. A Public Service Announcement (PSA) is a 'spot' message which is broadcast as a public service to the community. PSAs come in many varieties and are often produced by the station itself as a public service. Major market television stations in America receive an average of 100 PSAs a week from non-profit organizations seeking free publicity for either an event or a service. PSAs can also be mini-programs such as the kind I was offering KTVU from the women prisoners. The number of PSAs aired each week is 'promised' in the license renewal and a certain number may not be 'ghettoed' into the middle of the night but must be assigned to day parts.
28. On one occasion, the California Neo-Nazi Party asked for equal time to express their views after a documentary was aired, criticizing them for their anti-historical position. ('The holocaust never happened!') After much debate, KTVU agreed to allow them to speak on the air. In response to this controversial move, Ian Zellick was presented with an award by Temple B'nai Emanah in San Francisco. The Jewish congregation believed that by airing the Nazi opinions, KTVU was helping to expose their lack of education and general stupidity. Many told Zellick that had the same thing occurred in 1936, it would have made a difference. I was the producer of the program and to this day I still wonder if we did the right thing.
29. See note 28.
30. By 1984, several members of the League were getting rather sophisticated in their ability to produce television programs. On more than one occasion, they succeeded in getting outside financial support for some of their television projects. In this way, some League members used KTVU as a training ground, hoping to go into independent production at a later time.
31. The Fairness Doctrine was the FCC tenet which required stations to seek out and provide programming on significant issues no matter how boring! Under President Ronald Reagan, the FCC voted to abolish the Fairness Doctrine because it was considered government interference with free enterprise. The argument held that with the new technologies of cable and satellite penetration, a multiplicity of market options made the Fairness Doctrine unnecessary. In other words, there were now so many channels available, one could get whatever type of information one wanted, just by zapping through the options. *The fallacy in this reasoning, of course, is that very few channels will purposely produce informational programming on topics that are important, but boring to large numbers of people.* Indeed, economic survival is now dictating programming choices on all channels, including the network affiliates. News directors carefully choose subjects for 'in-depth' specials and avoid topics which might result in low viewership. They cannot afford to have three seconds of boredom or the viewer will zap to another channel. The result is that topics such as 'sexual child abuse'

163

will be treated in a primetime special, but never subjects such as nuclear waste material or the greenhouse effect.

The Fairness Doctrine also prevented propaganda and one-sided arguments from being broadcast. It is especially in radio that we now see the result of relaxing this protection. As of this writing, radio station KSFO in San Francisco, for example, includes in its station breaks the message: 'KSFO – In your heart, you know Newt is Right!' Referring to neo-Conservative Newt Gingrich, such a flagrant misuse of the airwaves would have been impossible under the Fairness Doctrine.

Sometimes the Fairness Doctrine is confused with the Equal Time Amendment. The second applies only to political candidates and is still enforced by the FCC.

32. Advocacy journalism is controversial because it departs from the traditional model of objective reporting. It is gaining new momentum in Europe, however, as journalists try to cope with increasingly difficult phenomena of 3 million homeless, 18 million unemployed and 50 million living in poverty. In Brussels, May 6-7, 1994, the Directorate General, Five (DG V) of the European Commission hosted a two day conference on 'Journalism and Social Exclusion: New Approaches.' European journalism schools were encouraged to teach advocacy journalism on behalf of the poor, homeless and other disenfranchised populations in Europe.

33. American television journalists are seldom trained in mass communication studies, yet most of them instinctively know that television in a commercial model is regulated by the lowest common denominator. Although this might be regretted, it is usually respected as an immutable law of American commercial television. Television journalists who choose TV news, therefore, must defend their policy of programming for the average person. Before the advent of cable and satellites, 'the average person' had fewer choices and stations could afford to take risks. Today, traditional *regional* newscasts on the network affiliates are slaves to consumer research, resulting in a kind of censorship. Boring but important stories simply do not get on the air. 'Commercial TV doesn't inform us about the effects of clear-cutting in national forests,' writes Betty Ann Bruno to the author, January 30, 1995. And 'commercial TV rejected Sesame Street and Barney initially as concepts that "had no popular appeal".'

34. In American television jargon, a 'talking head' is an 'on camera' interview with sync-sound. TV journalists are always wrestling with the ratio of 'talking heads' to 'voice over' narration and pictures. The use of 'heads' comes in and out of vogue and is currently *chic* once again. In the seventies, however, American TV journalists were just beginning to change from the traditional BBC model of cutting pictures first and then putting in the voice 'on top,' or voice-over. This resulted in a passionate love for pictures and accentuated the perception of 'old-fashioned' when looking at 'talking heads' just at the time when low budget productions could afford nothing else.

35. Rosy Chu was a graduate of the Broadcast Communication Department at San Francisco State University. I attended the same courses on a graduate level towards an M.A. degree. This education was 'state of the art' at the time, yet almost entirely theoretical with little practical experience. There was no practical internship, as there is for example in Danish programs. The other CA producers had no training at all in television production. Most of them arrived at KTVU, therefore, with virtually no training.

36. Sales personnel at a commercial TV station are motivated by the size of the commission they can get. The cost of a 30 second sponsor spot is linked to the program in which it appears, or to be more precise: in which it 'interrupts.' In fact, *The Saturday Night Special* often got 3 rating points, which is the same as the rating points on a regularly scheduled morning talk show on a competing channel. A '3' would certainly justify

commercials, but the sales department never wanted to support the programs due to their controversial nature. Their failure to do so has been hotly debated over the years. One explanation is that certain members of the sales department coveted the weekend time slots and wanted CA programming to disappear altogether. It was Roger Rice's successor, Bill Schwartz, who protected the weekend positions from an angry sales staff who saw them as wasted opportunities to make money.

37. KTVU's management knew that we loved our work as advocacy journalists. In retrospect, however, we were badly exploited as a result. Most of the full-time producers worked no less than fifty hours a week, and yet we were paid salaries between 40 and 50% of what the news journalists were earning. The station's justification was that we spent station revenue, but did not generate any in return. We did not have a union and therefore, unprotected, had no power to negotiate higher salaries. I left KTVU in 1984 in order to earn a higher salary, which I did three times over, plus winning regional Emmys along the way. But I never again had as much fun or satisfaction as I did as a community affairs journalist.

38. Ian Zellick, letter to the author from Oakland, California, February 27, 1995. All of us in the department lived on the cutting edge. Our faces were known to the public and none of us could escape small incidents of harassment. Most of us had unlisted telephone numbers. I was often targeted because I was 'white' in a department that was dominated by ethnic and racial minorities. Between 1974 and 1976, I was also targeted because I was a heterosexual women doing a program about women's issues when many of my viewers were lesbian separatists. I recall being picketed on the University of California campus because of an editorial I wrote in the *Daily Cal* defending a male studio guest I had invited to *A Woman's Choice*. Ian Zellick once returned from lunch to see pickets outside the station calling him 'running dog' and a 'lackey of capitalist imperialists' because he had refused to allow a militant community group to use an FSM to advertise an illegal demonstration. In addition to public harassment from unsatisfied members of the community, there were bomb scares. Between 1973 and 1979 it was not at all unusual to be evacuated from the building during normal working hours because an anonymous telephone call reported that a bomb had been planted inside the building in retaliation for something said on one of KTVU's programs. This happened so often that soon we stopped taking it seriously.

Popular Music
into the Seventies:
From Rock to Pop to Punk

Henrik Bødker

While the end of the 60s has in many ways been conceived of as a cultural closure it has nonetheless come to stand for much more than simply a change in the 'structure of feeling' and its 'cultural shape.'[1] The transformation of the 60s into the 70s has evolved into a focal point around which divergent views on the space for democratic expressions in a culture of mass production have come to revolve. The various attempts to politicize culture in the 60s gave an additional boost to the continuing discussion on the production, dissemination and consumption of mass-produced cultural commodities, a subject that has dominated much twentieth-century intellectual debate in America, and the 1960s are also 'the sub-text of so many of the current debates.'[2] Many post-sixties histories of popular music are thus invariably interwoven with aspects of 'the politics of the popular.'[3] This is especially evident in the history of rock, the kind of music which during the 60s turned into 'the ubiquitous ingredient of American popular culture.'[4] Whether it still is depends to a large extent on who you ask and what you take the term 'rock' to mean (a subject to which I shall return).

'Like most history, that of rock music has now developed its own narrative pattern, repeated from text to text,' and in this 'story' the fault line between the 60s and the 70s, in one disguise or the other, figures rather prominently.[5] This transformative 'moment' has, indeed, found its own definitive event, the free rock concert in Altamont, California, in December 1969 during which a member of the audience was stabbed to death by Hells Angels, who ironically enough were employed to keep order for the day. This apparently happened while the Rolling Stones were playing 'Sympathy for the Devil;' and the event, in terms of the music, the murder, and the geographical and historical location, has thus proved a gold mine for rock historians in search of appropriate symbolism. Altamont has accordingly been singled out as the 'Waterloo' of the 60s and has come to signify the '*rapid* shift from the ideal to the real' (my emphasis) both in the world of rock and in the (youth) culture at large, two spheres which, looking back, seem to have been virtually synonymous and inseparable.[6] In subsequent interpretations of this rapid shift from the 'ideal' to the 'real,' an unambiguous 'ideal' connection often seems to have been made between rock's capacity for expressing counter-cultural values in the 60s and its aesthetics and authenticity. The 'real' 70s have thus been seen as having eroded not only this 'ideal' connection but also its three components. It is this notion of erosion and dissolution that has turned the 60s into 'a safe haven for cherished ideals,' and it is consequently this perception, particularly as applied to popular music, that I intend to discuss and qualify in this article.[7]

An abundance of quotes, some of which indeed are rather catchy, from both living and dead rock legends, and journalists, have been used to support this notion of a move from 'white light' into virtual darkness, explosion to implosion, authentic to superficial and/or commercial; and the list of hard-edged dichotomies could be extended. The underlying consensus is well known and oft repeated: the apparent explosion of creativity, authenticity and rebelliousness had exhausted itself by the end of the 60s, which consequently meant that all later rock developments (apparently derived from other 'qualities') were destined to be superficial, commercial derivatives. This obviously raises the question of rock's 'original' source: is it black blues or gospel, white folk or country music or (predominantly white) rock 'n' roll? The answer to this is obviously rather complex and will in effect determine at what stage, if at all, one perceives the music to have been severed from this 'authentic' source. This question is constantly addressed within the never-ending discussion as to whether whites can, or should, play the blues.

Leaving aside, for the moment, the question of authenticity, one can safely claim that the 60s have been turned into the 'gilded cradle of rock culture,' accompanied by 'a modern miniature-version of Genesis that tells of the decade where all rock was created.'[8] Later rock users have thus been stuck in a 'post'-world. What Raymond Williams said about the canonization of Modernism applies rather well to the 'wedding' of the 60s and what is often perceived to be 'real,' 'authentic' rock:

'Modernism' is confined to this highly selective field and denied to everything else in the act of pure ideology, whose first, unconscious irony is that, absurdly, it stops history dead. Modernism being the terminus, everything afterwards is counted out of development. It is *after*; stuck in the post.[9]

Sixties rock has in fact been labelled modernist, in contradistinction to which post-sixties rock can be distinguished as post-modernist.[10] With connotations of an alienated modernist artist with a 'protopolitical vocation and terrorist stance' as opposed to a post-modern artist producing cultural texts inescapably enmeshed in the ideology of consumerism and indeterminacy, this division seems to fit in nicely with the perception of the dichotomy outlined above.[11]

And yet it has also been argued, conversely, that popular music *per se*, and especially sixties rock, is post-modern in its eclectic mixture of genres as well as its disregard for conventional cultural distinctions. Much has in fact been said about postmodernism's 'explanatory relationship with regard to pop music,' much of which eventually hinges on divergent ideological approaches to popular and/or mass culture and the concept of postmodernism.[12] On closer examination, however, it proves rather difficult to uphold this (partly chronological) division between modern and postmodern popular music. But even in spite of this, there arguably are certain affinities regarding the various mechanisms underlying the construction of the 'highly selective field[s]' of Modernism and Sixties Rock.

While this does not mean that there is no truth at all to the claim that the 60s were a 'hard act to follow' (something often said about the Rolling Stones), one is not obliged to accept completely the story of the glorious 60s and the atrocious 70s. That I, for one, do not, can partly be explained by the circumstance that my most active and formative years as a user of popular music took place in Europe in the 70s. Although predictions about the global village have partly been proven right, there was, and still is, a certain time lag in the European reception and application of American popular music. For that reason, and since the general 'structure of feeling' was/is different in Europe and in addition not directly affected by the same events in history as that of America, it could be argued that the 60s – as a culturally progressive rock decade – lasted longer in Europe than in the US, where it arguably also continued well into the 70s. European users in the 70s were thus relatively late in letting go of the 'cultural' 60s. This is merely to point out that 'decades' of production do not necessarily coincide with decades of reception and usage. Rather than attempting to date these geographically different decades more precisely, however, I intend to touch upon another relevant aspect of the perceived notion of the end of the 60s as a fall from grace.

That people who actually experienced the sixties in terms of popular music hold up a debased and corrupt present, i.e. the post-sixties world of popular music, against some irretrievable and admirable past is of course only human – we all incline towards nostalgia from time to time. And how could they not if they indeed were 'there' and the 'story' is to be believed ('did the sixties ever happen?' one might ask).[13] What has happened, however, is that many of the people who had their most intensive interactions with popular music during the 60s have found their way into positions from which, with varying degrees of vested interests, they can discuss these matters in public, e.g. from within record companies, magazines, radio and television, and such people have consequently played a key role in the canonization of classical, sixties rock.

But the mechanism behind this perception does not limit itself to the (grand-) fatherly parlance of 'when-I-was-young' in record reviews: it has been, and

168

will continue to be, at work within academic cultural criticism. Matthew Arnold held up stable pre-industrial (feudal) society in contrast to the 'anarchy' arising at his time, i.e. democracy and/or popular culture; this crusade was later joined by F.R. Leavis, who lamented the disappearance of moral values in the face of a continuously growing popular culture, which to him was presumably everything outside *The Great Tradition*. At the same time Richard Hoggart (in *The Uses of Literacy*) was longing for the 'organic' working-class culture of the 30s as opposed to the artificiality of the 50s, while John Crowe Ransom clung desperately to his 'Old South' in his struggle against encroaching industrialism; and these days, new names are constantly added to the list of critics who tend to look back to 'community and unmediated communications.'[14]

But even in light of this to some extent complicating mechanism, it hardly seems possible to discuss the popular music of the 70s without somehow relating it to that of the 60s, which in terms of rock music was after all a highly formative decade. It is obviously impossible completely to escape one's social, geographical and historical location when approaching the cultural shape of a certain period which, in addition, partly will have to be seen in relation to the period that it succeeds. The inherent danger, however, is that you often end up contrasting the incompatible entities of nostalgic memories (even myths) on the one hand with 'facts,' or contemporary 'evidence,' if you like, on the other; and I do recognize the pitfalls involved in turning the mechanism just described above on its head by juxtaposing (nostalgic) memories – my perception of the seventies – with my selective 'construct' of the 60s. I acknowledge that 'all isolated or discrete cultural analysis always involves a buried or repressed theory of historical periodization;'[15] but I am nonetheless convinced that it is possible to steer clear of using periodization as

a rhetorical creation, a way of constructing a historical 'other' that allows us to define a desirable past by contrasting it to a past (or to denigrate the present by contrasting it to a past).[16]

especially since I totally agree with the claim that

[d]eeply imbedded in popular culture and in academic sociology, the nostalgic attitude tends to replace historical analysis with abstract typologies – 'traditional' and "modern" society, gemeinschaft and gesellschaft – that interfere with an imaginative reconstruction of our past or a sober assessment of our prospects.[17]

And since 'the wide-spread use of the term "post-modern" has led to a crisis in the whole notion of historical and artistic periods,' it would seem only natural to take a closer look at some aspects of rock in terms of the contrastive view of the 60s and 70s.[18] What I wish to do is simply to approach the 'great divide' between the 60s and the 70s from a different location (in terms of

169

time, space and academic 'platform') from that which underlies much of the established rock narrative. It is, however, not my aim to overthrow the established ('artistic'?) hierarchy between the two decades, but rather to address, on a somewhat aggregate level, certain underlying structural changes which have informed what might be interpreted merely as 'fluctuations in public taste' or a change of aesthetics.[19] This approach will, I hope, help to explain and moderate the contrastive view in terms other than simply a lack of creativity and authenticity in the rock community of the 70s.

Speaking in decades obviously in itself furthers the mental construct of opposites. I do not completely reject the idea that the (arbitrary) division of time somehow affects our psyche, and thus our production of cultural 'texts,' and that a decade is more than 'just a chronological span but a period measured by its association with particular fads, fashions, crazes, styles or – in a less ephemeral way – a certain spirit or *kulturgeist*.'[20] What we often find interesting in cultural history are events/breaks which we can then invest with our perception of wider structural changes; and it is after all rather difficult to write history as a continuum, although beneath the various rock histories it obviously exists somehow. We are, though, condemned to force both lived experiences and recorded culture into some sort of conceptual system, and here, especially with regard to the writing of cultural history, the division of time into decades comes in rather handy. But since I do not intend to approach the history of rock into the 70s in terms of artists and record releases, which of course can be dated and analysed, but rather in terms of the music's 'respective contexts of use' and usages, I find exact dates somewhat unimportant.[21] Various usages of rock (here seen from the audiences' point of view) obviously do not change overnight; 'similar' usages may occur in different locations with a time lag, and particular usages may exist long after the related music styles have faded from lack of media exposure, and thus be considered 'dead' according to artist- and music-related history. But although a history of the music's contexts of use may differ from more conventional 'text'-oriented history, the two histories obviously correlate and develop in a dialectical pattern; the musical content, to some extent, determines the range of usages of which a particular style can be the centre, and as various usages/practices may generate new musical styles.

My approach is thus tied into the problematic of how rock music produces its 'meaning,' and the separation of 'text' (in a wide sense) and 'context' in this respect is somewhat artificial, since to a large extent they feed into each other. On an overall analytical level, the distinction is, however, possible. Within the 'text,' rock produces its signification through a number of relatively independent signs, 'written, spoken, sung, played, gestured,' which then combine to present the aggregate 'textual' meaning of rock.[22] But as the centre of cultural practices, and I am here thinking specifically of youth and adolescent usages, rock is obviously imbued with contextual 'meaning.' What

170

rock ultimately 'means' will then be the result of a complex interaction between 'text' and context, and this obviously opens up a number of different points of entry from which one can commence one's (hermeneutic) search for 'meaning.' The 'lack' so often associated with the popular music of the 70s has often been located within the 'text' and has thus somehow been perceived perhaps as a lack of 'meaning' altogether. But what so often has been described wholly in terms of qualitative changes within the 'text' can also, at least partly, be explained by shifting relations between 'text' and context and/or general changes in both production and consumption which ultimately had a great impact on the 'production' of meaning for the phenomenon at large.

What to me seems so interesting and alluring about the 60s with regard to popular music – and what is the cause of nostalgia for those who were there, I suspect – is the association of a non-linear, anti-rational, and thus somehow 'revolutionary' consciousness with the profit-driven mechanisms of the 'culture industry.' And it is exactly this 'association' which is interesting, yet so contradictory. A 'political' evaluation of this coalition of commodity and 'revolutionary' values lies outside the scope of this paper, although I do wish to point out that, at least in my view, a 'revolutionary' vision is not necessarily belittled by its association with a cultural commodity. What I here mean by counter-cultural values is a set of notions which run counter to those of the mainstream, especially with regard to personal freedom, work ethics and the importance attributed to a rationality-driven economic progress. I have deliberately used the terms 'association' and 'attachment' since I believe that these values to a large extent were connected to the music through its highly visible usage rather than being inherent in the music's various forms of expression. There were obviously both music and lyrics that could be interpreted as containing more or less explicit counter-cultural (and political) expressions and ideas, and these should not be overlooked. It could be argued, however, that the bulk of the music that helped glue together the various sub-groups making up the 'counter-culture' in the 60s was perceived to be counter-cultural simply because it became the focal point of various youth- and drug-related practices rather than because of the direct expressions of ideas which somehow challenged the political and cultural status quo. This is not to say that the artists themselves were not considered – by the audience, that is – part of the loosely defined 'rock' community in opposition to what was often referred to as the Establishment; how the various artists positioned themselves in this politicization of culture is, of course, another matter. But in the early/mid-60s, it seemed as if rock 'metamorphosed in such a rapid fashion from the popularity of folk music, that a very suspicious person might ask if seemingly safe groups like the Kingston Trio were not, in fact, the Red Guards of the hippie cultural revolution.'[23]

171

Approaching the question of authenticity from the users' point of view, on the other hand, raises somewhat different but related questions; most of us deal with derivatives in the sense that we relate to the various styles of music through their, to some extent mediated, commercial manifestations, which may be more or less 'authentic' with regard to their source. What most of us have in common – both American and European users – is that most of the time 'everything comes to [us] second-hand through television' or via records.[24] In addition, very few of us share the cultural contexts which gave rise to the various expressions (not all of which can, however, be attributed to specific cultural contexts). But does that necessarily make our reception less 'authentic'? Was the cultural chord which resonated within British working-class youths when exposed to the music of the Rolling Stones less authentic because their music was a mediated white middle-class response to black blues? And less authentic than what? Speaking of 'authenticity' we must thus distinguish, I will argue, between that of expression and source on the one hand, and that of reception on the other, two 'levels' of authenticity that are hopefully, but not necessarily linked. This must be kept in mind when discussing the 60s/70s 'dichotomy' in terms of popular music.

In terms of rock as a cultural 'practice,' however, it seems safe to claim (even allowing for the obfuscation of diversity that time produces) that its unifying role, as well as its effectiveness as a bearer of a set of ideas which was a product of a relatively attitudinal consensus among rock users, was at its peak sometime during the latter part of the 60s. Rock continued to function as a common denominator for a variety of divergent communities, but its ability to unite doubtless dwindled gradually as the 60s turned into the 70s. The Beatles, for instance, managed at one stage to be the almost single focal point of the entire international popular music community, something which was later to become increasingly difficult. A number of different but interrelated changes with regard to both production and consumption coalesced to inflate the stratification of the supply of popular music into more or less divergent categories each competing for the honour of being the most visible and vigorous genre.

The loosely defined 'revolutionary' ideology of the 60s, which comes rather close to what is often referred to as 'the ideology of rock,' began to seem less attractive for an increasing number of rock users. The (utopian) sentiment which had characterized many rock gatherings seemed more and more difficult to adhere to as the 'the profusion of money and leisure time ... enjoyed by such groups as teenagers and "lumpen proles"' was increasingly encroached on by the more tangible demands of the surrounding world. And as the age span of the rock audience increased, a new generation of rock users started to air new demands not so easily met by a complacent rock community and/or 'industry' so sure of its 'amplified' sixties formula in which the adjective 'super' had become so central.[25] The generational divide to which the phenomenon at large owed its existence had now moved inside the sphere of rock itself. With the 'extension' of youth, or what also quite aptly has been called 'the deconstruction of youth,' the dichotomy between adolescent/user and parent/non-user became increasingly difficult to uphold. Rock could thus no longer, at least with the same ease, function as a common banner of the discontented.[26]

The overall 'meaning' of rock which during the 60s had partly been the result of a relatively strong consensus among the most visible rock users was thus no longer sustained, not only because the consensus lost its grip among 'old' rock users but also because new audience segments with competing ideas of what rock was (or should be) found their way onto the scene. What has often been perceived as a loss of authentic expression in the music and the artist was therefore arguably just as much a waning 'authentic' belief in the greater role of rock among large parts of the audience, a change that obviously was eventually reflected in the divergent musical expressions that emerged in the course of the 70s; until the advent of punk, perhaps.

What I have just outlined above may sound as if I am of the opinion that 'producers dance [entirely] to the consumers' tune,' but what happens on the demand side is obviously linked to, and to a certain extent caused by, changes on the production and supply side.[27] The only way this development can be observed, however, when looking back, is obviously through an examination of what actually was bought and listened to, and/or what genres were the most visible in the mass media. This does not, of course, present a complete picture of the various and divergent usages of rock that continued beneath the aggregate level of the charts and music magazines. These usages, and spaces, are, however, also influenced by developments in the industry, and it could be argued that the increasingly multifarious and omnipresent entertainment industry was slowly appropriating, or at least encroaching on, these less visible usages as the 60s turned into the 70s. This can partly be explained by the increased professionalization and conglomeration of the industry.

Very determined not to miss out the second time around (having been left behind by small independent companies when rock 'n' roll took off in the 50s), during the 60s the music industry gave the artists on their roster relatively free hands to experiment. This can partly be explained by the fact that the record market had expanded rapidly ever since the advent of the Beatles, who single-handedly boosted overall record sales enormously. Faced with an ever-expanding pie, the record companies were less reluctant to turn away new opportunities and artists which might turn out to be profitable; emphasis was placed more on cashing in on the many new developments, and as long as things went so well there was no need for overall changes. What did change, however, was the set-up of the music industry. Ever since the middle of the 60s an increasing number of both horizontal and vertical mergers had resulted in the almost oligopolistic situation which characterized the market in 1977, when only five companies controlled around '70 per cent of the turnover of the capitalist world market in records and cassettes.'[28]

This development meant a division of labour within the record companies which made it increasingly difficult for the artist to remain in control of the final product, and the prospects for successful communication between the creative and the managerial levels were consequently diminished. Without a relatively homogenous community of users to sustain any overall 'meaning' of rock, mainstream rock seemed more and more left to its own 'industrial' devices, and it began to appear a hollow enterprise with no visible core apart from the remnants of an incorporated sixties ideology lurking behind the scenes. The audience became more and more divided into various segments with no apparent force to imbue the larger phenomenon of rock with any significance. This obviously also had to do with increasingly professional marketing strategies which made it possible to direct various genres more precisely at various audience segments, as well as a more heterogeneous audience, two developments which to some extent go hand in hand. Reduced largely to its 'textual' meaning it was as if meaning itself evaporated, or became reduced to a signification of business relations, or surface.

During the sixties, rock's commercial nature was well hidden by its usage: the inherent capitalism of rock coincided very well with the spreading of hippie wisdom, the counter-culture. But 'because [rock] had no way of linking up to grand mythic dimensions, it (in the 70s) lacked the charge much inferior music had some years earlier.'[29] Whether sixties rock is 'inferior' is, of course, a matter of dispute. But by the second half of the 70s, the rock record's aura as a commodity had diminished to the extent that it was almost stripped bare of its social significance. I realize that the dominant ideology's ability to reproduce itself in various patterns extends beyond the 'surface' meaning attributed to cultural commodities, but as far as the 'power relations' between industry and consumers are concerned with regard to the 'surface' meaning of rock, I think that the divergent industry/consumer relations of the 60s and 70s are rather important.

Having been appropriated by the mainstream, and only able to refer back to previous readings, rock's ability to carry any social significance had been eroded. When the music blended in with the background it lost its gravitational force on elements on the social/attitudinal fringe, and thus its potential as a disruptive sign. When rock as commodity lost its 'aura,' when appropriated by middle-class youngsters who no longer sought confrontation (as was the case with the adolescents of the counter-culture), it lost something to define itself against, since middle-class culture 'simply *is* the overall culture.'[30] Now it actually represented what it had set out to deconstruct, namely bland mainstream pop (although by this time, of course, mainstream mores had arguably been slightly altered).

It would obviously be easy to conclude this brief outline of certain developments in the music business and audience into the 70s by affirming the general perception that artistic authenticity in the 60s gave way to the industrial production of artifice in the 70s. The overall changed 'power relations' between business and audience – from a more homogenous audience facing an expanding and diversified industry to a heterogeneous audience facing an oligopolistic industry – shifted the burden of attributing the music any real (public) significance to the industry, a task that even the best marketing department could not carry out as successfully as various more or less united user communities (assisted by the mass media and the music industry) had been able to in the 60s. There is no doubt, however, that the music kept on 'meaning' something authentic to its users even though these were not in a position to brandish their particular interpretations outside their own communities.

Even though the general perception of rock had changed, I doubt whether the general motivations for playing rock had changed that much from what had driven Bill Haley and his peers to play rock 'n' roll in the 50s and Mick Jagger and his contemporaries in the 60s. What drove people onto the rock scene was probably to be found along a continuum, saturated with star ambitions, ranging from purely economic incentives to a deeply felt urge for self-expression – although the audience, and perhaps even the musicians, of the sixties placed more emphasis on the latter. Although there is no direct link between creativity and authenticity, it could be claimed that a great deal more creativity was needed in the 70s to get the audience to keep consuming music at the growth rate that had characterized the 60s.

The various ways in which different audience groups – divided by age, race, sex, and to some extent politics – made use of rock had, by the mid-seventies, broadened in scope to the extent that generation clashes within the rock world itself broke out into the open. The highbrow/lowbrow division which previously had been enforced on the popular music debate by 'non-users' (elitists) who contrasted popular music to products of 'refined,' elite culture, was now to be employed by genuine rock users at both ends of the age scale. Much of the criticism that had been directed at popular music in general was now, through a differing musical practice, to be turned against mainstream rock in much the same way that the counter-culture had turned these arguments against mainstream pop in the 60s; and the most vital and notable rejection of big-business rock to come of the 70s, was, of course, punk, which could be said to have cut the history of rock in half, or perhaps, turned it upside down, to the extent that the 'relation of past to present [often] is defined, above all, by the contrast between simplicity and sophistication.'[31]

Contrary to popular wisdom, punk did not rise out of a grass-roots context of unemployed anarchistic youths with no apparent future, although it very soon was appropriated by such. It rose, like so many other rock developments, out of a bohemian, art-school context. It was, in fact, a musical expression of a particular (anti-)art philosophy, Situationism, which was rooted in 'the anti-art of Surrealism and Dada' and which 'proposed a "revolution of everyday life" in order to disrupt the everyday life of capitalism.'[32] Although mainly associated with Britain, some disagreement exists as to which side of the Atlantic the genre actually developed. What seems certain, though, is that punk, although it may have looked like a misbegotten animal suddenly set loose, was not conjured up out of the blue. The punk 'approach' had been anticipated, at least musically, in the 'protopunk' of the American garage bands, and in the 'stripped-down sound' of for instance the Who and the 'non-seriousness' of the artifice-celebrating David Bowie.[33] Establishing the precise American/British ratio in punk, however, as was the case with the black/white ratio of rock 'n' roll, is secondary to the significance of the revolt against the complacency of the mid-seventies music industry. And with the transatlantic link of the anti-art radical-cum-manager, Malcolm McClaren, who orchestrated the formation and approach of the Sex Pistols in 1975, punk turned into an allied assault on musical and technical virtuosity, expensive studio productions and big live events, all aspects directly linked to the approach of 'progressive' rock and which had become so entrenched in the music industry.

As severe criticism moved inside the world of rock, the usual roles were reversed: having turned mainstream, the proponents of progressive rock now found themselves in a defensive, rather than offensive, position. Punk music, in the view of the mouthpiece of progressive rock, *Rolling Stone*, had no staying-power in comparison with the music of the Beatles, Bob Dylan and other big sixties names. It was hailed, however, 'because it offered the authentic rock 'n' roll buzz.' But the overall reception of punk did in fact echo many of the outcries that had greeted both jazz and rock 'n' roll.[34] 'Non-music' was the sentence that was passed, and punk was in fact – in its raw simplicity, its 'one chord wonders,' its do-it-yourself approach and its emphasis on live performance – a total negation of the contemporary rock aesthetic according to which rock music should be judged on merits closely connected to expensive studio production.[35] But it was not only musical aesthetics that were challenged – '"actually we're not into music," [said] one of the group [the Sex Pistols] afterwards. "We're into chaos."'[36] By confronting the rigidity of the centralized industry and its products, punk rock reinvigorated many of the elements that had been part of rock from its very beginning. It was in fact 'a unique example of the contradictory relationship of social, cultural, aesthetic and commercial factors to which rock owes its existence.'[37] But whereas the musical 'rebellion' of the 60s was assimilated rather smoothly into a very responsive industry, punk was partly incompatible with the set-up of the music industry in the 70s; this ultimately meant that it was never fully assimilated in its nascent form.

176

But arguing that rock, pop and punk are separable entities – as I tentatively and for the sake of argument set out to do – is in fact rather contentious. None of these broad classifications are, in fact, defined 'positively,' in the sense that to a large extent they are defined by what they are not, i.e. against some 'other(s).' I am not saying that 'the textual specifics of [these] genres are merely redundant' but simply pointing out that these groupings to some extent also are defined by other factors, one of these being their contexts of use.[38] The somewhat loose genre of rock has thus 'come to be understood by its listeners as a single body' much more than being defined in clear musical terms, and it is consequently to a large extent kept together as a genre by its more or less homogenous body of users, and this actually applies to all three categories.[39] In addition to the use, and reuse, of earlier musical developments, these 'genres' consist of a nucleus made up of (shifting) music/performer/audience relations, or perhaps correlations, which centre around various musical practices characterized by a certain level of 'commitment' of, and importance for, the user, and his/her definition of the music in terms of what it is not. This 'encapsulation' is furthermore dependent on the 'overdetermined relations between the music and a variety of other social, cultural, economic, sexual, and discursive practices.'[40] The user will, therefore, constantly have to readjust his/her perception of what constitutes the genre, or *his/her* genre, as both internal and external factors change; but whereas outsiders may have difficulty in determining what belongs and what does not, the committed user will always be able to tell. As a modification to this, it could be argued, however, that users of rock, and especially those with some sort of roots in the 60s, have never had any difficulty in defining music as pop, a description normally applied to popular music that they do not listen to.

But if the boundaries of these categories in terms of musical expression and contexts of use are somewhat unstable, their relations to 'the politics of the popular' are even more so. Linking sixties rock with mass cultural democracy (perhaps even revolution), seventies pop with mainstream hegemony, and punk with (futile) working-class rebellion/anarchy would be far too simplistic. The cultural power of popular music comes to a large extent from its contextual usages, and the visibility and character of these are obviously dependent on the users' shifting needs and ability to use popular culture as a means of communication. The importance attributed to the 60s in this respect can partly be explained by the fact that so many white middle-class adolescents had not only the urge, but also the leisure time and spending power to make rock into a highly visible aggregate sign. However, this was a practice that many smaller groups and minorities had been, and continue to be, engaged in, but because of a lack of both numbers and money they have never really attracted the interest of the music industry and/or the media. These groups have therefore never been able to imprint their divergent interpretations on the larger phenomenon of rock to the same extent that affluent white middle-class adolescents were able to in the 60s. '[C]apitalism still marks the boundary within which social and political goals are pursued,' and this has certainly always been the case for the politicization of popular music. 'This is surely one of the continuities between the 60s and the 70s.'[41]

Notes

1. The term 'the structure of feeling' is Raymond Williams's; 'cultural shape' is from Stanley Cohen, *Folk Devils and Moral Panic* (Oxford: Oxford University Press, 1972), 10.
2. Douglas Tallack, *Twentieth-Century America: The Intellectual and Cultural Context* (London: Longman, 1991), 331.
3. John Storey uses 'The Politics of the Popular' as the title of the last chapter of his *An Introductory Guide to Cultural Theory and Popular Culture* (Hemel Hempstead: Harvester Wheatsheaf, 1993), 181.
4. Robert Pattison, *The Triumph of Vulgarity: Rock Music in the Mirror of Romanticism* (Oxford: Oxford University Press, 1987), 12.
5. E. Ann Kaplan, *Rocking Around the Clock: Music Television, Postmodernism, and Consumer Culture* (New York: Methuen, 1987), 9.
6. Camille Paglia, *Sex, Art and American Culture* (New York: Basic Books, 1992), 212.
7. Grant McCracken, *Culture & Consumption* (Bloomington: Indiana University Press, 1988), 106.
8. Per Juul Carlsen, 'Rock 'n' Roll Forever,' in Niels Frid-Nielsen and Ole Lindboe (eds), *Medieeksplosionen* (Copenhagen: Gyldendal, 1992), 68, (my translation from Danish).
9. Raymond Williams, *The Politics of Modernism: Against the New Conformists* (London: Verso, 1989), 34-35.
10. This distinction is argued by Fredric Jameson in 'Postmodernism, or the cultural logic of late capitalism' in *New Left Review*, 146, (1984), 54.
11. Fredric Jameson in the foreword to Jean-François Lyotard, *The Postmodern Condition: A Report on Knowledge* (Minneapolis: University of Minnesota Press, 1993), xviii.
12. Storey, 173.
13. Gerald Howard (ed), *The Sixties: Art, Politics and Media of our Most Explosive Decade* (New York: Paragon House, 1982), 9.
14. Tallack, 321.
15. Fredric Jameson, *Postmodernism, or, the Cultural Logic of Late Capitalism* (Durham: Duke University Press, 1991), 3.
16. Michael Gorden (ed), *Johns Hopkins Guide to Literary Theory and Criticism* (Baltimore: Johns Hopkins University Press, 1994), 587.
17. Christopher Lasch, *The True and Only Heaven* (New York: W.W. Norton, 1991), 14.
18. Gorden, 587.
19. Lasch, 110.
20. Cohen, 10.
21. Peter Wicke, *Rock Music: Culture, aesthetics and sociology* (Cambridge: Cambridge University Press, 1990), 74.
22. Dave Laing, *One Chord Wonders: Power and Meaning in Punk Rock* (Milton Keynes: Open University Press, 1985), ix.
23. Warren Hinkle, 'A Social History of the Hippies,' in Howard, 221.

24. Paglia, 214.
25. Howard, 15.
26. Lawrence Grossberg, 'Is there Rock after Punk?' in Simon Frith and Andrew Goodwin (eds), *On Record: Rock, Pop & the Written Word* (London: Routledge, 1990), 118.
27. Paul Wannacott and Ronald Wannacott, *Economics* (Tokyo: McGraw-Hill, 1982), 445.
28. Wicke, 118.
29. Ray Cocks, 'Rock Hits the Hard Place,' *Time*, February 15, 1982, 79.
30. Stuart Hall and Tony Jefferson (eds), *Resistance through Rituals: Youth subcultures in post-war Britain* (London: Hutchinson & Co, 1976), 62.
31. Lasch, 241.
32. Laing, 126.
33. Laing, 22-24.
34. Simon Frith, *Sound Effects: Youth, Leisure and the Politics of Rock 'n' Roll* (London: Constable & Co, 1983), 176.
35. The main title of Dave Laing's *One Chord Wonders: Power and Meaning in Punk Rock.*
36. Jim Miller (ed), *The Rolling Stone Illustrated History of Rock & Roll* (New York: Random House/Rolling Stone Press, 1976), 89.
37. Wicke, 138.
38. Andrew Goodwin, 'Popular Music and Postmodern Theory,' in John Storey (ed), *Cultural Theory and Popular Culture* (Hemel Hempstead: Harvester Wheatsheaf, 1994), 415.
39. Pattison, x.
40. Pattison, 115.
41. Richard Crockatt as quoted in Tallack, 316-17.

Images of the Past, Present and Future: Hollywood Portraits of Bicentennial America

Elsebeth Hurup

Time past and time future
What might have been and what has been
Point to one end, which is always present.

T.S. Eliot (1935)[1]

The past and the future are functions of the present. Each generation has its private history, its own peculiar brand of prophecy. What it shall think about past and future is determined by its own immediate problems. It will go to the past for instruction, for sympathy, for justification, for flattery. It will look into the future for compensation for the present – into the past, too. For even the past can become a compensatory Utopia, indistinguishable from the earthly paradises of the future, except by the fact that the heroes have historical names and flourished between known dates. From age to age the past is re-created.... Anywhere, anywhere out of the world. We make our exit, forward or backward, by time-machine.

Aldous Huxley (1935)[2]

A narrative set in the past or the future will always say as much, if not more, about the present than the period it ostensibly portrays. For example, Westerns of any given period, though nominally set in the 19th century, have reflected concerns, issues and beliefs that were prevalent or in a state of conflict at the time of their production. John Ford's celebration of a mythic Wyatt Earp who cleans up the town of Tombstone to make it a fit place for decent folks in *My Darling Clementine* (1946) coincides with America's perception of its historic role, just then re-confirmed in World War Two. The Cold War Western may present Indians as stand-ins for the contemporary enemy, the communists, as in *Rio Grande* (1950). At the same time, fervid anti-communist witch-hunts give rise to doubts as to the virtues of the civilization supplanting the wilderness in films such as *High Noon* (1952). Under the impact of the Civil Rights movement, Indians are seen as victims of white brutality: *Soldier Blue* and *Little Big Man*, both 1970, mark the point of no return for the treatment of Native Americans on the silver screen. As evidenced by the popularity of *Dances with Wolves* (1990), we now prefer to daydream about their way of life as an appealing alternative to the alienation and rootlessness of white civilization.

Likewise, futuristic fantasies of the fifties are concerned with the threat of communism in the guise of infiltration from outer space (*Invasion of the Body Snatchers*, 1956) or with the atomic bomb (*On the Beach*, 1959). Man's increasing dependence on machines is ominously reflected in the sixties in the shape of the murderous computer HAL 9000 in *2001: A Space Odyssey* (1968). In the seventies, before *Star Wars* (1977) ushered in the 'feel good' space opera, the dominant view of the future parallels contemporary fears of nuclear annihilation, pollution, overpopulation and depletion of natural resources. The dystopian visions unanimously exclude democratic government, with violent anarchy or totalitarian rule as the sinister alternatives, as in *THX-1138* (1971), *Soylent Green* (1973) and *Rollerball* (1975).

Just as the present is superimposed on Hollywood's representations of the past and the future, the past is reflected and, sometimes, the future is anticipated in films set in the present. The theme itself may be the passage of time (*Save the Tiger* and *Summer Wishes, Winter Dreams*, both 1973); old genre conventions may appear in new combinations (*Silver Streak* and *Taxi Driver*, both 1976); old stories may be updated (*King Kong* 1933/1976; *A Star Is Born* 1937/1954/1976); well-known actors may continue to do what they have always done or add new facets to their screen personas, and future stars may make their debuts in films that initiate new trends.

At first glance, *The Shootist* (Don Siegel), *The Outlaw Josey Wales* (Clint Eastwood), *Taxi Driver* (Martin Scorsese), *Rocky* (John Avildsen) and *Logan's Run* (Michael Anderson) do not have much in common, except that all the titles refer to individuals. Two are Westerns, set at either end of the traditional time frame for the genre (Civil War to turn of the century); two are present-day stories, and one is set in 2274. However, they were all released in 1976, and, in combination, they provide an outline of many of the issues occupying the nation at this particular juncture. Not coincidentally, their protagonists are all outsiders and misfits struggling to regain a foothold in a complex world. In 1976 America was in the midst of an identity crisis, seeking to come to terms with changes and transformations that had taken place over the previous decade. The status attained in World War Two as the proud leader of the free world had been badly tarnished in the debacle of Vietnam; with assassinations, civil unrest, political scandals and a troubled economy on the homefront, Americans were forced to re-evaluate their self-image as the most virtuous and blessed people on earth.

Taking advantage of film's capacity to serve as a time-machine, the following will use the five films as stopovers on a tour of the past, present and future as depicted by Hollywood in the Bicentennial year. The films chosen reflect a sense of endings and new beginnings that was felt in the nation at large. These beginnings, however, do not so much constitute a new approach to the problems of the day as they explicitly or implicitly signal a yearning to restore lost values, which perhaps most clearly – and paradoxically – is demonstrated in the futuristic *Logan's Run*.

The Last Western: *The Shootist*

His name was J.B. Books and he had a matched pair of .45s with ivory grips and something to behold. But he wasn't an outlaw. Fact is, for a while he was a lawman. Long before I met Mr. Books, he was a famous man. I guess his fame was why somebody was always after him. The wild country had taught him to survive. He lived his life and herded by himself. He had a credo that went, 'I won't be lied to and I won't be laid a hand on; I don't do these things to other people and I require the same from them.'

From the opening sequence of *The Shootist*

22 January 1901. John Bernard Books (John Wayne), aging and ailing gunfighter of nationwide fame, rides into Carson City, Nevada, where his old friend, Dr. Hostetler (Jimmy Stewart) confirms a diagnosis of terminal cancer. With less than two months left he takes up lodgings at the boardinghouse of widow Bond Rogers (Lauren Bacall) and her teenage son Gillom (Ron Howard). As the rumor of Books' presence and his impending demise spreads, Books has to deal with a variety of people trying to capitalize on his death: gunmen who attempt to assassinate him to acquire fame; his former love and a newspaperman hoping to cash in on writing colorful accounts of his life; an undertaker (John Carradine) planning to exhibit Book's corpse; a barber, who sees good money prospects in selling samples of Books' hair as souvenirs; and above all, the blustering marshall Thibido (Harry Morgan) who, concerned with progress and taxpayers' money, just can't wait to see Books dead. The initially hostile Mrs. Rogers takes a liking to him, and he manages to temper her son's youthful infatuation with machismo. Taking his cue from Dr. Hostetler, who warns him that his condition will ultimately become extremely painful, Books stages a showdown at a saloon with three villainous types, preferring to die in style, with his dignity intact. Having killed his opponents, Books is shot in the back by the bartender, who in turn is killed by Gillom. Before dying, Books nods with approval as Gillom tosses the gun across the room.

The Shootist may be considered a revisionist Western, most notably expressed in its disillusioned stance toward the virtues of civilization and the fact that the hero is dying of cancer, but more importantly, it is an elegiac tribute to its aging star and the past glories of the genre. The lamentation for the passing of the Old West is simultaneously a lamentation for the passing of

Old Hollywood in general – personified by Wayne as well as Bacall, Stewart and Carradine – and for the passing of the Western in particular. This is made explicit in the four sequences that open the film.

A traditional panoramic view of the archetypal Western Landscape in which the equally archetypal Man on Horseback materializes, is followed by a flashback sequence which fuses the real-life legend of John Wayne with that of the fictitious John Books: a montage of black-and-white footage from old Wayne Westerns presented by a voice-over (by Ron Howard) as the personal history of Books.[3] The next sequence returns to the Great Outdoors where Wayne/Books expertly, if a bit less adroitly than in his prime, disposes of a would-be robber. Finally the film cuts to the first glimpse of Carson City: a pole with telephone wires next to an undertaker's sign, introducing the twin themes of progress and endings. The camera then pulls back to reveal ornate Victorian houses lining a bustling street complete with a horse-drawn trolley. In this environment (which, above all, is characterized by restricted space) J.B. Books, 'the most celebrated shootist extant,' a man, whose 'church has been the mountains and solitude,' is going to spend the remaining days of his life.

The American experience may be said to be a series of moments when innocence is perceived to be lost, although one may ask, like Arthur Schlesinger, 'How many times can a nation lose its innocence?'[4] Be that as it may, if optimism since the decline of orthodox Puritanism had become 'the chief effective religion,' as Leslie Fiedler stated in the sixties, by 1976 that religion also looked to be on the verge of extinction, as the events of the previous decade had led to yet another loss of innocence.[5] The transition from (mythic) frontier individualism with a code of honor to urban, materialistic middle-class conformity as it is portrayed in *The Shootist* was mirrored by America's transition from self-assured and admired economic, political and military leader of the world to a nation riddled with domestic problems and a tarnished international reputation three-quarters of a century later. By 1976, the larger-than-life hero, in Hollywood and elsewhere, had become an anachronism. The legendary movie-star of the Big Studio days was aging and lesser breeds had taken his place: antiheroes had begun dominating the screen in the sixties, as time-honored traditions and revered institutions, one by one, were questioned, examined and ultimately discarded. Politicians had, seemingly without exception, become villains; and with the defeat in Vietnam, not even the war hero could be counted on to provide a model worth emulating. America, crime-ridden, with pockets of poverty throughout the land, dependent on foreign energy supplies to keep its multitude of machines and technologically advanced gadgets going, was not quite the picture-perfect civilization that the nation had aspired to on its westward course of empire.

It is in this context that the disillusionment of *The Shootist* is to be seen. Throughout the film there are numerous verbal as well as visual references to the advanced technological and industrial state of civilization – doorbells, bathrooms with running water, telephones, electric fans, a creamery delivery service, overnight dry cleaning service, cars. The saloon, appropriately named 'The Metropole,' is a huge, elegant affair with plush furniture and a well-dressed, orderly clientele: a far cry from the rowdy, rustic atmosphere of the stereotypical frontier saloon. Books rides to his final showdown on the trolley and is informed by the driver that there is a time schedule to be kept.

Marshall Thibido's praise of the accomplishments and continuing progress of his city is understandable, but with the hindsight of 1976 it serves to emphasize the gap between the centuries-old dream of perfection in the New World and the reality of the twentieth century. Benjamin Franklin once expressed his desire to experience the future:

> I have sometimes almost wished it had been my destiny to be born two or three centuries hence. For invention and improvement are prolific, and beget more of their kind. The present progress is rapid. Many of great importance, now unthought of, will before that period be produced; ... if the art of physic shall be improved in proportion with other arts, we may then be able to avoid diseases, and live as long as the patriarchs in Genesis; to which I suppose we should make little objection.[6]

Compare with this Marshall Thibido's gleeful dismissal of the primitive past:

> Books, this is nineteen-nought-one. The old days are gone and you don't know it. We've got a waterworks, telephones and lights and we'll have our streetcar electrified by next year and we've started to pave the streets. Oh, we've still got some weedin' to do but once we're rid of people like you we'll have a goddamn Garden of Eden here. To put it in a nutshell, you've plain plum outlived your time.

Books has indeed outlived his time, but the very stature of the man, in physical deportment as well as character, in comparison to the diminutive marshall and his insulting braggadocio ('what I'll do on your grave won't pass for flowers'), leaves no doubt that the exchange is not a happy one. We are also given to understand that although Books' fame rests on the somewhat dubious accomplishment of his having killed thirty men, not one of them did not deserve his fate. Thus Books has done his part in making the West safe for civilization – which has freed Thibido from any obligation to engage in combat in the line of duty as well. And the behavior exhibited by most of the upright denizens of Carson City underscores the irony in Thibido's proclamation of a 'goddamn Garden of Eden.'

The ambivalence toward the blessings of civilization and the equally ambivalent attitude toward the wilderness that characterize American cultural history were in the Western resolved through the mediating hero, who, while maintaining his individualism – and thereby associating himself with the wilderness – lent a budding civilization a helping hand, whereupon he returned to nowhere in particular at film's end. The question of whether cleaning up the town was actually worth his while did not seriously arise until the beginning of the fifties. In both *The Gunfighter* (1950) and *High Noon* (1952) space is severely restricted, and both are structured according to the ticking away of time (*High Noon* with the added distinction that the film's time equals real time). In both, the threat is perceived to be coming from the outside, in the shape of villains approaching town, but it soon becomes apparent that these villains are only stand-ins for the *real* peril: the complacency and cowardice of the townspeople who are shown to be unworthy of the hero.[7]

This is taken a step further in *The Shootist,* in which the enemy/villain has become wholly internalized, i.e. the cancer eating away at Books' dignity and strength. As the town itself, with its advanced state of civilization and its inhabitants determinedly turning away from the virtues of simplicity and moderation so that they fall somewhat short of the idealized citizens of the classic Western, Books' illness comes to stand for the pettiness and material-ism of citified life as opposed to the supposedly higher moral stature gained in the wilderness, and Thomas Jefferson's remarks in *Notes on the State of Virginia* come to mind: 'It is the manners and spirit of a people which preserve a republic in vigor. A degeneracy in these is a canker which soon eats to the heart of its laws and constitution.'[8] The day-by-day account of Books' final week is thus in a very real sense a count-down of the last days of the Old West and with it (as Turner would heartily agree) those characteristics that have made America unique among nations.

The passing of this glorious era in American history is tied to that of the Victorian Age. On arrival in Carson City, Books buys a newspaper announcing the death of Queen Victoria. During the following week he reads the entire newspaper: he wants to know everything that happened on January 22 1901, 'an important day in my life.' Books' epitaph for 'old Queen Vic' is also his own: 'Maybe she outlived her time, maybe she was a museum piece. But she never lost her dignity, she never sold her guns. She hung on to her pride and she went out in style. Now there's a kind of old gal I'd like to meet.'

Not only does Books embody the mythic qualities of the West, his personal history is linked to the western expansion in general: in the year of his birth, 1843, John Charles Frémont and Kit Carson (for whom Carson City was named) set out on the expedition along the Oregon and California Trails that came to mark the final opening of the West.[9] By the time of Books' death, American territorial expansion, except for a few minor acquisitions, was completed. In less than a century, from the Louisiana purchase in 1803, American territory had more than quadrupled and had expanded beyond the continent.

At this particular juncture, a fictional compensation for the loss of the Old West was already underway, laying the foundation for John Wayne's unique position in American cultural history in the twentieth century. In the foreword to his novel *The Virginian: A Horseman of the Plains* from 1902, Owen Wister was sad to note how rapidly the horseman had vanished:

He rides in his historic yesterday.... And yet [he] is so near our day that in some chapters of this book, which were published separately at the close of the nineteenth century, the present tense was used. It is true no longer.... Time has flowed faster than my ink.

He continued, 'a transition has followed the horseman of the plains; a shapeless state, a condition of men and manners unlovely as that bald moment in the year when winter is gone and spring not come, and the face of Nature is ugly.' What he could not have known was that technological developments would soon help revive this 'last romantic figure upon our soil' and, largely recreated according to Wister's specifications, he would ride again and again throughout the twentieth century. In 1903, only a year after the publication of *The Virginian*, Americans saw the thrill of Edwin S. Porter's *The Great Train Robbery*, popularly known as the first Western (all eleven minutes of it).[10] Another four years and Marion Robert Morrison was born; under the somewhat less unwieldy (and more manly) name of John Wayne he would come to be seen as an authentic representative of the Old West, despite the fact that he had never, so to speak, set foot in it.[11]

Like a Möbius strip, *The Shootist* takes us backward and forward in time. The passing of the Old West implicitly involves a contemplation of America's mythic golden age before the onset of full-blown civilization. Similarly, the passing of the Classic Western implicitly and explicitly involves Wayne's illustrious career, which spans more than four decades.

Wayne was a staunch defender of conservative politics, stemming from a deep-felt belief in the values of frontier America. From his breakthrough as the Ringo Kid in *Stagecoach* in 1939 till his death (of cancer) in 1979, he became a national institution who eventually made redundant efforts at distinguishing between the man and the characters he portrayed.[12] John Wayne was John Wayne was John Wayne. As Roger Ebert aptly put it: 'John Wayne grew, role by role, into the most mythic presence in American movies.... Wayne was up there on the screen, squinting into the sun, making decisions, ready for action. For my generation, while presidents came and went, John Wayne merely grew a little more thoughtful.'[13] When, in 1964, he had successfully battled cancer ('I licked the big C,' as he said), the very idea of John Wayne being ill was, according to Joan Didion, disturbing: 'when John Wayne rode through my childhood, and perhaps through yours, he determined forever the shape of certain of our dreams. It did not seem possible that such a man could fall ill, could carry within him that most inexplicable and ungovernable of diseases. The rumor struck some obscure anxiety, threw our very childhoods into question. In John Wayne's world, John Wayne was supposed to give the orders.'[14] It was therefore fitting that in *The Shootist* he played a dying man who decided to call the shots himself, to die in action rather than to suffer a slow and increasingly painful deterioration of body and spirit.[15]

No one, except perhaps Wayne himself, knew at the time that this was to be his last film. As such it serves as a fitting obituary for the man – and the genre: Pauline Kael was only slightly premature when in 1974 she pronounced the Western dead.[16] In fact, eight Westerns (out of 14 new productions) plus the reissued spoof *Blazing Saddles* from 1974 made it into *Variety's* chart for 1976, and it looked for a short while as if the genre was staging a comeback. But by 1977 Kael was proven right; during the Western's golden age, the mid-fifties, the genre constituted an entire fifth of Hollywood's output. In 1977 the figure was down to two per cent (from nine per cent the previous year) and on average Westerns have made up a mere one per cent in the period 1977-1993, the lowest figure since 1939 when John Wayne became a star. It is hard to escape the thought that the Western indeed is so bound up with his persona that when he died, the genre died, too.[17]

And yet, Wayne did have an heir. The most popular of the Westerns to come out in 1976 was directed by the only actor who could seriously be considered the new Wayne, Clint Eastwood.[18] Interestingly, almost appropriately, *The Outlaw Josey Wales* is, despite the violence and mayhem liberally distributed throughout the film, a story of reconciliation and new beginnings.

The Old West Revived: *The Outlaw Josey Wales*

I suppose that mangy, red-bone hound's got no place to go either. He might as well ride along with us. Everybody else is.

I guess we all died a little in that damn war.

Clint Eastwood as Josey Wales

The family of Missouri farmer Josey Wales (Clint Eastwood) are murdered by 'Redlegs,' a band of Union marauders led by Captain Terrill (Bill McKinney), and Josey joins a band of renegade Confederates pursuing the Redlegs. The Civil War ended, Josey alone declines the invitation to surrender and witnesses from a distance the cold-blooded massacre of his disarmed friends as they are pledging their loyalty to the Union. Single-handedly Josey attacks the army camp, guns down numerous soldiers and rescues the wounded Jamie, who later dies. Fletcher (John Vernon), who unwittingly led his Confederate band into the trap, is ordered to help Terrill track down Josey. As he consistently dodges attempts to capture him, by bounty hunters and the official search party alike, Josey's reputation grows. Along the way he becomes the somewhat unwilling leader and protector of an ever-expanding assortment of strays: Lone Watie, an old Cherokee (Chief Dan George); Little Moonlight, a young Navajo girl; Grandma Sarah (Paula Trueman) and her granddaughter Laura Lee (Sondra Locke), the survivors of a Kansan pioneer family taken prisoners by a band of *comancheros*; Chato, an old Mexican; Travis, an unemployed cowboy; and – a dog. Having settled on a piece of land in Texas, the little community is threatened by Comanches, but Josey successfully negotiates a truce with the

Indians. When Terrill and Fletcher finally catch up with him, Josey kills Terrill, and Fletcher decides to end the war by deliberately not recognizing Josey. He can now return to farming, together with Laura Lee and the extended family he has garnered on his quest for justice.

With *The Outlaw Josey Wales* we return from the confined spaces of an urbanized West in *The Shootist* to the West of the Great Outdoors. We also return from the end of the West to its beginning, to the period when the western expansion entered its most vigorous phase. Simultaneously traditional and revisionist, epic and realistic, and with a hero both larger than life and human, *Josey Wales* incongruously but successfully fuses the progressive, manifest destinarian ideology of the Classic Western with the stylized nihilism of Sergio Leone's so-called *Dollars* trilogy (1964-1967), which launched Eastwood as the foremost revisionist Western Hero.[19] As the laconic Man With No Name, Eastwood plays a cynical loner, concerned only with his own survival in a depraved world, a violent antihero who is not overly observant of the Code of the West which demands waiting for the opponent to draw first.[20]

These traits are also found in Josey Wales, but it is made perfectly clear *why* he acts the way he does. His actions are conditioned by circumstances: they are not reflections of his character, as witness his grief at the graves of his family; his dejected comment to Lone Watie, 'When I get to liking someone, they ain't around long;' and the tender romance with Laura Lee that almost makes him forget his mission.[21] He may be labelled an outlaw, but in the context of a U.S. Senator giving the orders to massacre surrendering Confederates, the designation is at best meaningless. Although Josey's trail is abundantly littered with corpses, the only violent confrontation he is actively seeking – to revenge his family – keeps eluding him. Instead, with exasperating regularity he finds himself in situations that can only be solved by the gun. Still, toward the end, he negotiates a truce with Comanches threatening his newfound 'family.' Moreover, the violence is undercut by the comic interludes featuring Lone Watie, who serves as the traditional sidekick to the hero, and Grandma Sarah's equally comical no-nonsense approach to everyone around her, including Josey. There is considerable irony in the fact that the loner is never given the opportunity to be left alone, and that the violent avenger winds up as the head of a movement of reconciliation.

In a sense, *Josey Wales* is a road movie on horseback. The roots of the genre, popular since the sixties, can be traced back to Mark Twain's *The Adventures of Huckleberry Finn*, with the journey down the Mississippi as a metaphor for Huck's inner journey toward insight and maturity. In *Easy Rider* (1969), the two protagonists set out 'to find America' but are killed in the process, a fate that also befalls the outlaw heroes *Bonnie and Clyde* (1967). This disillusionment is reversed in Josey Wales' odyssey, which leads to redemption as he rediscovers his true self as a farmer and member of a community.

Lone Watie, his function as sidekick notwithstanding, is portrayed with dignity and respect; the fact that he lost his wife and children on the Trail of Tears is duly noted but not melodramatically belabored. For this reason his wry observations of the relationship between whites and Cherokees are so much more poignant: 'They call us the civilized tribe. They call us civilized because we are easy to sneak up on. The white man has been sneaking up on us for years.' Lone Watie himself is unable to sneak up on Josey, no matter how hard he tries. His comment that it 'seems like we can't trust the white man' is amply borne out throughout the story, with the twist that white men cannot trust each other either. The majority of the whites are portrayed as vain, prejudiced, and opportunistic or dull-witted, brutal or greedy. (Even Grandma is equipped with a set of prejudices: she doesn't much care for anybody not from her home-state of Kansas, but in due course she rids herself of these notions.) In essence, the justification for Josey's acts of violence is not far removed from those of the traditional town tamer. Instead of cleaning up the town, Josey seems to be cleaning up the entire country.

That is not to say that Indians generally are shown to be innocent and noble alternatives to white civilization. The Navajo girl was captured by the Cheyennes and raped by an Arapaho. The only reason Laura Lee is spared from rape by the *comancheros* is that she is to be sold off to Cheyenne chief Black Kettle, who wants undamaged goods.[22] Faced with an imminent Comanche attack, Josey has to instruct his friends in the tactics of warfare, with Grandma telling Lone Watie 'We'll show these redskins ... no offense,' to which he replies, 'None taken.' This exchange is comically reversed when the little community comes under attack from Terrill's band. As the Indian attack never materializes, Josey's instructions ironically come in handy in the defense against *whites*.

Comanche chief Ten Bears is a reasonable man, on the warpath only because he is tired of the white man's broken promises. In the meeting between him and Josey, the film's reconciliatory and ultimately anti-violent message is articulated, with the Civil War and the Indian Wars standing in for issues of a post-sixties America, complete with distrust of government, countercultural notions of living in harmony with the land, and, in Richard Slotkin's words, 'the concepts of mutual deterrence and détente ... so prominent in the diplomacy of 1973-77':[23]

Josey – I came here to die with you – or live with you. Dyin' ain't so hard for men such as you and me. It's livin' that's hard. When all you've cared about has been butchered or raped. Governments don't live together. *People* live together. With governments you don't always get a fair word or a fair fight. Well, I've come here to give either one – or get either one from you. I came here like this so you'll know that my word of death is true and my word of life is then true. The bear lives here, the wolf, the antelope, the

Comanche. And so will we. Now, we'll only hunt what we need to live on, same as the Comanche.... The sign of the Comanche, that will be on our lodge. That's my word of life.

Ten Bears – And your word of death?

Josey – It's here in my pistols, there in your rifles. I'm here for either one. I'm just givin' you life and you're givin' me life. And I'm sayin' that men can live together without butcherin' one another.

Ten Bears – It's sad that governments are chieved by the double-tongues. There is iron in your words of death for all Comanches to see. And so there is iron in your words of life. No signed paper can hold the iron. It must come from men. The words of Ten Bears carries the same iron of life and death. It's good that warriors such as we meet in the struggle of life or death. It shall be life.

The End of the West theme that came to dominate the genre as the sixties wore on, played out in varying shades of the blues from Peckinpah's bloody *The Wild Bunch* and Hill's tragi-comical *Butch Cassidy and the Sundance Kid* (both 1969) to Siegel's elegiac *The Shootist*, is reversed in *Josey Wales*. The West is once again seen as a viable location for a new beginning, and the discredited Turnerian thesis of the West as the cradle of American democracy is given a new lease on life. But whereas Turner's West – and the Classic Western – was Anglo-American and male-dominated, though in actual fact it was a veritable cultural cross-roads, Eastwood, on the other hand, portrays a multicultural community in which Anglos, Indians and Mexicans, Southerners and Yankees, old and young, men and women, are equals, working together toward a common goal.[24] In particular, the women are not reduced to just playing damsels in distress. True, Josey saves the three women from dire situations, but in the end they contribute to saving him – from Terrill's hunting party as well as from a future as a drifter. The superhuman hero would not have survived had it not been for Grandma Sarah's determination, Laura Lee's skills in handling a gun and the efforts of the other members of his band of outcasts. Included in the new community are also the three remaining residents of what used to be a thriving mining town: a bartender, a gambler and a dancehall girl.

From the ashes of a war-torn nation (past and present), whose ideals and ambitions have been laid waste by war and internal strife, a new America will rise. There is a place for everyone, including the Lone Hero, who, traditionally, is supposed to ride off once the community's prospects of survival and a golden future are secured. But just as Josey Wales did not ride out of nowhere, the way Shane and numerous other Western Heroes have made their entry, he does not disappear to nowhere after his redemptive task has been performed. The last frame does show him riding into the sunset, but this is the final twist in the film's play on the conventions: he is riding *toward*, not *away from* the farm that will be his future home. Thus, the film suggests that it *is* possible to go home again and that the process of healing necessitates involvement by all, including Lone Heroes.

In his earlier Westerns Eastwood had shattered the Code of the West and the image of the traditional Western Hero so effectively that in *Josey Wales* some critics were unable to see beyond what they considered the formulaic Eastwood violence. A typical example was *Variety's* review of the film: 'It is nothing more than a prairie 'Death Wish' in which the protagonist soon emerges more psychotic than wronged, despite the over-loaded backdrop of Civil War antagonisms, Indian repression and other cardboard excuses shoehorned into the script.'[25] Another review attempted a definition of the appeal of John Wayne as opposed to Clint Eastwood:

> What is attractive about a male figure who carries no genuine authority? ... Think about it. Say John Wayne tells you to wipe your feet before you enter the saloon. Maybe you don't want to wipe your feet, but there must be a good reason for it or John Wayne wouldn't tell you to do it. John Wayne might beat you up if you don't.... But mostly he wants you to, and you want to please him. John Wayne is tough, but he's fair, and what the hell, maybe he reminds you of your father. So you wipe your feet. Even though you've subordinated yourself, you're comfortable, for John Wayne's authority is earned authority. But if Clint Eastwood tells you to wipe your feet, you sullenly wipe your feet because you know that if you don't, he'll kill you. Eastwood has never earned the right nor the respect to tell you what to do. He just has a gun.[26]

Yet if we compare the characters of Josey Wales with that of another Confederate soldier who refused to surrender, Ethan Edwards (John Wayne) in Ford's *The Searchers* (1956), it is Ethan who comes out as a near psychotic, so obsessed with his hatred for the Indians, who have kidnapped his niece, that he spends seven years searching for her with the intention of killing her if he finds her. At the crucial point, his resolution falters, but having brought her back to civilization, Ethan wanders off alone, unable to fit into the community. There is no redemption for him, he is forever destined to 'wander between the winds.' In *Josey Wales* Eastwood softens his screen persona into a more humane and sociable character. Thus, with *The Shootist* and *Josey Wales*, Wayne and Eastwood seem to have switched roles, although this point eluded John Lenihan when he compared the two:

> Wayne's victory usually spelled some hope for the preservation of traditional frontier values, in spite of the certain, undesirable accompaniment to civilization. Eastwood's Westerns became every bit as despairing as the tragic variety with respect to their vision of an irreparably depraved social order. He may avenge, punish, or merely survive, but without the assurance that his triumph is socially meaningful.[27]

Wayne's victory in *The Shootist* is at best ambiguous, not only because he dies, but mainly because the civilization supplanting the frontier is shown to be tainted. Conversely, Eastwood's triumph as Josey Wales does not so much consist in the fact that he rids the world of a number of unsavory characters than in his acceptance of his socially meaningful role as member of a pluralistic community founded on respect, even love. Eastwood himself has in recent years become respected as a filmmaker and is now viewed as the Grand Old Man of American film, particularly since the popular and critical success of his *Unforgiven* (1992).[28] As for the Western, it has seemingly become the American equivalent of *Hamlet*, the performance that stars aspire to at least once in their career.

The Culmination of the Sixties Film: *Taxi Driver*

> ... here is a man who would not take it anymore.... Here is a man who stood up against the scum, the cunts, the dopes, the filth, the shit. Here is someone who stood up.

> Faster 'n you, son-of-a-bitch.... Saw you comin' ... shit-heel. I'm standin' here. You make the move. You make the move. It's your move.... Try it.... You talkin' to me? You talkin' to me? ... Well, I'm the only one here. Who the fuck do you think you're talkin' to?
> Robert De Niro as Travis Bickle

New York City, the present. Unable to sleep nights, Travis Bickle (Robert De Niro), an introverted loner and Vietnam veteran, takes a job as a night cabbie in the seediest sections of the big city and spends his free time going to porno movies and writing entries in his diary. Disgusted with the 'scum' around him, Travis dreams of the rain that will someday wash it away. A date with a reluctant but intrigued Betsy (Cybill Shepherd), who works for the glib, populist presidential candidate Palantine, ends in rejection as Travis takes her to a hard-core movie. As the purifying rain is not forthcoming, Travis becomes obsessed with saving Iris, a twelve-year-old runaway streetwalker (Jodie Foster). He turns himself into a killing-machine and, failing to assassinate Palantine at a rally, he seeks out Iris's pimp Sport (Harvey Keitel) and some of his cronies. A horrifying bloodbath ensues, in which Travis is badly wounded. A few months later, he is back on the job, hailed as a hero for having eliminated the criminals and ensuring Iris's return to her parents. He is last seen driving off in his cab.

Taxi Driver is one of the most significant films to come out of the seventies. Though drawing on or alluding to a variety of styles and genres, including the Classic Western and *film noir*, as well as the vigilante and disaster movies of the early seventies, *Taxi Driver* comes across as a semi-documentary account of the descent into madness of an ordinary American. At the same time it is the culmination of the sixties film with its antihero, graphic violence and ambiguous, open ending.[29]

While many critics called the film a masterpiece, some were ardent in their rejection: 'Travis is not an interesting character, we know nothing about him ... New York City is totally distorted.... *Taxi Driver* is neither entertainment nor art. It is a rambling, unfocused, one-dimensional wallow in cheap sensationalism.'[30] Andrew Sarris found 'much to like ... if one doesn't mind the disorder in the narrative.' What he did mind was 'its life-denying spirit, its complete lack of curiosity about the possibilities of people.'[31] However, the fact that we know nothing about Travis not only serves to place him in a long line of American heroes whose obscure origins and detached demeanor come with the territory, so to speak; it also contributes to the unsettling realization that a loner's isolation is not necessarily voluntary; that in real life, contrary to monomythic conventions, this isolation may lead to destructive rather than redemptive violence, and that there often is no telling a madman from the guy next door.[32]

Just as the eyes of T.J. Eckleburg in *The Great Gatsby* 'brood ... over the solemn dumping ground' of the valley of ashes, a metaphor for human corruption and the defilement of the American Dream, Travis's eyes in the rear-view mirror are observing the wasteland of New York half a century later.[33] To him the nocturnal, neon-lit city is 'like an open sewer,' populated by 'animals' that 'come out at night – whores, skunk pussies, buggers, queens, fairies, dopers, junkies ... sick, venal.' This is not the wholesome irritation of Wyatt Earp (Henry Fonda) upon arrival in the rowdy Tombstone of *My Darling Clementine* (1946), 'What kind of town is this?' It is the reaction to a New York City which is both grossly misrepresented and all too easy to believe as it confirms deep-seated misgivings about the big city as a hotbed of degeneracy and corruption: New York City is merely the extreme manifestation of the depravity hinted at in the Carson City of *The Shootist*. Civilization has disintegrated into a new state of wilderness, in which the villains are more elusive and difficult to identify, and, consequently, the Western-style solution of single combat is inadequate to solve the problem.

This is the mythic city landscape of the *film noir* of the forties and fifties. A drama of existential alienation and paranoia, the classic *noir* often employs a laconic, matter-of-fact voice-over narration by its protagonist, and the bleak and cynical mood is amplified through the use of deep shadows, oblique camera angles and the oft-parodied wailing of a lonely sax as the wind sweeps autumn leaves down a deserted street at night. Paul Schrader, who wrote the script for *Taxi Driver*, saw the style as appropriate in capturing the tenor of the seventies: 'As the current political mood hardens, filmgoers and filmmakers will find the film-noir style of the late forties increasingly attractive. The forties may be to the seventies what the thirties were to the sixties.'[34] Consequently *Taxi Driver*, which in part was inspired by the diaries of Arthur Bremer, the would-be assassin of George Wallace in 1972, uses the elements of the voice-over (Travis reading from his diary), the score (by Bernard Herrmann, who scored Welles' *Citizen Kane* and several of Hitchcock's greatest, including *North by Northwest* and *Psycho*), and the pervading red of neon floating in the darkness and reflecting on surfaces, into which the ambience of the old black-and-white predecessors is successfully translated.

While uneasily rooting for Travis, as we share his nausea, we are increasingly aware of the futility of pinning our hopes on his ability to solve his – and by extension our – problem.[35] Things don't add up. Despite his condemnation of the venality of the city, Travis takes Betsy, whom he sees as the epitome of angelic purity, to a porno movie, and when she reacts with fear and disgust, he tries to explain that he does not know about other movies. He writes deceptive letters to his parents about his 'important business in the city,' leaving no address. He incessantly pops pills and swills liquor. Preparing for a showdown that is only vaguely – if at all – defined, he equips himself on the black market with an impressive array of weapons, including a Magnum of *Dirty Harry* fame, and, having taken the first steps toward a redefinition of himself as vigilante, he rehearses a confrontation with an imaginary adversary in the famous mirror scene: 'Are you talking to *me*?' – a variation on the Virginian's 'When you call me that, *smile!*' and Dirty Harry's 'Go ahead, make my day!'

But Harry Callahan, whose vigilantism is 'justified' by the bureaucratic inefficiency of a big city police department, is a law enforcer who 'merely' bends the rules to accomplish what he is trained to do. Travis, on the other hand, is a private citizen who has acquired deadly skills in the service of his country, skills that he now plans to employ on the homefront. The fact that Travis is a Vietnam veteran is not elaborated, it is left open to interpretation whether the war has in any way contributed to his state of mind. Yet Travis's one-man war may resemble the one Americans fought in Vietnam – a lost cause from the very beginning, due to the failure to accurately identify the issues (and the enemy) involved. The principle of destroying the village in order to save it has a peculiar applicability in Travis's urban jungle. His rigorous regimen of exercise to render himself fit for the task ahead is in effect a perversion of the fitness movement of the seventies, and, further, of Franklin's thirteen-point program for self-improvement. By mounting weapons on sliding devices attached to his arms he turns himself into a walking killing machine. He builds himself up – physically as well as mentally – for destruction which, as a farewell note indicates, includes his own annihilation, possibly because he is aware that he himself is part of the problem, although the film is none too clear on this point.

If, in the End of the West Westerns, the victim of civilization is the individual, *Taxi Driver* suggests that civilization may be the victim of the frustrated individual. Although Travis's rage in the end 'only' leads to a murdering rampage through a brothel whereby some expendable types are disposed of (as in *The Shootist*), the fact that he, apparently without reflection, first turns up to shoot Palantine and then, without missing a beat, seeks out a new target at the other extreme of the social structure, carries a disturbing implication, borne out in real life: that a madman bent on destruction may be totally indiscriminatory when he takes aim.[36]

I disagree with James Monaco's dismissal of *Taxi Driver* as mere old-fashioned entertainment:

> So what's a film noir doing at a time like this? Mainly turning back the clock politically and artistically.... [D]epriving a contemporary assassin of a context of contemporary sensibilities makes the film a hodgepodge. It's just as much an entertainment machine as *Rollercoaster* or *Meteor*; it's an individualist's disaster movie.[37]

There is a crucial difference between the cardboard types of the disaster movies, who are characterized only according to their respective roles as villains, victims and rescuer-heroes, and Travis, who is shown to belong in all three categories. What makes *Taxi Driver* more haunting than action-packed images of burning skyscrapers or crashing airplanes is the question that if Travis is not categorically one or the other, neither totally insane nor completely 'normal,' then how is one to recognize him for what he is – a walking time-bomb? As stated by one critic:

> The true horrors of life are more banal than most movies are willing to admit. They don't arise from killer sharks cruising the shores of summer islands or huge gorillas locking the Empire State Building in matte shot embrace.... Because real horror erupts from people, from you and me, when some fact of life throws a kink into our brain waves and we quietly set out to murder the world for it.[38]

In addition, if D.H. Lawrence, upon reading Cooper, was right in his conclusions that the archetypal American hero (Deerslayer) is 'silent, simple, philosophic, moralistic and an unerring shot' and that the 'essential American soul is hard, isolate, stoic, and a killer,' descriptions that are tailor-made to fit Travis, then Travis is a plausible representative of his society and his actions, though extreme, are consistent with his cultural background.[39]

David Boyd has persuasively demonstrated this in his comparison of *The Searchers* and *Taxi Driver*. Both are captivity tales (the former more obviously so than the latter) and their main characters, Ethan Edwards and Travis Bickle, both 'like to regard themselves as guardians of their society's values against the threat of alien intruders, yet neither really belongs to his society.'[40] In fact, both move with ease in 'enemy' territory. The conflict between the two antithetical worlds is internalized, with the two men the actual embodiments of that conflict:

> neither Ethan nor Travis can safely be dismissed as simply an aberrant individual. However severely alienated from their respective societies, both are also, nevertheless, paradoxically representative of those societies, and their private psychosis therefore symptomatic of a more general social malaise. Each, significantly, is not an isolated madman, but rather one of a series [of mad people appearing throughout the two films].... Both are representatives of societies seething with barely repressed sexuality, violence and racism, and it is therefore perfectly, if ironically, appropriate that both are, ultimately, if only temporarily, acclaimed as heroes by those societies.[41]

As such, Travis's job as taxi driver may be seen as a metaphor for America itself: a sense of direction has been replaced by the aimless moving in circles, going and going but getting nowhere. And when cowboy Travis shaves his head and metamorphoses into a Mohawk who seeks to rid the urban wilderness of its savages, the American Dream is shown to be in its final stages of disintegration. A description of the phenomenon, while specifically related to American literature, is apt in this connection:

> It seems no time at all since North American novelists were trying to capture something called the American Dream, that strange sense of promise, of infinite space and possibility, which continued to hang like a cloud of dust over the New World long after the Old World had passed furiously across it in a westerly direction. There was a pause, during which hints of trouble were given, disillusioned cowboys appeared to be milling about, before all of a sudden the whole population seemed to go into a flat spin, and amid general symptoms of hysteria the novelists began trying to capture the American Nightmare.[42]

The shattered sense of direction, the confusion at the complexities of modern life, were reflected in both form and content of a number of American films (influenced by the French New Wave) from the sixties on. Thomas Schatz lists a series of dominant oppositions between what he calls 'classical and modernist strategies' in American film:

Classical	Modernist
primacy of the tale	primacy of the telling
(story as product)	(story as process)
standardized technique	innovative technique
straightforward	ironic
director disguises presence	director acknowledges presence
(invisible narration)	(self-reflexive narration)
screen as transparent window	screen as opaque surface
'realism'	artifice, stylization
passive, unself-conscious viewer	active, self-conscious viewer
(viewing as subjective act)	(viewing as objective act)
(viewer engaged)	(viewing 'distanced')
(story tells itself)	(viewer constructs the story)
(viewer as consumer)	(viewer as producer)
(viewing as play)	(viewing as work)
closed text	open text
(hermetic space)	(porous space; fiction-reality interface)
(three-act structure; closure)	(unstructured; open-ended)
linear plot: causal logic	plotless: free association
motivated, consistent characters	inscrutable characters
(disclosure via exposition)	(information withheld)
primary conflict(s) obvious	conflicts ambiguous (or nonexistent)
conflict(s) resolved	conflict(s) unacknowledged or irreconcilable
(supports the status quo)	(questions the status quo)[43]

Obviously, as Schatz also points out, these oppositions are not mutually exclusive: 'all films are to some extent both classical and modernist, thus falling somewhere between these two poles.' In *Taxi Driver,* the modernist strategies are far more apparent than the classical. Cinematic reflexivity and a semi-documentary form combine to involve the viewer as *co-producer* of the story. The telling becomes a *process,* in which each piece of information must be evaluated in relation to both the film's universe and to real life (*open text, fiction-reality interface*). *Information is withheld,* thus making the protagonist *inscrutable.* The conflict is *ambiguous* and remains *unresolved* as the *ironic* ending leaves it *open* to intepretation whether Travis will erupt again or whether his frustrated energy has been spent once and for all. And finally, the *director's presence* is tangibly *acknowledged* as Scorsese (in an extended homage to Hitchcock?) appears as one of Travis's customers, an insanely jealous man who fantasizes about killing his unfaithful wife with a .44 Magnum.

While the modernist strategies to a certain extent continued to play a role in American filmmaking, the late seventies saw an increasing tendency to discard experiment and complexity in favor of old-fashioned, straightforward story-telling. One such film was the sleeper hit of 1976, *Rocky.* A big-city movie like *Taxi Driver,* it suggested that there was a way out of the impasse: all that was needed was to turn around and go back to the fork in the road and choose the other direction. And the popularity of that movie amply demonstrated that Americans were ready for such a message; a message that, ironically, was clothed in – violence.

A Larger-than-Life Antihero: *Rocky*

We're a couple of coconuts. You're shy and I'm dumb.
Sylvester Stallone as Rocky Balboa to girlfriend Adrian

Philadelphia, the present. Thirty-year-old Rocky Balboa (Sylvester Stallone), also known as 'The Italian Stallion,' is pursuing a third-rate boxing career when, out of the blue, he is given a chance in the big league. The contender for the world heavyweight championship has been injured; the reigning champion Apollo Creed (Carl Weathers) is reluctant to cancel the match scheduled for Philadelphia and decides to pick a local boy as his opponent. Rocky accepts the challenge and goes into intensive training, although he is aware that he cannot possibly win. With an astonishing display of will power he proves a worthy contender: Creed retains his championship, but Rocky is no less a winner, managing to stay on his feet till the very end, having won seven of the fifteen rounds. As the audience is cheering and reporters are trying to interview him, Rocky wails for his girlfriend Adrian (Talia Shire), who makes her way through the crowds and falls into his arms.

The setting of *Rocky* is only quantitatively different from that of *Taxi Driver*. While Rocky Balboa's rundown neighborhood in Bicentennial Philadelphia has not sunk to the same level of sleaziness and depravity, it is nevertheless a squalid environment in which an assortment of blue-collar workers stuck in a daily grind, aimless losers and small-time crooks go about their business, without much hope (or ambition) for improvement in their circumstances. Yet in American success mythology this is exactly the place to go looking for the qualities that characterize one of America's most beloved heroes, the poor boy who makes good. Where *Taxi Driver* focuses on alienation, frustration and destruction, *Rocky* promotes the faith in human potential and redemption through (structured and legitimate) violence, but also through love. It is a film about the return of the vanishing individualist, to paraphrase Leslie Fiedler, and about the rebirth of the core values that have made America strong and can make her so again.[44]

Rocky is a larger-than-life antihero, whose immediate forbears include Marlon Brando's Terry Malloy in *On the Waterfront* from 1954 ('I coulda been a contender'); Ernest Borgnine as *Marty* (1955), and the real-life Rocky Graziano, whose rise from juvenile delinquent and convict to renowned boxing champion was celebrated in *Somebody Up There Likes Me* (1956), with Paul Newman as Graziano. There are even parallels to Gary Cooper's Thomas Jefferson Deeds in Capra's *Mr. Deeds Goes to Town* (1936), the main difference being that Deeds is a small-town innocent who is respected at home, whereas Rocky is – and paradoxically so – a streetwise innocent who is also a bum.[45]

And yet, Rocky is a decent bum. He admonishes a teenage girl to quit hanging out on street corners, carries a drunk off the street and cannot bring himself to employ harsh measures as collector for a loan shark. He woos the mousy, painfully shy Adrian with tender patience (and is rewarded when eventually, in fifties Hollywood fashion, she lets her guard down, removes her glasses and turns into a beauty); he is endearingly attached to his turtles Cuff and Link and his goldfish Moby Dick; and despite the contempt of the gym manager Mickey – 'You fight like an ape. You'll never amount to anything' – he good-naturedly plods on, taking pride in the fact that his nose has never been broken. In short, loser though he is, Rocky is endowed with the virtues of the Jeffersonian natural aristocrat and he proves himself a worthy disciple of the Franklinesque work ethic and self-improvement school.

Both Travis Bickle and Rocky Balboa are lonely, both display the same tenacity in wooing the girl of their dreams, both are concerned with the welfare of under-age girls, and both prepare themselves physically and mentally for a 'showdown' to render their lives meaningful. But whereas the absurdity of certain events in *Taxi Driver* heightens the realism of that film and makes it a valid social commentary on life in contemporary urban America, the realism of *Rocky* subdues the absurdities inherent in the plot and makes the film a seemingly plausible model for the rebirth of an older and better America. That model takes the shape of the essential American version of the Cinderella story, the Horatio Alger tale of the orphaned bootblack's ascent up the social ladder in the big city. All the major elements are present: the street-kid with a heart of gold, lesser characters as foils to highlight his potential as hero, a lucky break (the appropriately named Apollo Creed who descends as a *deus ex machina* and picks Rocky out of obscurity), and our hero's determination to improve his life.

Rocky's chances of winning the match are slim, but since this is not his main goal it does not matter. Following the Alger tradition he seeks respectability rather than fame and fortune. It is characteristic of the movie's values that even though he will receive a handsome $150,000 for his participation in what is essentially a publicity stunt for Apollo Creed, this gets only passing attention and there is no mention of the money as the motivating factor: 'All I want to do is go the distance.... When that bell rings and I'm still standing, I'll know for the first time in my life, see, that I weren't just another bum from the neighborhood.'

A veritable catalog of American values, *Rocky* was a fitting Bicentennial contribution to the resurrection of America as the Land of Opportunity. Patriotism, innocence, community spirit, individualism and the work ethic were promoted by a hero who was a throwback to the good old days before Hollywood became 'artsy.' Stallone himself said,

> I am at the beginning of a new style of actors. Hollywood had the stage types in the '30s. Then it developed its own bigger, broad-shouldered type of acting – Kirk Douglas and Vic Mature and Burt Lancaster. Then it kind of went into the woodwork and started coming out with the cerebral types.... [N]ow again we are going to see the communicative actor, the actor who will be a hero, the actor who will inspire confidence and, ah, imitativeness in his viewers. Positiveness![46]

Rocky was in fact a double Alger, with life imitating art. The story of Sylvester Stallone's dogged pursuit of happiness was the stuff myth is made of: despite an impressive collection of rejection slips for previous screenplays, an undistinguished acting career, a pregnant wife and $106 to his name, he adamantly refused to back down and let a more prominent actor play the lead in the film once his script (allegedly written in three and a half days) had been accepted.[47] Then unqualified triumph as the low-budget production within weeks stormed to the top of the box-office charts, earned 10 Academy Award nominations (two for Stallone as Best Actor and for Best Original Screenplay) and won three Oscars: Best Picture, Best Director and Best Film Editing.[48]

The cautious optimism of the first *Rocky* mirrored the general spirit in 1976. In May of that year, the *U.S. News & World Report* stated in its semiannual 'Mood of America' survey that

There's a readily discernible upturn in morale nearly everywhere. People are less gloomy about their own circumstances, more confident about the future. Compared with similar interviews conducted last autumn – when the recession was going full tilt and defeat in Vietnam still tasted bitter – Americans have made a remarkable comeback.[49]

The article ended by quoting a New Jersey barber: 'The American people are strong enough to do anything, once they decide they are right and stand up.' Apparently he knew what he was talking about: in the four sequels Rocky metamorphosed into an all-out winner, as the shell-shocked seventies gave way to the can-do eighties.

In *Taxi Driver* the city is uniformly bleak. As Rocky's prospects take a turn for the better, the depressing dinginess of his south side environment is contrasted with a much brighter view of Philadelphia in the sequence that ends with his triumphant flight up the steps to the Museum of Art. This is a magnificent, Greek-style structure, entirely appropriate as the Olympus to which Rocky, by his innocent acceptance of a phoney challenge, rightfully gains access. But far from isolated from the community in his quest, he is shown running through a busy street where someone throws him an apple and everyone cheers him on. In the same sequence he runs along a sunlit stretch of water, a vivid contrast to the drab harbor area where we first meet him. Thus the movie suggests that the city is not necessarily a corrupting environment that holds unfortunate souls in an iron grip. On the contrary, there is beauty and warmth to be found by those who are willing to break out of their despondency. This shift toward a more positive view of the city was manifest by 1978, as summed up by Scot Haller:

Where have all the floozies gone? Where are all the urban crazies and walking failures of yesterday? Not so many months ago American movies were pelting their audiences with scenes of murder, rape, robbery, and other seedy spectacles of city life. But in the past year or so the urban misfit, a character who seemed well on the way to becoming an essential element of the 1970s cinema, has nearly disappeared from the screen. Suddenly, the city streets aren't nearly as mean as they once were, and the citizens no longer resemble Cain.[50]

Haller listed the following titles as evidence of the new trend according to which cities were cast as 'havens of hope and right-minded heroes:' *Saturday Night Fever, The Turning Point, The Goodbye Girl, An Unmarried Woman, Annie Hall*. The following year, 1979, saw Woody Allen's tribute, *Manhattan*, famous for its lyrical poster shot of Allen and Diane Keaton in silhouette against the Queensboro Bridge.

What was most surprising about *Rocky* was the reaction of the critics, the great majority of whom were – *enchanted*. In Roger Ebert's assessment, the movie's appeal stems from the fact that it 'involves us emotionally, it makes us commit ourselves: We find, maybe to our surprise after remaining detached during so many movies, that this time we *care*.'[51] While some called it sentimental and schmaltzy (but nevertheless charming), others praised its 'honesty, unpretentiousness and stark social realism' or saw it as a 'deeply stirring affirmation of human aspiration, of strength of character, and of simple decency.'[52] Even *The New Yorker's* Pauline Kael, renowned for her caustic pen, was favorably inclined:

> *Rocky* is shameless, and that's why – on a certain level – it works. What holds it together is innocence.... There's a bull-necked energy in [Stallone], smoldering.... In his deep caveman's voice he gives the most surprising, sharp, fresh shadings to his lines.... [He] has the gift of direct communication with the audience.[53]

It was as if the critics, along with the rest of the population, had become fed up with the confessionals of self-doubt and anxiety that had marked so many film productions in the previous decade. Said one critic: '*Rocky* ... believes in values that most movies don't believe in anymore. It believes in the American Dream.... It even believes in happy endings.'[54]

Among the few dissenting critics, I. Lloyd Michaels was perhaps more prophetic than he could possibly have imagined when he expressed his concern 'for the immediate future of American commercial film':

> Already, we are hearing cries for the revival of 'Capra-corn.' After the enormous popularity and considerable achievement of Coppola's two *Godfather* films, the brilliant debuts of Scorsese's *Mean Streets* and Malick's *Badlands*, and the psychological complexity of performances like Pacino's in *Serpico* and Caan's in *The Gambler*, the most honored American movies of the past two years have been *One Flew Over the Cuckoo's Nest* and *Rocky*, both characterized by banal moral themes, one-dimensional macho heroes and utterly nondescript direction. Within the same time span, only Altman's *Nashville* seems worthy of serious attention. It is undoubtedly too soon to call these disturbing developments a trend, but it is certainly not too early to warn against lowering critical standards so far as to encourage more movies like *Rocky*.[55]

Everything about *Rocky* – from its production and promotion over audience appeal and critical acclaim to its inclusion in the Oscar Hall of Fame and Stallone's instant stardom – combined to make it what French director Francois Truffaut has called an *event sociologique*. Its impact on Hollywood lasted well into the eighties, most tangibly in the success of the increasingly bigger-budgeted sequels and Stallone's other character, Vietnam veteran John Rambo, who got to win the Vietnam War this time, and who counted President Reagan among his fans: 'Boy, after seeing *Rambo* last night, I know what to do the next time [Americans are taken hostage]'.[56] The Rocky and Rambo series were rituals of heroics and hero worship, on the strength of which most notably Austrian immigrant Arnold Schwartzenegger in the eighties would add yet another chapter to the book about making it big in America.

Nostalgia for the Present: *Logan's Run*

> Sometime in the 23rd century, the survivors of war, overpopulation and pollution are living in a great domed city, sealed away from the forgotten world outside. Here, in an ecologically balanced world, mankind lives only for pleasure, freed by the servomechanisms which provide everything.
> There's just one catch: Life must end at thirty unless reborn in the fiery ritual of carrousel.
>
> Opening titles to *Logan's Run*

The year is 2274. Quincentennial festivities would be in the planning, except that the United States as we know it no longer exists. A hedonistic society of young people, governed by a computer and shielded by gigantic domes, is what is supposedly left of the nation. Each citizen carries implanted in his palm a crystal that changes color at various stages of life; when it turns black, at age 30, it is time for the ritual of 'renewal.' Skeptics, who accurately perceive the ritual as a sophisticated method of extermination, seek to escape the city in search of a place called Sanctuary. Logan 5 (Michael York) and Francis 7 (Richard Jordan) are Sandmen, entrusted with hunting down and killing these 'runners.' As the number of runners is on the increase, Logan is assigned the task of finding Sanctuary to destroy it. He teams up with a runner, Jessica 6 (Jenny Agutter), and after many hazards they reach the outside, chased by Francis who senses that Logan has second thoughts about his mission. Logan and Jessica realize that the outside is not polluted and that the life clock no longer has any power over them. In the ruins of Washington D.C. they meet an old man (Peter Ustinov), who introduces them to the concepts of marriage, family, natural death and burial. Logan is attacked by Francis, who refuses to listen to reason, and Logan is forced to kill him in self-defense. Determined to bring the truth to the people in the city, Jessica and Logan return, accompanied by the Old Man. Logan is captured and subjected to interrogation; his insistence that there is no Sanctuary eventually causes the computer to short-circuit, 'input contrary to established facts. The answer does not program.' A chain reaction of destruction follows. The inhabitants of the city flee and meet the Old Man waiting outside – the first old person they have ever seen.

In his review of the film, Jay Cocks of *Time* complained that the 'portrait of an oppressive futuristic society looks no more menacing than the California beach culture run riot. Everyone is bland and pretty, decked out for pleasure in outfits that look like togas designed by Frederick's of Hollywood.'[57] However, the willing submission to the pleasure principle of the citizens in *Logan's Run* may not seem very dystopian precisely because it is a phenomenon that is not far removed from contemporary reality.[58] Norman Mailer, in his *Presidential Papers* from 1964, went so far as to use the term *totalitarianism* to describe what he saw as a disturbing trend in the transformation of the

American landscape: 'We learn little from travel, not nearly so much as we need to learn, if everywhere we are assaulted by the faceless plastic surfaces of everything which has been built in America since the war.' Speaking of suburbs, he said, 'To live in leisure in a house much like other houses, to live in a landscape where it is meaningless to walk because each corner which is turned produces the same view, to live in comfort and be bored is a preparation for one condition: limbo.'[59]

Limbo, or inertia, is exactly what characterizes the domed city. As in the present-day shopping mall there is no change of seasons.[60] All of the inhabitants look the same – young and pretty; nobody is handicapped, overweight, or in any other way deviant from the norm. They all dress the same, in colors that correspond to their particular age-group (the color of their crystal). What little individuality there is disappears at the end, when they enter the carrousel: all are wearing masks and white robes. Compare Mailer's warning: 'The essence of totalitarianism is that it beheads. It beheads individuality, variety, dissent, extreme possibility, romantic faith, it blinds vision, deadens instinct, it obliterates the past.... We are left with less and less sense of the lives of the men and women who came before us.'[61]

Two months after the opening of *Logan's Run*, Tom Wolfe coined the label – 'the "Me" Decade' – that ever since has served as a short-hand definition of the period.[62] A month later, Christopher Lasch outlined the ideas that were to inform his widely discussed examination of contemporary American society, *The Culture of Narcissism* from 1979. In his critique, Lasch echoed Mailer: 'To live for the moment is the prevailing passion – to live for yourself, not for your predecessors or posterity. We are fast losing the sense of historical continuity, the sense of belonging to a succession of generations originating in the past and stretching into the future.'[63]

In essence, *Logan's Run* is a visualization of Lasch's thesis. What the film explicitly formulates as the only viable means to prevent a future such as the one portrayed corresponds to Lasch's nostalgic yearning to restore values that are in the process of disintegration in contemporary America. Life in the city is admirably devoid of disease, pollution, starvation and crime, but the freedom from want and fear comes at the price of a corresponding lack of individuality and a sense of purpose in life, something that is further exacerbated by the inevitable termination at age thirty. As the Old Man says when told that everyone knows when his or her life will be over, 'Takes all the fun out of dying.' Reproduction is carried out in test-tube facilities; divorced from emotion and biological purpose, sex is reduced to an antiseptic, organized pastime. Thus the concepts of love, family and personal, not to mention collective, history no longer exist. It is a 'live fast and die young' culture which, unconcerned with representative government, religion, ethics, and morality, reflects contemporary voter apathy, materialism and the cult of the self. The pre-occupation with staying young and fit that became pervasive in the seventies has in *Logan's Run* merely been taken to the logical conclusion of termination before the onset of bodily decay.

Once outside the city, Jessica and Logan experience a rebirth in nature: frolicking in a lake, surrounded by lush vegetation, they discover that their crystals have turned white, and they make love, in the true sense of the word. The change in mood is accentuated by the score: in the city the music is dissonant, electronic and metallic; in nature it becomes soft, harmonious and includes the romantic tinkling of bells. In their new incarnations as the proverbial American Adam and Eve Logan and Jessica retrace American history from the discovery of the continent and the notion of the unspoiled wilderness as a Garden of Eden through the War of Independence and the founding of the republic to the emancipation of the slaves. The *natural* principle of democracy is symbolized by a Washington D.C. whose picturesque ruins, overgrown with ivy, have entered into an harmonic and organic symbiosis with nature, in contrast to the domed city which appears as an alien element in the landscape. However, the Old Man living with his cats in what we recognize as the Senate is unaware of the original function of the place. Yet he is able to provide a few mythic fragments of American history: rummaging through some dusty paintings, he alludes to George Washington, 'Father said one of these people never told a lie. I don't know which one.' He does know that the place belongs to the people, 'It says on one of these walls: "All the people all the time shall not" [sic].' We have already been introduced to Lincoln when Logan and Jessica stand face to face with his statue at the Memorial; later Logan is studying his portrait on the Senate floor.

When Logan kills Francis, his weapon is a pole carrying the Stars and Stripes. The symbolism is unmistakable: the flag of the free is an effective weapon against the agent of oppression. The evocation of the War of Independence and the emancipation of the slaves is complemented by the obvious biblical reference to Moses leading the People of Israel out of Egypt in the shape of the Old Man. Placed on a background of a pool and cascading water, he awaits, whitebearded and staff in hand, the exodus from the domed city.

Logan's conclusion that Sanctuary does not exist, that it is only 'something that people wanted to be because they did not want to die' is, on a deeper level, contradicted through these references to biblical and *American* mythology. Thus the film effectively serves as a reminder of America's unique status as sanctuary for all the world and its divine mission which in the film's present have been forgotten and which, subtextually, contemporary Americans are warned not to lose sight of. As Susan Sontag said in 1977: 'Just wait until now becomes then. You'll see how happy we were.'[64]

The original source for the film was William F. Nolan and George Clayton Johnson's novel of the same title from 1967.[65] While sharing the premise of a society of people not allowed to live beyond a certain age and renegades looking for sanctuary, the film and the novel part ways in a number of important aspects. In the novel, the story takes place some 150 years earlier, in 2116. The totalitarian system is the outcome of a youth rebellion called the Little War, rooted in the 1960s and culminating worldwide in the year 2000. In order to ensure that the authority of age has forever been eliminated, people are supposed to check into a 'sleep shop' at age 21. Obviously the inspiration is drawn from the youth revolt which was escalating all over the western world when the novel was published. The film, on the other hand, came at a time when youngsters were once more pursuing mainstream goals. Accordingly, the explanation for the system within the city is more vaguely defined, having to do with survival in the aftermath of nuclear war, pollution and overpopulation.

In the novel, people are not confined to a domed city but move freely around the world, all the continents of the globe being linked by an elaborate underground transportation system. Washington D.C., destroyed by a nuclear bomb during the Little War, has turned into a veritable jungle inhabited by tigers and snakes; it merely functions as one of the deserted stopovers for Logan and Jessica. At the end, after an action-packed 24 hours, they reach their final destination in the Florida Keys where a passenger rocket is waiting to take them to an abandoned space station near Mars, 'a small colony now, still crude, cold, hard to live on.' To see them off is Francis, the legendary leader of the renegade organization, who says to Logan, 'Someday you and Jess and the others will be able to come back – to a changed world. A good, strong one' (147).

It is particularly on these points that the film deviates from its source. That the story takes place on the North American continent is only of minor importance in the novel; it could have taken place anywhere in what we know as the western world. The film makes the story specifically American, not only by playing on the classic American binary opposition of city *vs* country (the domed, computer-driven city may be seen as the ultimate machine in the garden), but most notably by emphasizing the founding principles of life, liberty and *worthy* pursuits of happiness, realized through democracy and firmly anchored in the institution of family. As for the ending, the novel merely promises that some day things will change, and in the meantime Logan will be a refugee among other refugees; whereas in the film his role has been transformed into that of the mythic individual, who, despite initial reluctance, takes it upon himself to save the community.

Andrew Tudor has noted the similarity between *The Planet of the Apes* (1968) and *Logan's Run* in their use of, respectively, the half-buried Statue of Liberty and Washington D.C. in ruins: they function, he says, 'as triggers of instant nostalgia, allowing us to regret the good old present before it's gone.'[66] Undoubtedly the film seeks to alleviate the disillusionment caused by the lies and corruption of sixties and early seventies administrations by presenting the infinitely more menacing specter of a society *founded* on lies and perpetuated through impersonal government by a machine. Through the invocation of cherished old presidents, Johnson and Nixon thus come to be seen as aberrations, anomalies in an otherwise virtuous and noble system – after all, Founding Father Washington could not tell a lie, and what essentially came out of Watergate – according to popular wisdom – was the reassurance that the System Works.

Most critics were not amused by *Logan's Run*, but it was reasonably popular with the audience and earned enough in rentals to secure a position as one of the top 25 movies of 1976.[67] In retrospect, it is clear that the feel-good message of *Logan's Run* was a harbinger of things to come. In the latter half of the seventies, old-fashioned science fiction entertainment in the *Flash Gordon* and *Buck Rogers* mold experienced an unprecedented boom, ending the genre's status as B-film material only.

Conclusion

So far as Hollywood was concerned, 1976 was the sixties' last hurrah.

J. Hoberman (1985)[68]

When *Variety* summed up the year of 1976 as seen from the box-office, the magazine was unable to identify any particular trend in the movie business. The list testified to 'a scattering of miscellaneous fare' with a 'variety of violence' and a 'variety of comedy.'[69] Indeed, to use five films, of a production totalling more than 150, as a barometer of the nation's mood in that year is a perilous undertaking. There is an almost infinite number of variables involved in the production, distribution, promotion and popularity of a given movie. However, to the extent that movies in general reflect their time, the five films in combination do mirror the divergent trends in society at large – the aftermath of the upheavals of the preceding decade and the growing optimism and confidence that, at least on the surface, were to become the trademarks of Reagan's America. In 1976, horror still appealed to a large segment of the audience, whereas the disaster cycle of the previous years was running out of steam. Dirty Harry Callahan was still busy cleaning up San Francisco in *The Enforcer*. But although *Network* claimed that Americans were 'mad as hell' and were 'not gonna take it anymore,' (as Travis Bickle proved was a valid threat), *All the President's Men* demonstrated that the System Works (which *Outlaw Josey Wales* and *Logan's Run*, each in its own way, also sought to confirm). Comedies were in abundance; in one in particular, *The Bad News Bears*, there were shades of *Rocky*, as a hopeless Little League baseball team, led by one of the preeminent child stars of the seventies, Tatum O'Neal, was improbably coached to victory by near-alcoholic Walther Matthau.[70]

Had *Logan's Run* been made in the sixties, the emphasis would probably have been different, as it was in the novel that inspired the film. At a time when the movement to abolish tradition, fueled by resentment toward Washington, was gathering momentum, a reminder to preserve (as symbolized by Washington in ruins) rather than to overturn would not have sat well with the young who made up the majority of the audience. Nor would *Rocky* have been taken seriously, whereas *Taxi Driver* in all likelihood would have found a spot in popularity next to *Bonnie and Clyde* and *Easy Rider*. The reconciliatory message of *The Outlaw Josey Wales* relied on the end of U.S. involvement in Vietnam and the general attenuation of domestic confrontation, which did not come about until the mid-seventies. John Wayne's death in *The Shootist* had already been foreshadowed by his death in *The Cowboys* from 1972, in which he, deserted by his ranch hands, was forced to take on eleven boys as wranglers on a cattle drive. He passed on the spirit of the frontier to the kids so effectively that, upon his death at the hands of a brutal outlaw, they became violent avengers. That movie condoned violence, whereas in *The Shootist*, only four years later, part of Books' last week was spent on curbing young Gillom's fascination with guns and machismo.

The general sense of both disillusionment and hope was perhaps expressed most clearly in the election of Jimmy Carter. The candidacy of a virtually unknown Southern Baptist and peanut farmer would under different circumstances have been considered a joke (as indeed it was in some quarters in the beginning). But 1976 was a watershed year in which anything could happen. It is one of the small ironies of that year that the Bicentennial was presided over by Gerald Ford, the only non-elected president in history. Another was the emergence on the national political scene of a former Hollywood actor and Democrat-turned-Republican who only four years later swept the peanut farmer from power. The election of Ronald Reagan ushered in a period of renewed optimism and national pride that may be compared to the fifties when another grandfather presided over the nation. The more things change, the more they stay the same.

Notes

1. 'Burnt Norton' (1935), ll. 44-46.
2. Aldous Huxley, 'On the Charms of History and the Future of the Past' in *Music at Night and Other Essays* (Hamburg: The Albatross, 1935), 114-115.
3. These include *Stagecoach, Red River* and *Rio Bravo* (the latter was actually in color).
4. Arthur M. Schlesinger, Jr., *The Cycles of American History* (Boston: Houghton Mifflin, 1986), 10.
5. Leslie Fiedler, *Love and Death in the American Novel* (New York: Scarborough, 1966), 27.
6. *The Writings of Benjamin Franklin*, ed. by Albert Henry Smyth (1905-07). Here quoted from Peter Freese, *'America': Dream or Nightmare? Reflections on a Composite Image* (Essen: Die Blaue Eule, 1994), 115.
7. Yet as early as *Stagecoach* (1939), the manifest destinarian virtue of the townspeople is questioned, most pointedly in the self-righteousness of the 'Petticoat Brigade.'
8. Thomas Jefferson, 'Query XIX: Manufactures.' *Notes on the State of Virginia* (1781-82).
9. Incidentally, 1843 also saw the birth of President McKinley, who was assassinated in – 1901.
10. Film historians George Fenin and William Everson assign the honor to W.K.L. Dickson's *Cripple Creek Bar-Room* from 1898. See their *The Western: From Silents to the Seventies* (New York: Grossman, 1973), 48.
11. See Richard Slotkin's discussion of the phenomenon of John Wayne in his *Gunfighter Nation: The Myth of the Frontier in Twentieth-Century America* (New York: HarperPerennial, 1993), 512-520.
12. *Stagecoach* was actually Wayne's 60th film.
13. *Roger Ebert's Video Companion*, Microsoft Cinemania '95.
14. Joan Didion, 'John Wayne: A Love Song' (1965). In *Slouching Towards Bethlehem* (New York: Touchstone, 1979), 30.
15. *Playboy*, May 1971: 'I licked the Big C. I know the man upstairs will pull the plug when he wants, but I don't want to end my life being sick. I want to go out on two feet – in action.'
16. *The New Yorker*, 25 Feb. 1974: 'A few more Westerns may straggle in, but the Western is dead.' Here quoted from the reprint in Pauline Kael, *Reeling* (1976), 283.
17. Critics were divided over *The Shootist*. Judith Crist of the *Saturday Review* called it a 'tediously pretentious and vapid melodrama' (21 Aug. 1976, 45). At the other end of the spectrum, *Variety* hailed it as 'one of the great films of our time,' praising John Wayne's 'towering achievement' in a film which was 'simply beautiful, and beautifully simple ... quiet, elegant and sensitive.' At the same time *Variety* was concerned that audiences might be misled by expectations based on Don Siegel and John Wayne's previous efforts: 'This is by no means the formula summer shoot-em-up.... If the film does not get itself across to the public, few of the wrong people, and none of the right ones, will ever know' (28 July 1976). This insight turned out to be prophetic; while not quite a box-office flop, *The Shootist* only made it to the no. 50 spot on *Variety's* top-rental chart for 1976.
18. *The Outlaw Josey Wales* was so popular that it figures as no. 38 on Joel W. Finler and David Pirie's adjusted-for-inflation list of 'All-Time Hit Westerns.' David Pirie (ed), *Anatomy of the Movies* (London: WHS Distributors, 1981), 208.
19. *A Fistful of Dollars* (1964), *For a Few Dollars More* (1965) and *The Good, the Bad and the Ugly* (1967), all released in the U.S. 1967.

20. See Jenni Calder, *There Must Be a Lone Ranger: The American West in Film and Reality* (New York: McGraw-Hill, 1974), 137: 'Leone's version of the West is total anarchy with scarcely any room for heroism.'

21. Lone Watie drily remarks, 'I've noticed when you get to *dis*liking someone they ain't around long either.'

22. At this point in time the real-life Black Kettle was busy recovering from the Sand Creek Massacre (1864) and the tribe was starving due to the disappearance of the buffalo.

23. Slotkin, *Gunfighter Nation*, 632.

24. Yet blacks are conspicuously absent, a curious omission, given the theme of reconciliation and the achievements of the Civil Rights movement. From the early seventies on, blacks became more visible in Westerns, which brought the genre in closer alignment with historical fact. Eastwood made up for the omission in his *Bronco Billy* (1980) which featured him as a contemporary ex-convict and former shoe salesman from New Jersey turned latter-day Buffalo Bill, touring the West with his Wild West Circus. His troupe consisted of an assortment of losers and outcasts, including a Native American and a black man.

25. *Variety*, 30 June 1976. The movie did receive favorable reviews as well: 'a full-scale saga of great impact' (*Los Angeles Times*, 14 July); 'a thoroughly likeable film' (London *Sunday Times,* 8 August); 'What is remarkable about the film ... is the skill with which Eastwood gives [its] theme a resonantly full orchestration while at the same time silencing any propensities to pretension or sentimentality lurking in the script' (*Monthly Film Bulletin*, August).

26. Jeff Millar, 'Outlaw Josey Wales,' *Film Heritage* 12:1 (1976), 38.

27. John Lenihan, *Showdown: Confronting Modern America in the Western Film* (Urbana: University of Illinois Press, 1980), 173.

28. See David Thomson, 'Forgiven,' *The Independent on Sunday*, 22 Aug. 1993, 16: 'He is at his snow-capped peak in films; and he is one of the most admired, and least questioned, public figures in America.'

29. That is not to say that antiheroes and graphic violence disappeared after *Taxi Driver*, but the darker nuances of the antihero's existential dilemma faded, and he increasingly appeared in mild-mannered comedies such as Woody Allen's *Annie Hall* and *Manhattan*. The violence of the revived superhero was either 'clean' as in the *Superman* and *Indiana Jones* series or, as in the *Rambo* films, it was excessive but postulated to be patriotic and therefore redemptive.

30. Marcia Magill, *Films in Review*, March 1976.

31. *Village Voice*, 16 Feb. 1976.

32. 'The American monomyth begins and ends in Eden. Stories in this genre typically begin with a small community of hard-working farmers and townspeople living in harmony. A disruption of harmony occurs, and must be eliminated by the superhero [who remains detached from the community he is called to save], before the Edenic condition can be re-established in a happy ending.' Robert Jewett and John Shelton Lawrence, *The American Monomyth* (Garden City, New York: Anchor Press, 1977), 169-70.

33. F. Scott Fitzgerald, *The Great Gatsby* (1925), ch. 2, second paragraph.

34. 'Notes on Film Noir.' *Film Comment* (Spring 1972), 180. Here quoted from James Monaco, *American Film Now: The People, the Power, the Money, the Movies* (New York: Plume, 1979), 181.

35. For an excellent analysis of how the movie manipulates audience expectations of Travis

as a Western Hero, see Robert B. Ray, *A Certain Tendency of the Hollywood Cinema, 1930-1980* (Princeton: Princeton University Press, 1985), 349-360.

36. In August 1966, student Charles Whitman ensconced himself in the bell tower of the University of Texas and, firing at random, killed 13 and wounded 33. The tragic incident was the subject of a TV movie in 1975, entitled *The Deadly Tower*, with Kurt Russell as Whitman.
37. Monaco, *American Film Now*, 158.
38. William Gallo, 'Taxi Driver,' *Film Heritage* 11:3 (Spring 1976), 28.
39. D.H. Lawrence, *Studies in Classic American Literature* (1924; Harmondsworth: Penguin, 1971), 66 and 68.
40. David Boyd, 'Prisoner of the Night,' *Film Heritage* 12:2 (1976-77), 26.
41. *Ibid.*, 29-30.
42. Henry Tube, 'Poisoned Wells' (review of *Mr. Sammler's Planet* by Saul Bellow). *The Spectator*, 18 July 1970, 44.
43. Thomas Schatz, *Old Hollywood/New Hollywood: Ritual, Art, and Industry* (Ann Arbor: UMI Research Press, 1983), 232.
44. Leslie Fiedler, *The Return of the Vanishing American* (London: Jonathan Cape, 1968).
45. Frank Capra himself said that *Rocky* was the kind of movie he would like to have made (Martin Kasindorf, 'Rocky KO's Hollywood,' *Newsweek*, 11 April 1977, 39). However, Capra's turf was the affluent middle class, and it is doubtful if he would have been able to portray the gritty, inner-city world as realistically as John Avildsen did, despite *Rocky*'s fairy-tale plot.
46. Kasindorf, 'Rocky KO's Hollywood,' 40.
47. The producers wanted Burt Reynolds or Robert Redford in the starring role. See Susan Sackett, *The Hollywood Reporter Book of Box Office Hits* (New York: Billboard Books, 1990), 246.
48. The production costs were just under $1 million; by the end of 1977 (the film was released in November of 1976) rentals for the U.S. and Canada were in excess of $55 million. By comparison, hit no. 2, *A Star Is Born,* brought in 'only' $37 million.
49. 17 May 1976, 21.
50. Scot Haller, 'New Views of the City,' *Horizon*, March 1978, 23.
51. *Roger Ebert's Movie Companion*, Microsoft Cinemania '95.
52. Marcia Magill, *Films in Review*, Jan. 1977, 56; Judith Crist, *Saturday Review*, 27 Nov. 1976, 40.
53. 29 Nov. 1976. Here quoted from the reprint in Pauline Kael, *When the Lights Go Down* (New York: Holt, Rinehart and Winston, 1980), 213-14.
54. Frank Rich, *New York Post*, 22 Nov. 1976, 18.
55. *Film Criticism* 1:3 (Winter 1976-77), 41. Other unimpressed critics included Richard Schickel (*Time* 13 Dec. 1976, 96-97), who complained about 'the conceit [the film] employs to lift Rocky out of the clubs and into the big arena for his title challenge,' and Vincent Canby of the *New York Times* (22 Nov. 1976, C19) who called it 'fraudulent,' 'latent[ly] racis[t],' 'a sentimental little slum movie' and characterized Stallone's acting as that of 'an unconvincing actor imitating a lug.'
56. This was one of Reagan's mishaps with a microphone. The unfortunate statement was made in June 1985 during a sound check prior to Reagan's announcement that the 39 Americans taken hostage in Beirut had been released. See Paul Slansky, *The Clothes Have No Emperor: A Chronicle of the American Eighties* (New York: Fireside, 1989), 133.
57. Jay Cocks, 'Also Ran,' *Time*, 26 July 1976, 68.

58. Saul David, the producer of *Logan's Run*: 'When you make this kind of film, depending on your wit or your temperament, you extrapolate from what you've got in the present to what you think may happen in the future. In other words, you take all the tendencies you see around you now – juvenile delinquency, sexual licence, you name it – and you project those things to the future, simply exaggerating them.' *American Cinematographer*, June 1976; here quoted from John Brosnan, *Future Tense: The Cinema of Science Fiction* (London: Macdonald and Jane's, 1978), 243. Whereas the Cold War informed Orwell's *1984* (1949) and continued to inform the bulk of Hollywood's future fantasies into the 1970s, *Logan's Run* leans to Huxley's point of view in *Brave New World* from 1932. Orwell's vision was one of an externally imposed oppression which controlled people through the infliction of pain. Huxley depicted a society so in love with the comfort and amusement provided by technology that it was controlled through the infliction of pleasure: 'An Orwellian world is much easier to recognize, and to oppose, than a Huxleyan.' Neil Postman, *Amusing Ourselves to Death: Public Discourse in the Age of Show Business* (New York: Viking Penguin, 1985), vii-viii and 156.

59. Norman Mailer, *The Presidential Papers* (London: Andre Deutsch, 1964), 178.

60. The city scenes were, in fact, shot in a shopping-mall in Dallas.

61. Mailer, *The Presidential Papers,* 184-85.

62. Tom Wolfe, 'The "Me" Decade and the Third Great Awakening,' *New York,* 23 Aug.1976, 26-40.

63. Christopher Lasch, 'The Narcissist Society,' *New York Review of Books*, 30 Sep. 1976, 5.

64. Susan Sontag, 'Unguided Tour,' *New Yorker*, 31 Oct. 1977, 42.

65. New York: Bantam, 1976. Page references are included in the text.

66. Quoted in Michael Wood, 'Kiss Tomorrow Hello,' *American Film* 2:6 (1977), 17.

67. It also spawned a short-lived TV series, 1977-78.

68. J. Hoberman, '1975-1985: Ten Years that Shook the World,' *American Film*, June 1985, 38.

69. 5 January 1977, 14.

70. The ten-year-old daughter of actor Ryan O'Neal was the youngest ever to receive an Oscar for Best Actress for her role in *Paper Moon* (1973). Shirley Temple received an *honorary* Oscar at the age of six in 1934. The other child star of the seventies, Jodie Foster, was nominated as Best Supporting Actress (*Taxi Driver* 1976) but lost to Faye Dunaway (*Network*).

Abstracts

'That's What I Like about the South:' Changing Images of the South in the 1970s
(John G. Cawelti)
Responding to the transformations of modernization, urbanization, prosperity, and Civil
Rights in the post World War II period, the South gradually evolved new myths which
would profoundly influence the way in which the rest of the United States perceived its
history and culture. Two different myths had a very strong influence in the 1970s. Though
these myths were connected by their insistence on the crucial relevance of the Southern
historical experience for the rest of the nation, they were very different in the way they
understood Southern history and the lessons it offered.

The myth of the South as last stronghold of traditional American values proclaimed that
because the South had retained its rural culture longer than the rest of the country it still
adhered to certain moral and cultural values associated with traditional American culture
such as honesty, simplicity, dedication to family and kinship, strong ties to local communities and a continuing faith in 'old-time religion.' However, as the South increasingly
modernized during the decade there was increasing doubt about the persistence, even in the
South, of anything resembling traditional values.

The myth of the South as tragic exemplar had been first articulated in the 1920s and
1930s in several of the important writers of the Southern renaissance, and particularly in the
work of William Faulkner. In the 1960s and 1970s this myth was central to the work of a
new generation of Southern and African American writers, as illustrated in the novels of
William Styron and Toni Morrison. This view of Southern history as characterized primarily
by tragedy, defeat, and the encounter with human evil and limitation offered thoughtful
Americans of the 1970s and 1980s a deeper sense of the ironic ambiguities of the American
dream, a greater awareness of the racial and ethnic conflicts that had often been overlooked
in the celebration of American democracy, and a realization of the degree to which
oppression and suffering were as much a part of American history as progress and
abundance.

Declension and Renewal: New England's Shifting Mood in the 1970s (David E. Nye)
In the 1970s New England as a whole stagnated economically, with almost no growth in
population. Called the 'Frost Belt' in contradistinction to the 'Sun Belt' of the South and
the Southwest, and the 'Rust Belt' of the Middle West, many companies left the region for
warmer climes where costs were also lower. The oil shortages and high prices were
particularly serious for New England. Nevertheless, a look at regions within the region
shows considerable variation, as certain high-tech industries, notably computing, developed
rapidly.

Aside from economics, the region faced a crisis of identity. Once it had seen itself as the
center of American intellectual life. Its history had seemed to represent the American
experience. In the 1970s, however, it began to seem idiosyncratic. Its politicians, e.g.
Senator Muskie from Maine, were not able to be nominated for the Presidency. Its writers,
who once believed they spoke for the nation, were ill-disposed to write as regionalists. Its
many private universities found themselves challenged both by newer private schools
elsewhere and by land-grant institutions with lower tuitions and ambitious faculties. By the
end of the decade New England was chastened in mood and down-sized in its expectations.

Nevertheless, New Englanders retained a sense of tradition, superior cultural institutions, and a high-tech industrial base. If no longer at the center of American economic and cultural life, it remained a vital and resourceful region, that by 1984 had lower unemployment, more popular universities, and higher house prices than most of the rest of the nation. Thus the 1970s may be seen as a time of readjustment, when New England discovered it was only a region, and not the United States in microcosm.

Searching for an Old Faithful America: National Park Tourism in the 1970s (Robert Matej Bednar)
This article analyzes tourism in the American national parks in the 1970s by reconstructing and interrogating the period discourse regarding the parks and tourism. The article uses the works of 1970s journalists, preservationists, cultural critics, anthropologists, environmental-behavior researchers, and National Park Service officials as sources to tell the story of Americans struggling to determine what the national parks would and should mean in a rapidly changing America. The picture of national park tourism that emerges here is one in which people who had come to the parks searching for an Old Faithful America to re-orient themselves in the anxious 1970s found that the new American 'social landscape' that many had hoped to have left at home had followed them to the 'natural landscapes' of the parks as well – leading to a confusing park experience for all involved. If we remember that this experience of disorientation was simply a microcosm of the dominant discursive experience of 'malaise' in American social life in general in the 1970s, then we find that the national parks – instead of being isolated from American society as many desired – not only reflected the dominant trends of the day, but were also some of the most problematic places where these trends played out.

Love and Will: **Rollo May and the Seventies' Crisis of Intimacy** (Robert Abzug)
The 1970s experienced a collapse of traditional sources of authority about self, and in their place substituted various psychotherapies and psychology-based explanations of the world. Among these latter, one of the most enduring has been Rollo May's best-selling *Love and Will*, which sought to define the sources of social and personal renewal amid a delegitimized and disintegrating public consciousness. This article explores the reasons for the book's popularity and its various arguments, and notes that it was one of the last popular books to draw upon the full range of the Western tradition in making its arguments. This last point, I argue, also underlines an increasing poverty of reference experienced in the culture that is one of the unmistakable marks of the 1970s.

Jimmy Carter and America: Memory/Hope versus Nostalgia/Optimism (Charles Bussey)
The American faith in Progress promotes a sense of optimism which cannot deal with disappointment. It is an ideology which discourages planning for the future and fosters a way of life which is indifferent to both the past and the future. In other words, it depends upon a nostalgic view of the past which, as Christopher Lasch wrote, is an abdication of Memory, or history. Despite the hold which the false gods of Nostalgia and Optimism had on Americans, there was in the mid-1970s a certain disillusionment pervading the United States. Jimmy Carter tapped into that disillusionment and skillfully made his way to the Presidency. My contention is that Carter failed to win a second term because of his effort to promote Hope and Memory as opposed to Nostalgia and Optimism. The American people showed their preference for Ronald Reagan, a man who encouraged a 'no limits' approach to the future and a 'nostalgic' view of the past. Carter's understanding of the past and the future focused on a morally demanding state of mind. He understood the concept of limits. Reagan simply promoted a 'feel good' attitude. Nonetheless, as the Carter years recede from

the emotions of the 1980s, his tenure as President is beginning to be viewed more positively. In part this reevaluation is normal and might be attributed to Carter's post-presidential life, which clearly demonstrates service to others as opposed to a life of ease and acquisitiveness. On the other hand, it is just possible that Americans are beginning to understand the distinction between Hope/Memory and Optimism/Nostalgia. If that is the case, Carter deserves credit for teaching Americans something about the way they think.

The Crooked Path: Continuity and Change in American Foreign Policy, 1968-1981 (Dale Carter)

The course of US foreign relations during the 1970s led at one level from détente to confrontation. Beneath such manifest Cold War contours, however, American diplomacy followed a more crooked path, one whose twists and turns are best understood by reference to the late 1960s and 1970s: the era of Republican Richard Nixon.

At that time, Washington was coming to terms with the costs of the Cold War and the limits of power symbolized by the Vietnam debacle. Pursuing withdrawal from South East Asia and détente with the Communists, it sought under Nixon to sustain containment on the cheap; redefining relations with major allies, it endeavored to restore US economic supremacy. The President's conservative and liberal critics may have fostered and exploited his fall in 1974. Yet the liberals who helped Democrat Jimmy Carter into office soon afterwards sought less to undo Nixon's work than (in the shape of Trilateralism) to stabilize and extend it. Conservatives who attacked both Nixon and Carter in turn found it hard to recreate or sustain the pre-Vietnam order Nixon had helped dismantle. Even as the dissolution of détente fostered Ronald Reagan's rise to power at the end of the decade, Nixon's influence lived on. Within a few years, the Great Communicator would be following, literally and metaphorically, in his Republican predecessor's footsteps.

Sixties Activism in the 'Me Decade' (Douglas T. Miller)

The purpose of this article is twofold. First, it challenges the common assumption that there exists a sharp dichotomy between the politicized sixties and the personalized seventies. The post-Vietnam seventies has been described as a period of excessively selfish narcissism, the 'Me Decade.' Yet the hedonistic search for personal fulfillment was not unique to the seventies but grew quite naturally from the sixties counterculture. Furthermore, political activism did not end with the Vietnam War. Although the political pursuit of change became less vociferous in the post-Vietnam, post-Watergate years, it nevertheless remained an important feature of American life.

The second aim of this article is to refute those scholars who debunk the social movements of the sixties as having had few lasting legacies. Such critics frequently cite the post-sixties careers of a few well-known New Leftists who 'sold out' to the establishment as proof of the superficial nature of their activism. But as this article indicates, the great majority of sixties activists continued to play important roles in the social movements of the seventies and more recent times.

'Power to the People' through Television: Community Access in a Commercial System (Nancy Graham Holm)

The seventies saw the development of public access to the airwaves in America. Within the commercial system of American broadcasting, various television stations throughout the nation were challenged to 'give up' certain hours to community programming as a public service. This challenge was demanded as an official threat to license ownership by organized community groups who used the Fairness Doctrine as the legal basis for their demands. The San Francisco market was a major player in this experiment; specifically the

214

independent, unaffiliated station, KTVU. Throughout the seventies, until the abolition of the Fairness Doctrine under Reagan in the mid-eighties, KTVU was a model to the country for community affairs programming. Up to six hours of programs a week covered topics that affected the changing demographics of the San Francisco Bay Area, giving voice to the under-represented segments of society whose social, economic and political issues seldom, if ever, appeared in news and public affairs programs.

Popular Music into the Seventies: From Rock to Pop to Punk (Henrik Bødker)

The popular music of the 70s is often denigrated by a comparative perspective through which the decade's music is largely defined in terms of an absence of certain 'authentic' qualities. This notion partly relies on the perceived existence of an idealized, temporal quality where authentic (and/or progressive) sentiments were allowed to flow uninhibitedly into mass-produced cultural commodities. By shifting the focus away from the musical 'text,' this essay suggests that the wider contexts of reception and modes of production need examining in order to qualify the contrastive perspective between the popular music of the 60s and the 70s. What so often has been interpreted wholly in terms of a waning of authenticity and quality in the popular music of the 70s can thus be partly explained as a result of certain generational, attitudinal and institutional changes. This is not to suggest that textual specifics are unimportant, but merely to direct the attention towards some of the larger frameworks within which popular music acquires its 'meaning(s).'

Images of the Past, Present and Future: Hollywood Portraits of Bicentennial America (Elsebeth Hurup)

The Bicentennial year of 1976 was a time for reflection on American history in general and the immediate past in particular. America was in the midst of an identity crisis, seeking to come to terms with changes and transformations that had taken place over the previous decade. A sense of endings and new beginnings was reflected by a number of movies released in that year. The new beginnings, however, did not so much constitute a new approach to the problems of the day as they explicitly or implicitly signalled a yearning to restore lost values. Through analyses of two Westerns, *The Shootist* (John Wayne's last) and Clint Eastwood's *The Outlaw Josey Wales*, the essay traces the decline and attempted resurrection of the Western genre. Next, two films set in the present are compared and contrasted: the brooding sixties-style *Taxi Driver*, and the sleeper hit of the year, *Rocky*, an old-fashioned story of perseverance and success against all odds in the big-city slum. Finally, the futuristic fantasy *Logan's Run* is demonstrated to be an improbable exercise in nostalgia for the present and a harbinger of the 'feel-good' science fiction trend that arose in the late seventies with the phenomenal success of the *Star Wars* series.

The Contributors

Robert Abzug is Professor of History and American Studies and Director of the American Studies Program at the University of Texas at Austin. He has taught at UCLA, Berkeley, and the University of Munich, and has been at Texas since 1978. He is the author of several books, among which are *Cosmos Crumbling: American Reform and the Religious Imagination* (1994), *Inside the Vicious Heart: Americans and the Liberation of Nazi Concentration Camps* (1985), *Passionate Liberator: Theodore Dwight Weld and the Dilemma of Reform* (1980). Abzug is presently working on a biography of the American psychologist Rollo May, one that will focus on the interplay of religion and psychology in modern American culture.

Robert M. Bednar is an Instructor of English in the Department of English at Southwestern University, Georgetown, Texas, and a Ph.D. student in American Civilization at the University of Texas, where he is completing his dissertation. The article included here is a chapter from that dissertation – *Images of the Land of Images: Contemporary Visions of the American West* – which analyzes the contemporary use of images of iconic western landscapes in literature, film, photography, advertising, and National Park Service interpretive facilities. A self-proclaimed 'tourist of tourism,' he has traveled extensively in the American West studying tourist interactions with natural landscapes.

Charles Bussey is Professor of History at Western Kentucky University. He has edited *America's Heritage in the Twentieth Century* (1978) and has published articles on twentieth century America. He is currently working on a biography of Julius B. Richmond, President Carter's Surgeon General. In addition he serves as a consultant with the Franklin and Eleanor Roosevelt Institute and was a Fulbright Senior Lecturer at the University of Aarhus 1993.

Henrik Bødker holds a B.A. in Business Communication from the Aarhus School of Business, 1987. After holding full time positions as budget assistant in Aarhus and market analyst for a major international company in London, he became a student at the University of Aarhus in 1989 and graduated in 1994. His Master's thesis dealt with various aspects of rock music. He has worked as a teaching assistant at the Aarhus School of Business, and is currently enrolled in the Ph.D. program at the Center for American Studies, University of Odense, working on a project on the role of products as intermediaries in the cultural exchange between the U.S. and Europe.

Dale Carter is Associate Professor of American Studies at the Department of English, University of Aarhus. He is the author of *The Final Frontier: The Rise and Fall of the American Rocket State* (1988) and editor of *Blood on the Nash Ambassador: The Selected Essays of Eric Mottram* (1989) and *Cracking the Ike Age: Aspects of Fifties America* (1993). His teaching and research interests focus on American society, culture, politics and foreign relations since the 1930s.

John G. Cawelti is Professor of English at the University of Kentucky. The author of seven books, including *Apostles of the Self-Made Man* (1965), *The Six-Gun Mystique* (1970; rev.

216

ed. 1984), *Adventure, Mystery and Romance* (1976) and *The Spy Story* (1987), he has published widely in the fields of American literature, cultural history and popular culture. Cawelti has served on the Board of Trustees of the National Humanities Faculty, as a consultant to the National Endowment for the Humanities, and a President of the Popular Culture Association. He is currently working on books on the African American writer Leon Forrest, a third revised edition of *The Six-Gun Mystique* and on changing images of the South and the West in American culture.

Nancy Graham Holm holds M.A.s in American History (UC, Berkeley 1970) and in Broadcast Communication Arts (San Francisco State University 1972). Beginning as a freelancer at KTVU in 1974, she was a staff producer at the station from 1976 till 1984. She was News and Public Affairs Manager at KBHK in 1985, and Editorial and Public Affairs Director at KPIX 1986-91. Since 1991 she has been Head of the TV section at the Danish School of Journalism.

Elsebeth Hurup received an M.A. in English and History of Art from the University of Aarhus in 1984. She was Visiting Lecturer in Danish at the University of Michigan, Ann Arbor, 1987-89, and has taught courses in translation, English language and American Studies at the universities of Aarhus and Odense. Her contribution to the present collection is a chapter from her doctoral dissertation, *Marching Backward into the Future: American Nostalgia and the 1970s*, which is currently under adjudication. At present she is co-authoring a volume on the cinema of Scandinavia in Greenwood Press's Reference Guides to the World's Cinema series. The volume is scheduled for publication in 1997.

Douglas T. Miller is the professor of American intellectual history at Michigan State University and has written extensively on nineteenth- and twentieth-century U.S. history. Among his many books are *Jacksonian Aristocracy*; *Henry David Thoreau*; *Frederick Douglass and the Fight for Freedom*; *The Fifties* (with Marion Nowak); and *Visions of America: Second World War to the Present*. His latest book is entitled *On Your Own: Americans in the Sixties* (1996). In 1979-1980, Professor Miller was the senior Fulbright lecturer at the Universities of Copenhagen and Odense. In 1987-1988, he held the John Adams Chair in American Civilization at the University of Amsterdam.

David E. Nye is Chair of the Center for American Studies, Odense University. He attended Amherst College and the University of Minnesota, completing his Ph.D. in American Studies in 1974. His many books include *Electrifying America: Social Meanings of a New Technology* (1990), winner of the Dexter Prize, and *American Technological Sublime* (1994). He is now writing a work on energy and the consumer society, under contract with MIT Press. Former president of the Danish Association for American Studies, he has been a member of the Danish-American Fulbright Committee since 1987.